FEMALE ADOLESCENT DEVELOPMENT

Second Edition

Edited by
Max Sugar, M.D.

*Clinical Professor of Psychiatry
at Louisiana State University Medical Center
and Tulane University Medical Center,
New Orleans, Louisiana*

BRUNNER/MAZEL Publishers ● New York

Library of Congress Cataloging-in-Publication Data

Female adolescent development/edited by Max Sugar—2nd ed.
    p. cm.
    Includes bibliographical references and indexes.
    ISBN 0-87630-715-2
    1. Adolescent psychology. 2. Women—Psychology. I. Sugar, Max.
BF724.F435 1993
305.23′55—dc20   92-41570
                                                                              CIP

Published by
BRUNNER/MAZEL, INC.
19 Union Square West
New York, New York 10003

Manufactured in the United States of America

10 9 8 7 6 5 4 3 2 1

To

the memory of

ABRAHAM JACOB and ANNIE
TEPPERMAN SUGAR

who provided the basics

Contents

Foreword

In the past 14 years the contributions of clinical, sociological, and biological research and practice have crystallized the need for a Second Edition of *Female Adolescent Development*. Though the editor remains the same, the author-contributors present state-of-the-art research and scholarly contributions, and discuss pressing questions that confront all the professionals concerned.

There is an understandable emphasis on healthy development, with a sophisticated psychoanalytic frame of reference for what is normative, also indicating the boundaries of and transitions to what is deviant. In this sense, the Second Edition demonstrates an awareness of how physical, psychological, social, cultural, economic, and historical perspectives are necessary for a full understanding of female adolescent development.

Peer-reviewed articles and the updating of scholarly books such as this one have an influence on national social policy, as indicated in the NIH's commitment to bringing about male and female equity in subjects studied by controlled biopsychosocial research. The feminist movement has dramatized how most large controlled studies of the past have concentrated on males and their health-illness states. Thus, not only the conditions studied but also the reasonable generalizations inferred have focused on males and have inherently downgraded the significance of female experience and development.

This Second Edition of *Female Adolescent Development* sustains the effort to redress the balance. Throughout this volume the changing roles of women in education, in the workplace, and in establishing a family are clearly recorded, without slipping into either the adversarial or the polarized postures that generations of scientific pressure may produce. Indeed, there are "safe" generalizations that are not ignored. These include biological and cultural diversity and differentiation; the greater tolerance for role interchange; and the risks and challenges confronting pregnant teenagers and single mothers. Of equal importance as changing background factors are: the impact of economic conditions; the advent of labor-saving devices for the household; the influence of computers on the daily lives of teenagers; the controversies about family planning and therapeutic abortions; and the efforts to put teenage pregnancies and continuing education into an attractive, workable policy-practice alliance. Perhaps the most dramatic, threatening change of context is in the advent and spread of AIDS and its association with the increase in drug and alcohol abuse and violence. Female adolescent expectations and experiences cannot avoid the influence of these apparent changing realities. Indeed, the velocity of history is increasing so rapidly that there is a paucity of rigorous studies examining the impact of these risk factors.

Other epidemiological realities that are alluded to include suicidal behaviors, eating disorders, socioeconomic-educational class differences, the increase of delinquent behaviors, and the impact of earlier and increasing sexual activities. The latter brings with it the substantial risk of sexually transmitted diseases.

The changing opportunities for young women have been paralleled by the changing roles and structures of the family with a higher divorce rate than in 1979. All in all, although this book updates students and experts, it is carefully presented to keep the reader prepared for new findings, for changing conditions, and for the elaboration and refinement of our knowledge and questions. Perhaps its greatest accomplishment is to emphasize explicitly and intrinsically that female adolescence commands its own line of development and that individual differences continue to be compelling in research, diagnosis, and treatment.

—Albert J. Solnit, M.D.

Preface

More than a decade has passed since the first publication of *Female Adolescent Development*. During that time our knowledge has been greatly expanded by extensive new research data and theoretical concepts. At the same time, far-reaching cultural and social changes have affected the development of young females in ways that we could barely conceive of in the late 70s. Therefore, this completely revised and updated edition is presented. This edition brings in eight new contributors who provide some new vantage points and ideas on female adolescent development. These reflect not only social and cultural issues but also involve maturation, cognition, ethnicity, female active engulfment, and the superego. We hope this edition will contribute further to a coherent, current, normative view of this developmental stage in females.

In Part I, Judith Dubas and Anne Petersen provide some correlation of biological and social development, particularly about effects of pubertal timing and the role of context. They underscore that there is now a less rigid view of the outcome of early-maturing girls compared to average or late maturers.

The data on cognitive development in girls, which have been updated by Dubas and Petersen, show that there are now no differences between males and females for math ability, except that males still have an advantage on mental rotation tasks. The authors present compelling explanations for the change.

In Part II, on Psychodynamics, Joan Zilbach homes in on primary femininity with the issues of active engulfment, interdependence on mother and others, reciprocal identification, and gender identity, along with the emotional effects of breast development and menarche. These are seen not as analogs of the male, but as aspects of a separate, specific, and different female developmental line.

Maj-Britt Rosenbaum emphasizes the revisions in body image and ego development in conjunction with physical alterations in adolescence along with the girl's continued striving for integration of body image, self-esteem, and sexuality.

Hyman Muslin and Jonathan Lewis consider superego development in the female as related to role models for females in each culture. In the current U.S. culture, there are many such role models. A view of different theories of the male vs. the female superego brings in notions about justice and care, but the authors conclude that, though the contents differ, the functions of the superego are the same for both sexes.

In his chapter on the ego-ideal in mid-adolescent girls, Vann Spruiell stresses the shift from narcissism to the capacity for object-love with lust and tenderness for a whole object of the opposite sex.

In Part III, on Psychosocial Issues, further social historical data are presented by Lyman Wynne and Laura Frader about female adolescents and their families, their development (with a particular view of bundling), and social class differences.

Pamela Sarigiani and associates point out that there are insufficient data on different cultural contexts and their influence on female adolescent adjustment to adolescence. However, the cultural effect is indirect, pervasive, and significant for the understanding of youngsters' development.

Graciela Viale-Val and Carrie Sylvester find that in spite of many societal changes in recent decades, females still are less delinquent than males. A major risk factor for delinquent girls appears to be the absence of a suitably protective, stable parent.

Alayne Yates has concerns about the positive results of the women's movement, such as independence, which leads some adolescents toward goals with excessive self-imposed demands that may eventuate in diminished relationships. This may result in a sense of emptiness, with possible clinical consequences.

Ethnic and socioeconomic factors are considered by Irving Berkovitz in his chapter on schools and their effect on female adolescent development. Depending on the size of the school, the teacher and counselor still have significant influence on youngsters. School is also important as a conveyor of societal values.

Finally, Max Sugar collates facts about adolescent motherhood and stresses various features of significance in the reproductive, educational, vocational, and maternal development of adolescent females. Although varying for each individual, the adolescent mother has a confounded and incomplete emotional development.

A further illustration of the expanding knowledge in the field is the research collating genital staging with Tanner's breast staging, just as genital staging is a part of Tanner staging for boys (Yordan & Yordan, 1992).

There are many questions that we hope future research will answer. For instance, the understanding of female sexual arousal patterns and responses remains incomplete. Researchers continue to explore this, especially since the vaginal photoplethysmograph came into use in 1975 (Darling, Davidson & Conway-Welsh, 1990; Hatch, 1979). Also, bone density increases about three times more in black than in white females at Tanner stages 4 and 5, and this seems to be related to the lower prevalence and incidence of osteoporosis and vertebral fracture in black women (Gilsang, Roe, Mora, Costin & Goodman, 1991).

In recent decades we have learned considerably more about adolescent female development and hope to continue this expansion in knowledge.

REFERENCES

Darling, C.A., Davidson, J.K., & Conway-Welch, C., 1990. Female ejaculation: Perceived origins, the Grafenberg Spot/Area, and sexual responsiveness. *Arch. Sex. Behav.*, 19:29–47.

Gilsang, V., Roe, T.F., Mora, S., Costin, G., & Goodman, W.G., 1991. Changes in vertebral bone density in black girls and white girls during childhood and puberty. *New Engl. J. Med.*, 325:1597–1600.

Hatch, J., 1979. Vaginal photoplethysmography: Methodological considerations. *Arch. Sex. Behav.*, 8:357–374.

Yordan, E.E., & Yordan, R., 1992. The Hymen and Tanner staging of the breast. *Adolesc. Pediatr. Gynecol.*, 5:76–79.

Acknowledgments

In addition to the contributors, there are a host of others to whom I am indebted for advice, support, and diligent efforts. Among these are my wife, Barbara, for her consistent encouragement, forbearance, and help so that I could work on this second edition; my secretary, Mrs. Dora V. Posey, whose capable endeavors helped smooth many issues; and, above all, the countless adolescents from whom the data derive.

Contributors

Irving H. Berkovitz, M.D.
Clinical Professor of Psychiatry
University of California (UCLA) Los Angeles
Member, So. California Psychoanalytic Institute/Society;
Los Angeles, CA

Phame M. Camarena, Ph.D.
Visiting Assistant Professor of Child Development
Department of Child Development and Family Studies
Purdue University
West Lafayette, IN

Judith Semon Dubas, Ph.D.
Assistant Professor of Psychology
Department of Psychology
College of William and Mary
Williamsburg, VA

Laura Frader, Ph.D.
Associate Professor of History
Northeastern University
Boston, MA

Jonathan D. Lewis, M.D.
Clinical Assistant Professor of Psychiatry
University of Illinois
Chicago, IL

Hyman L. Muslin, M.D.
Professor of Psychiatry
University of Illinois
Chicago, IL

Anne C. Petersen, Ph.D.
Vice President for Research and Dean of the Graduate School
Professor of Adolescent Development and Pediatrics
University of Minnesota
Minneapolis, MN

Maj-Britt Rosenbaum, M.D.
Associate Clinical Professor of Psychiatry
Albert Einstein College of Medicine
Director, Human Sexuality Center
Long Island Jewish Medical Center
New York, NY

Pamela A. Sarigiani, Ph.D.
Assistant Professor of Child Development
Department of Child Development and Family Studies
Purdue University
West Lafayette, IN

Vann Spruiell, M.D.
Clinical Professor of Psychiatry
Louisiana State University School of Medicine
Clinical Professor of Psychiatry
Tulane School of Medicine
Training and Supervising Analyst
New Orleans Psychoanalytic Institute
New Orleans, LA

Max Sugar, M.D.
Clinical Professor of Psychiatry
Louisiana State University School of Medicine
Clinical Professor of Psychiatry
Tulane University School of Medicine
New Orleans, LA

Carrie Sylvester, M.D., M.P.H.
Assistant Professor
Department of Psychiatry
University of Illinois at Chicago
Institute for Juvenile Research
Chicago, IL

Graciela Viale-Val, Psy.D.
Illinois State Psychiatric Institute
Chicago, IL

Lyman C. Wynne, M.D., Ph.D.
Professor and Chairman
Department of Psychiatry
University of Rochester Medical Center
Rochester, NY

Alayne Yates, M.D.
Chief of Child & Adolescent Psychiatry
University of Arizona College of Medicine
Tucson, AZ

Joan J. Zilbach, M.D.
Regional—Faculty, Boston
Fielding Institute, Santa Barbara, California
Training and Supervising Analyst
Faculty, Boston Psychoanalytic Institute
Boston, MA

PART I

BIOLOGICAL ISSUES

1 Female Pubertal Development

Judith Semon Dubas, Ph.D.
Anne C. Petersen, Ph.D.

Puberty has been labeled the most important biological event in development (Grave, 1974). It is second only to infancy in the rate of growth experienced by the individual and is characterized by rapid physical growth, large increases in levels of hormones, and the appearance of secondary sexual characteristics (Petersen & Taylor, 1980). During puberty the body is transformed from the physical appearance of a child to that of an adult. Individuals are acutely aware of pubertal changes and actively work to integrate these changes in their definition of self. The somatic changes become visible to parents, friends, and others, signaling the beginning of adolescence. Changes in pubertal status have been associated with changes on a number of psychosocial constructs such as self-concept, cognitive abilities, family relationships, and sexuality (e.g., Crockett & Petersen, 1987; Simmons, Blyth, Van Cleave & Bush, 1979; Steinberg & Hill, 1978; Tanner, 1962). In addition, the effects of pubertal development on certain behaviors are different for boys and girls (Petersen, 1988). Thus, pubertal development is an important life transition that affects the individual at the biological, psychological, and sociological levels.

While a variety of work regarding puberty has been conducted by physical anthropologists, pediatricians, endocrinologists, and social scientists, it is only within the past decade that models linking biological and psychosocial factors have emerged (e.g., Brooks-Gunn, Petersen & Eichorn, 1985; Gunnar & Collins, 1988; Petersen, 1988; Petersen & Taylor, 1980). Pubertal changes may have either direct effects on behavior or be mediated through social or contextual factors. In addition, environmental factors (such as diet, exercise, stress) may influence pubertal processes. Models have been developed that examine the

This chapter was supported in part by a grant from the National Institute of Mental Health, MH30252/38142 to Anne C. Petersen. The section reporting data from the Fels longitudinal sample appeared in the Female Pubertal Development chapter written by Anne C. Petersen in the first edition of *Female Adolescent Development* published in 1979.

3

interaction between environmental and biological factors rather than just focusing primarily on one or the other (Brooks-Gunn & Reiter, 1990). It is important, then, to understand the nature of pubertal development within a certain context and the association between pubertal events and psychosocial development in that context.

The purpose of this chapter is to present data on the biological development of girls from one of the major longitudinal studies of Human Development in this country. We examine the concurrent and longitudinal relations among and between stature, somatic, and menarcheal measures. We then compare these data to our more recent work in this area and to the work of other researchers. We conclude with a discussion of the relationships between biological development and psychosocial development in girls.

BIOLOGICAL DEVELOPMENT IN GIRLS

The best known and most comprehensive study of somatic growth and development in adolescence was conducted by Tanner and colleagues in England (Marshall & Tanner, 1969; Tanner, 1962, 1969). More recently, longitudinal studies of growth in a number of countries have been completed and a new volume has been published discussing the growth parameters of six additional countries along with menarcheal age data for almost all populations (Eveleth & Tanner, 1990; Marshall & Tanner, 1986).

The two major longitudinal studies in this country are the Institute for Human Development in Berkeley, California (Jones, Bayley, MacFarlane & Honzik, 1971) and at the Fels Research Institute for the Study of Human Development (Kagan & Moss, 1962). More recent longitudinal studies that include at least some growth markers not discussed in Marshall & Tanner (1986) include our longitudinal study of two cohorts of adolescents followed during sixth, seventh, eighth, 12th grades and at age 21 (Petersen, 1984) and a sample of adolescent girls followed from ages 10-15 to 17-25 (Brooks-Gunn & Warren, 1985a).

A major point to emerge from these studies is that puberty is not a single event. People think of menarche as the mark of puberty in girls. It is a milestone but represents only one event, and a relatively late one, in a lengthy and complex biological process which transforms a physically immature girl into a physically mature woman. In the following pages we review the basic process of pubertal development in girls and report data from a United States sample which examines the associations between the physical indices.

THE PROCESS OF PUBERTY

All of the components required for mature sexual functioning are present prenatally. The development of reproductive capacity is initiated prenatally when the neuroendocrine system develops. The system is then activated perinatally and then suppressed until about seven years of age (Petersen & Brooks-Gunn, 1988). Puberty refers to the period of rapid physical change involving endocrine and somatic development that results in reproductive maturity. For girls, this process begins anywhere between the ages of eight and eleven and takes an average between four and five years to complete (Tanner, 1962).

Endocrine Development

Studies of endocrine development in adolescence demonstrate the very strong correlation between increasing sex steroid levels and somatic and skeletal maturation. There are three major endocrine systems that undergo change during puberty: adrenal, gonadal and hypothalamal-hypopheseal (hypothalamus and pituitary) systems. The adrenal system matures earliest, resulting in increased androgen production by the adrenal glands (Grumbach, Roth, Kaplan & Kelch, 1974). Changes in the hypothalamus, the pituitary and the gonads (ovaries and testes), all work in synchrony in what has been called a negative feedback system. The hypothalamus directly controls the pituitary by secreting in rhythmic pulses gonadotropin-releasing hormone (GnRH). In response to these pulses of GnRH, the pituitary produces, stores, and secretes luteinizing hormone (LH) and follicle stimulating hormone (FSH). In response to LH and FSH, the gonads respond by synthesizing and secreting sex steroids (estrogens in girls) and producing ova. Hormone production is regulated by a negative feedback loop linking the gonadal steroids and the hypothalamus. When steroid levels rise to a certain threshold level, the hypothalamus responds by decreasing its output, leading to decreased hormone production by the pituitary and then by the gonads.

The onset of puberty is thought to result from a change in the operation of the negative feedback system. The setpoint of the ''gonadostat'' is low during childhood, but gradually rises to permit increasing concentrations of hormones to circulate (Conte, Grumbach, Kaplan & Reiter, 1980; Kulin, Grumbach & Kaplan, 1969).

Developmental Changes

Winter and Faiman (1973a) found that daytime levels of circulating gonadotropins (follicle-stimulating hormone and luteinizing hormone), estradiol, and progesterone are correlated with somatic and skeletal maturation in healthy female children and adolescents. Angsusingha, Kenny, Hankin, and Taylor (1974) obtained similar results comparing these same hormones, as well as estrone, to maturational stages. Of the two estrogens, estradiol most differentiated the sexes, suggesting its greater potency in terms of sexual development. Gupta, Attanasio, and Raaf (1975) studied, in addition to estrogens, the development of testosterone in both boys and girls. Testosterone did not show a rise throughout the development of pubertal phases with girls. Androstenedione, a less potent androgen, did show increments from Tanner stages 1 to 3 with a plateau thereafter. The ratio of estradiol to testosterone most differentiated the sexes, suggesting its usefulness for examining manifestations of endocrine influence as was proposed by Forest, Cathiard, and Bertrand (1973). Brooks-Gunn and Warren (1989) found moderate associations between estradiol, and testosterone with stages of breast development and pubic hair growth among a sample of 10- to 14-year-old girls (rs ranged from .45 to .60). These results suggest that the gonadotropins, estradiol, and progesterone are related to somatic development in female adolescents. While testosterone does not increase throughout development with girls, it may serve as an inhibitor of estrogen action and hence may possibly be important, at least for some girls.

Menarche

The endocrine changes associated with the onset of menarche, like those associated with all of puberty, are relatively slow and gradual, with menarche a relatively late marker rather than the total event. The hypothalamic mechanisms which control gonadotropin release mature gradually, with different maturational phases now apparent. Surges of gonadotropins and estrogens that occasionally attain ovulatory magnitude have been obtained in premenarcheal pubertal girls (Hayes & Johanson, 1972; Penny, Parlow, Olambwonnu & Frasier, 1977; Winter & Faiman, 1973a). Synchronization of gonadotropin and estrogen peaks does not occur, however, until menarche. Although endocrine patterns begin to stabilize at menarche, ovulation may not occur on a regular basis for several years (Winter & Faiman, 1973b; Penny et al., 1977).

Somatic Changes

Several changes in body shape, size and functioning are produced by the hormonal changes that occur during puberty. In particular, breast development appears to be influenced by estrogens while pubic hair development appears to be under the control of androgens. The development of these secondary sexual characteristics is a continuous process divided into five stages described by Tanner and depicted in Figure 1.1. Stage 1 indicates the prepubescent form while stage 2 indicates initial development. Stages 3 & 4 are intermediary stages reflecting increasing maturity while stage 5 indicates complete maturation.

Breast budding is typically the first secondary sexual characteristic to occur, beginning on the average at 10.5 years (Brooks-Gunn & Reiter, 1990; Malina, 1990). Breast development is usually complete by about age 15½, with great variations in rate. Pubic hair development usually begins next at about 11½

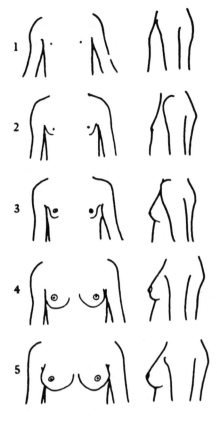

BREASTS

1. No breast development.

2. The first sign of breast development has appeared . This stage is sometimes referred to as the breast budding stage. Some palpable breast tissue under the nipple, the flat area of the nipple (areola) may be somewhat enlarged.

3. The breast is more distinct although there is no separation between contours of the two breasts.

4. The breast is further enlarged and there is greater contour distinction. The nipple including the areola forms a secondary mound on the breast.

5. Mature Stage Size may vary in the mature stage. The breast is fully developed. The contours are distinct and the areola has receded into the general contour of the breast.

PUBIC HAIR

1. No pubic hair.

2. There is a small amount of long pubic hair chiefly along vaginal lips.

3. Hair is darker, coarser, and curlier and spreads sparsely over skin around vaginal lips.

4. Hair is now adult in type, but area covered is smaller than in most adults. There is no pubic hair on the inside of the thighs.

5. Hair is adult in type, distributed as an inverse triangle. There may be hair on the inside of the thighs.

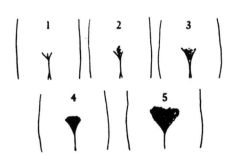

FIGURE 1.1 *The five pubertal stages for breast and pubic hair growth. (From W. A. Marshall and J. M. Tanner (1969), "Variations on the pattern of pubertal changes in girls," Archives of Disease in Childhood, 44, 291).*

years, although for some girls it may develop prior to or concurrently with breast development. Minimal adult distribution of pubic hair is present by age 14½.

Other changes that occur include increases in height, weight, axillary hair growth, and maturation of the uterus, vagina, and labia. The sweat glands begin to produce a characteristic odor and the sebaceous glands increase productivity, sometimes leading to the overproduction of oil related to acne (Petersen & Brooks-Gunn, 1988).

Initiation of the growth spurt occurs relatively early in the pubertal process with mean ages ranging from 8.7 to 10.3 years for girls (Malina, Bouchard, & Beunen, 1988). The peak growth in height (or peak height velocity) ranges from 11.4 years to 12.2 years in girls from North American and European samples (Malina et al., 1988). Growth continues until the ends of the bones fuse with the bone shafts (epiphyseal closure), halting all future growth. The peak gain in weight occurs after the height spurt. Characteristics of body composition and shape, such as lean body mass, body fat, and its distribution change with puberty, resulting in the characteristic appearance in girls of broader hips and fatty deposits in the breasts, hips, buttocks, and thighs.

Menarche (the first menses) is a late maturational event occurring in the United States at approximately 12.8 years for girls of European descent and 12.5 years for girls of African origin (MacMahon, 1973), about two years after breast buds and one year after peak height velocity. It should be noted that considerable variation exists in the maturational sequence of these measures. Peak height velocity may occur prior to the development of pubic hair and/or breast development in about one-fourth of girls (Brooks-Gunn & Reiter, 1990). In addition, there is marked variation in the tempo of development across the various measures. We now present data from one of the major growth studies which illustrates the pubertal process in girls.

THE FELS RESEARCH INSTITUTE STUDY

Method

These data were obtained from the Fels Research Institute for the Study of Human Development in Yellow Springs, Ohio. The data were collected for a study of the relationship between somatic growth and cognitive functioning in adolescents (Petersen, 1976).

Sample

Subjects in the Fels study came from the community in and around Yellow Springs, Ohio, a rural farming community with a small liberal arts college; they are mainly white, and middle and upper-middle class. The Fels longitudinal study was begun in the late 1930s and has continued until recent times. Biological data reported in the present paper were obtained from 99 females at three ages: 13, 16, and 18 years.

Measures

The biological data are of several kinds: ratings of somatic characteristics and secondary sex characteristic development, age at menarche obtained by self-report, and various parameters of growth in stature. Height and weight were also obtained to calculate a measure of mass (height/weight^2), but weight was available only for 50 subjects in the total sample, hence reducing the value of the mass variable.

The growth parameters—amount of growth in stature obtained during adolescence, peak height velocity during adolescence, and age at peak height velocity—were determined in a study of the parametization of growth curves (Bock, Wainer, Petersen, Thissen, Murray & Roche, 1973). Age at peak height velocity is a measure of age at peak pubertal development and is strongly related to age at menarche (r = .77).

The ratings of somatic characteristics were based on the adrogeny scale developed by Bayer and Bayley (1959). This scale is intended to measure secondary sex development of body shape on a continuum from extremely masculine to extremely feminine. Petersen (1973) expanded the scale to include nine rather than five points. Characteristics included in this rating scheme are surface modeling (relative muscle versus fat distribution), shoulder width, waist indentation, hip flare, buttocks shape, thigh form, interspace between legs, calf bulge, the average of the preceding eight somatic ratings, breast size, and overall shape. The ratings of secondary sex characteristic development (pubic hair distribution and breast development) were done according to the scale developed by Tanner (1962, 1969; see Figure 1.1). The pubic hair ratings were extrapolated beyond minimal adult distribution according to Petersen's (1973) scheme for females. The scale ranged from 1 (no development) to 8 (extensive distribution).

The ratings of somatic characteristics were conducted by two raters for the total Fels sample. Ratings were based on nude photographs taken in the three standard views (front, side, rear) at six-month intervals. First, all boys were rated and then all girls, a procedure which probably served to increase within-sex similarities and to decrease the continuity of the ratings between the sexes. The interrater reliability was examined both by Pearson product-moment correlations and specific reliability estimates (Lord & Novick, 1968). The two reliability measures produced similar results. The median reliability of the ratings was adequate at .64 for females.

TABLE 1.1
Means and Standard Deviations of Somatic Indices of Development[a]

Variable	Mean (sd)		
Adolescent Growth	30.4 (8.3) cm		
Peak Height Velocity	6.4 (1.1) cm/yr		
Age at PHV	11.0 (0.9) yr		
Age at Menarche	12.9 (1.2) yr		
	Age 13 mean (sd)	Age 16 mean (sd)	Age 18 mean (sd)
Muscles/Fat[b]	6.0 (1.0)	6.9 (1.0)	7.1 (0.8)
Shoulder Width[b]	5.6 (1.1)	6.3 (1.1)	6.5 (1.2)
Waist Indentation[b]	6.2 (1.2)	7.2 (0.9)	7.6 (1.0)
Hip Width $_b$	6.0 (1.2)	7.3 (0.9)	7.3 (1.0)
Buttocks Shape[b]	6.0 (1.2)	7.1 (0.8)	7.5 (1.0)
Thigh Shape[b]	5.9 (1.5)	6.8 (1.5)	7.3 (1.4)
Leg Space[b]	5.6 (1.5)	6.2 (1.7)	6.4 (1.8)
Calf Shape[b]	6.0 (1.3)	7.0 (1.1)	7.3 (1.1)
Average Rating[b]	5.9 (1.1)	6.9 (0.8)	7.2 (0.9)
Overall Shape[b]	6.1 (1.0)	7.1 (0.7)	7.4 (0.8)
Breast Size[c]	2.1 (0.8)	2.8 (0.8)	3.0 (0.9)
Pubic Hair[d]	3.5 (1.2)	5.2 (0.8)	5.9 (0.8)
Breast Development[e]	3.7 (1.3)	4.9 (0.4)	5.0 (0.2)

[a] n = 99, but some variables were missing observations at some ages
[b] Scales range from 1 (extremely masculine) to 9 (extremely feminine)
[c] Scales range from 1 (very small) to 5 (very large)
[d] Scale ranges from 1 (no development) to 8 (extensive distribution)
[e] Scale ranges from 1 (no development) to 5 (mature development)

Results

Table 1.1 contains summary statistics of the distributions of the somatic characteristics in females. The means follow the expected developmental sequence, becoming more feminine with age. Except with the Tanner breast development ratings, the variations between subjects on these measures are fairly stable across the three ages. The standard deviations of the Tanner breast development ratings approach zero as the subjects reach maturity, which we would expect. Since the earliest age at which these data were obtained is 13, they do not describe the beginning of puberty in girls. Indeed, average age at menarche, a relatively late pubertal event, is 12.9 years in these data. Similarly, the average Tanner rating for breast development is 3.7 at age 13 and reaches 4.9 (on a 5-point scale) by age 16. Thus, at age 13, most girls are at least in the midst of their pubertal development.

Intercorrelations of the Physical Variables

Tables 1.2, 1.3, and 1.4 display the correlations significantly different from zero among the physical variables at the three ages. We discuss these tables, considering the stature parameters, the somatic ratings, age at menarche, and the relations among them.

Relations Among Growth in Stature Parameters.

The relationships among the growth parameters are low to moderate for this group of females. Subjects who matured later tend to have shorter adolescent increments in height and experience slower growth in adolescence.

Relations Between Growth in Stature and Somatic Development.

Growth in stature occurring during adolescence consistently has very low relationships with other variables. The amount of growth in height during adolescence is virtually unrelated to development of other somatic characteristics. There are moderately low relationships of faster growth rates and earlier age of maturity to increasing development as measured by the various somatic measures. The number of relationships with growth rate and age at peak growth decrease over the three ages at which somatic development was measured. Furthermore, these relationships are strongest with the Tanner ratings measuring development of secondary sexual characteristics. These latter two results support the notion that the growth parameters are primarily indices of pubertal development and do not relate to differences among mature individuals.

Relations of Age at Menarche to Growth and Somatic Variables.

Age at menarche correlates .77 with age at peak height velocity; these two measures are similarly related to other variables. A major exception is that age at menarche, unlike age at peak height velocity, is unrelated to the adolescent stature increment. This result, together with the lack of relation of the adolescent increment to any of the somatic ratings, suggests that the relation between the two growth parameters is artifactually induced by the parameter estimation procedure.

Age at menarche shows slightly higher correlations than age at peak height velocity to the somatic ratings. On the other hand, like age at peak height velocity, age at menarche is decreasingly related to the somatic ratings by age 18.

Relations Among the Somatic Ratings.

The somatic ratings are consistently related in the positive direction, indicating that the parts of the body scored in this rating scheme tend to develop in a similar way in each individual. A comparison of the correlations of the body shape variables with the overall body shape ratings versus the average of the eight body shape ratings indicates which of the variables detract from the unity of these ratings. All of the leg ratings frequently diverge from the overall characteristic shape for females, suggesting that leg shape is less likely than the other

TABLE 1.2
Significant[1] Correlations Among Somatic Indices at Age 13

	Adol	PHV	APHV	AMen	Musc	Shol	Wast	Hips	Butt	Thi	Legs	Calf	AV	Oval	BSiz	PubH
Adol Incr																
Pk Ht Vel	.30															
Age at PHV	-.39	-.41														
Age at Men		-.47	.77													
Musc/Fat	.25	-.49		-.51												
Shoulder		-.39		-.33	.59											
Waist	.25	-.46		-.45	.54	.68										
Hip Width		-.51		-.50	.60	.77	.76									
Buttocks	.23	-.55		-.54	.57	.73	.74	.88								
Thigh Shape		-.40		-.42	.46	.57	.55	.73	.76							
Leg Space		-.28		-.23	.32	.45	.37	.56	.59	.86						
Calf Shape	.19	-.50		-.47	.46	.56	.58	.73	.76	.84	.69					
Av Body	.16	-.52		-.50	.63	.80	.78	.91	.91	.89	.76	.87				
Overall	.21	-.49		-.51	.56	.72	.80	.86	.84	.66	.50	.73	.86			
Breast Size	.31	-.55		-.61	.42	.47	.60	.64	.71	.57	.39	.59	.66	.62		
Pubic Hair	.32	-.54		-.65	-.30	.35	.48	.46	.49	.30	.43	.43	.44	.55	.69	
Breast Devel	.35	-.60		-.69	.41	.42	.62	.56	.58	.42	.24	.52	.56	.65	.80	.79

[1] r ≥ .16

TABLE 1.3

Significant[1] Correlations Among Somatic Indices at Age 16

	Adol	PHV	APHV	AMen	Musc	Shol	Wast	Hips	Butt	Thi	Legs	Calf	Av	Oval	BSiz	PubH
Adol Incr																
Pk Ht Vel	.30															
Age at PHV	−.39	−.41														
Age at Men		−.47	.77													
Musc/Fat			−.19	−.22												
Shoulder					.63											
Waist					.47	.46										
Hip Width		.17	−.23	−.23	.52	.50	.79									
Buttocks		.21	−.22	−.29	.64	.52	.63	.81								
Thigh Shape			−.26	−.35	.41	.27	.44	.58	.63							
Leg Space			−.21	−.25	.31	.16	.28	.45	.51	.84						
Calf Shape		.16	−.20	−.28	.49	.31	.46	.57	.62	.65	.59					
Av Body		.17	−.25	−.28	.68	.58	.70	.82	.85	.85	.77	.78				
Overall		.23	−.22	−.32	.65	.53	.61	.78	.78	.56	.49	.58	.79			
Breast Size		.18	−.24	−.29	.39	.31	.26	.47	.50	.50	.48	.37	.55	.50	.22	
Pubic Hair		.27	−.37	−.49											.18	
Breast Devel			−.28	−.26	.22	.16									.32	.41

[1]r ≥ .16

TABLE 1.4
Significant[1] Correlations Among Somatic Indices at Age 18

	Adol	PHV	APHV	AMen	Musc	Shol	Wast	Hips	Butt	Thi	Legs	Calf	Av	Oval	BSiz	PubH
Adol Incr	.30															
Pk Ht Vel		-.39														
Age at PHV		-.41														
Age at Men		-.47	.77													
Musc/Fat																
Shoulder					.73											
Waist					.58	.42										
Hip Width	.18	-.18	-.17		.69	.54	.78									
Buttocks	.18	-.16	-.20		.63	.54	.66	.87								
Thigh Shape		-.20	-.24		.49	.32	.43	.58	.64							
Leg Space			-.19		.42	.27	.29	.50	.56	.80						
Calf Shape		-.20	-.27		.55	.39	.47	.65	.61	.66	.55					
Av Body		-.18	-.21		.78	.64	.70	.87	.87	.83	.77	.78				
Overall		-.16	-.18		.78	.59	.75	.86	.81	.64	.56	.62	.88			
Breast Size			-.17		.41	.37	.18	.41	.44	.45	.49	.34	.51	.45		
Pubic Hair	.17	-.20	-.30													
Breast Devel		-.18	-.23				-.18								.29	-.21

[1]r ≥ .16

characteristics to be consistently related to overall body shape. This is also shown in the principal components analysis to be discussed later.

The Tanner ratings tend to be strongly correlated with each other and with the other variables having strong developmental components. These ratings stand in contrast to the breast size rating, which consistently relates to body shape ratings. Once maturity has been achieved, the function of the Tanner ratings is substantially reduced; this is clearly appropriate for the breast rating since there is no more variance upon maturity. There is evidence with females that by age 18 the pubic hair rating is beginning to reflect androgen influence. Growth of the body hair is one of the latest developmental processes to occur. The pubic hair rating originally correlated positively with all the feminine, estrogen-influenced variables; by age 18, however, these correlations become negative—though most of them are not significantly different from zero—thus giving mild support to the hypothesis that the pubic hair ratings should tend in a masculine and androgenized direction.

Components of Growth with Age

Table 1.5 shows the principal components (factors) of the measures for each age. At each age there is one primary component representing feminine development of most somatic characteristics. At age 13, this factor is also related to an earlier age of maturation. By age 18, earlier onset of puberty is only slightly related to more feminine characteristics.

The number of factors beyond the first general one increases with age. At age 13, there are two smaller factors. The first consists of slower rate of growth, later onset of puberty, feminine leg shape, and lower pubertal stage on the Tanner scales. This appears to be an immaturity factor. The third factor at age 13 consists of a longer component of adolescent growth in height, faster growth, earlier onset of the adolescent growth spurt, and lesser pubic hair development.

At age 16, the second factor is again an immaturity factor, but with no contribution from the leg-shape ratings. The third factor at age 16 appears to be muscle, shoulder, pubic hair, and breast development contrasted with leg shape. The fourth factor here is similar to the third at age 13—more and faster adolescent growth in stature together with less pubic hair development.

At age 18, we again see the immaturity factor; since physical maturity has been attained by this age in most girls, we may conclude that those who had a later onset of puberty are developing more slowly and by age 18 have not yet attained full maturity in breast development and pubic hair distribution. The third factor at age 18 relates a shorter adolescent component of stature to larger breast development. This makes sense since estrogen acts to close the epiphyses and curtail growth in long bones; in addition it stimulates mammary development. The fifth factor is similar but with the addition of later onset of menarche.

TABLE 1.5
Principal Components by Age

	Age 13			Age 16				Age 18				
	1	2	3	1	2	3	4	1	2	3	4	5
Adol	.33	-.60	.91	.31	-.56		.85		-.63	-.61		-.62
Phv	-.70	.41	.38	-.42	.73		.36		.81			
Aphv	-.71	.48	-.34	-.49	.70			-.31	.79			.38
Amen	.67			.71		.33		.80				
Musc	.75			.58		.50		.64			-.43	
Shol	.81			.69				.72				
Wst	.89			.85				.90				
Hip	.91			.87				.88				
But	.79			.77		-.46		.77			-.43	
Thi	.60	.43		.65		-.60		.69			-.49	
Leg	.82	.56		.73				.76		.34		
Calf	.89			.86				.91				
Ov	.81			.64				.57				
Bsiz												
TPh	.66	-.47	-.36		-.63	.31	-.37		-.50	.43	.51	.39
BDev	.77	-.41			-.43	.44			-.34	.42		.52
% Variance	53.1	12.4	8.7	38.6	14.4	9.0	7.9	39.2	14.3	7.9	7.2	6.5

The fourth factor at age 18 combines more shoulder width and masculine leg shape with extensive pubic hair distribution. It is likely that these variables are influenced by androgen.

Discussion of These Results

These ratings of somatic development appear to be measuring two related processes—growth to maturity and degree of response to endocrine influence. The first process, growth to maturity, is experienced by all individuals experiencing normal growth, though at different rates and with different results. The resulting degree of sexual differentiation appears to reflect a different response to endocrine influence. Marshall and Tanner (1969), in tracing the distributions of events of puberty, noted that the differences in the timing of various adolescent events were sometimes quite large. Pubic hair growth is the slowest of these events, with the final distribution of body hair in males not being attained until the mid-twenties (Rosenfield, 1972). This variation in timing of various characteristics may reflect different degrees of tissue responsivity to endocrine influence, different genetic timing mechanisms, and/or totally different processes for different characteristics. In addition to biological factors, environmental factors such as nutrition, illness, exercise also influence the pattern and rate of development. When one examines secondary sexual characteristics and other somatic measures, it is important to realize that the ratings obtained at younger ages are measuring both the status of growth and individual differences in final adult form of the body. By the age when most girls are physically mature (age 18), secondary sexual characteristics for immature girls and age at peak height velocity indicate the timing of a girl's pubertal maturation. The femininity of her somatic characteristics such as leg shape, muscle to fat distribution, etc. is no longer strongly associated with her timing of physical maturation.

Comparison with Other Data

Unfortunately, no other sources of data are available for comparison of the somatic ratings. The growth parameters, however, have been compared among four American samples (Thissen, Bock, Wainer & Roche, 1976). Statistical tests of the individual growth parameters revealed significant but small differences among the samples between the magnitude of the contributions of adolescent growth component and the velocity of growth. No differences among samples were found in the timing of the adolescent growth component. In a more recent sample of middle class girls in Newton, Massachusetts, Zacharis and Rand (1983) found the peak height velocity to be 7.8 cm/year, which is greater than the growth of the Fels sample (6.4 cm/year). The two samples are nearly identical on age at menarche:12.8 in the Newton sample and 12.87 in the Fels.

In our more recent study of an upper middle class sample followed initially in sixth, seventh and eighth grade, we find the age at peak height velocity (11.7 years) to be later than the Fels sample. Age at menarche is also later for this sample at 13.2 years. The ranges reported by Malina et al. (1988) earlier also report a later age at peak height velocity than the Fels sample, with most means clustering between 11.7 to 12.2 years in girls. The age at peak height velocity reported by Marshall and Tanner (1969) on the England Growth study conducted in Harpenden (using a method of fitting the growth curve by eye) found the mean for females to be 12.1 years of age. The average for the Fels sample (using a function minimization procedure) was 11.0 years of age. In comparing different methods of estimation of age at peak height velocity, Marshall and Tanner (1986) report that the double logistic function used by Bock et al. (1973) may be estimating age at peak height velocity too early. A more recent triple logistic function appears to give better fit to the data (Preece & Heinrich, 1981). Caution must be used in interpreting differences in age at peak height velocity across samples employing different estimation procedures.

Marshall and Tanner (1969) provide a source for comparison of the secondary sexual characteristic development ratings. They rated photographs of subjects in the Harpenden, England growth study and found that females had reached Tanner breast stage 4 by age 13.1. The Fels females had a mean breast stage rating of 3.7 at age 13, slightly behind the Harpenden girls. Harpenden girls reached a Tanner pubic hair rating of 4 by age 13, while the Fels girls had an average pubic hair rating of 3.5 at that age, again slightly behind the Harpenden girls. Also different are the ages at menarche for the two samples:13.47 in the Harpenden sample and 12.87 in the Fels sample. The comparison of age at menarche in the two populations suggests that the Fels girls are developing faster than the Harpenden girls, yet the Tanner ratings suggest that the Fels girls are developing more slowly. These discrepancies may be due to measurement errors or to real sample differences. It is also possible that there is no inconsistency here and the American girls are showing earlier menarche, but not earlier development in secondary sexual characteristics. The underlying endocrine processes responsible for these aspects of development are slightly different, although we would expect some greater amount of consistency.

Marshall and Tanner (1969) note that the sequence of development of these various characteristics may vary widely among individuals. Though the stages for each characteristic progress in an invariant sequence, the relationships among characteristics are highly variable. They further note that, contrary to earlier belief (Tanner, 1962), there is little tendency for the early or late maturers to differ in their rate of passage through puberty. Among the Fels girls, however, we noted that age at peak height velocity and age at menarche correlate—.41 and .47, respectively—with peak height velocity. In these data, then, earlier maturation is moderately related to a faster rate of growth in height. We again must consider the possible sources of the different conclusions, based on data from the Harpenden versus Fels samples. Marshall and Tanner (1969) correlated the mean age of beginning breast development and age at menarche with the age interval between the two. The correlation for the Fels data is based on stature development. Different measures, different estimation procedures, or sample differences are all possible sources of these differences. Hence, the conclusion about the relation between timing of maturation and its rate appears premature, at least with girls.

RELATIONSHIPS BETWEEN BIOLOGICAL AND PSYCHOSOCIAL DEVELOPMENT

In considering the association between puberty and psychosocial functioning, researchers have usually focused on one of two aspects: pubertal status and pubertal timing. Pubertal status refers to the current level of physical development experienced by the adolescent relative to the overall process of pubertal change, whereas pubertal timing refers to whether the adolescent's physical development is occurring on time, early, or late, relative to same sex peers. In examining the effects of pubertal status on a particular construct, we are interested in answering a developmental question (such as how relationships with parents change as individuals mature). In examining the effects of pubertal timing, we are interested in answering an individual differences question (such as, whether or not early maturers have different relationships with their parents than on-time or late maturers). Pubertal status or timing effects could be direct or they could be indirect, mediated by the social or psychological responses of the individual or other aspects of their environment (Petersen & Taylor, 1980).

There are three hypotheses concerning the effects of pubertal development on psychosocial changes that have received considerable attention (see Simmons & Blyth, 1987 for a review and discussion of others). The first hypothesis, called the "stressful change hypothesis," posits that all change is stressful. Puberty with its alterations in physical characteristics is a disruptive experience that may give rise to problems. Therefore, all girls, regardless of pubertal timing, will experience some distress, particularly at the time of most rapid change. The second hypothesis, the "off-time hypothesis," posits that events that are considered to be occurring out of synchrony, either earlier or later than expected, are stressful. Thus, both early and late developing girls may exhibit difficulties in adolescence. The third hypothesis, "the early timing hypothesis," predicts that early maturing girls may be particularly vulnerable to adjustment difficulties in adolescence, perhaps because of a mismatch between societal expectations for their behavior and their own levels of cognitive and emotional levels of maturity (e.g., Eichorn, 1975).

More recent conceptualizations of the effects of pubertal development on behavior consider the context in which such development occurs. For example, Caspi, Lyman, Mofitt & Silva (1991) report that early maturing girls exhibit more delinquent behaviors than on time or late maturing girls attending mixed-sex schools; yet this same association is not found in same-sex schools. We now briefly review the work that has examined the effects of pubertal status and pubertal timing on psychological functioning.

The Effects of Pubertal Status

In examining the associations of pubertal status and psychosocial variables, our research has found that advancing pubertal status was associated with enhanced body image and moods for boys, but decreased feelings of attractiveness for girls. As pubertal status advanced, both boys and girls became more interested in the opposite sex and conflict increased in girls' relationships with their parents (Crockett & Petersen, 1987; Dorn, Crockett & Petersen, 1988).

Cross sectional studies of the effects of pubertal status have also indicated that pubertal maturation is associated with increased aloofness, dissatisfaction, and conflict in the parent-child relationships (e.g., Hill, Holmbeck, Marlow, Green & Lynch, 1985a; Steinberg, 1987). This association is most apparent between mothers and daughters and during the midpoint of pubertal development (Hill, Holmbeck, Marlow, Green & Lynch, 1985b).

We have not found any association between pubertal status and cognitive abilities in our data (Dubas, Crockett & Petersen, 1990) even though cognitive development and cognitive abilities increase over the adolescent years. Others have proposed that pubertal development may have a disruptive effect on cognitive ability because of brain reorganization. Carey and Diamond (1980) find that there is a disruption in the ability to encode faces in the midst of puberty, but such an effect has not been replicated on other cognitive tasks (Diamond, Carey & Beck, 1983). We find no effects of pubertal status on school performance (Dubas, Graber & Petersen, 1991). Other researchers interested in the effects of puberty on cognition and achievement have focused on the effects of pubertal timing rather than pubertal status.

The Effects of Pubertal Timing

The possibility that timing of puberty is linked to advantages on intellectual tasks has received considerable attention from psychologists and educators (see Newcombe & Dubas, 1987 or Dubas, 1991 for a review). A recent meta analysis of the relationship between pubertal timing and intelligence found a small consistent advantage for early maturers (Newcombe & Dubas, 1987). Waber's (1976) hypothesis that sex differences in maturation rate explained sex differences in cognitive ability has not been supported (Linn & Petersen, 1985; Newcombe & Dubas, 1987). There may be a small effect of pubertal timing on spatial abilities favoring the late maturer, but the effect is vulnerable to the file drawer problem, that is, it would take a very few nonsignificant studies to render the overall effect nonsignificant. (See Chapter 2 on girls' cognition for a more detailed discussion.)

When pubertal timing effects are found on adjustment measures, in most instances, the results indicate negative effects for early maturing girls. Early maturing girls weigh more and are slightly shorter than their on-time and later maturing counterparts (Brooks-Gunn, 1988). Girls, in general, are secretive and reluctant to discuss menstruation when it first occurs, and early girls in particular report more negative experiences about menstruation (Brooks-Gunn & Ruble, 1982; Petersen, 1983). Early maturers have poorer body image than on-time or late maturers, are less satisfied with their weight, and have less positive feelings about their pubertal timing (Blyth, Simmons & Zakin, 1985; Dubas, Graber & Petersen, 1991; Duncan, Ritter, Dornbusch, et al., 1985; Tobin-Richards, Boxer & Petersen, 1983). Early maturing girls are also more likely to have eating problems lasting throughout adolescence (Brooks-Gunn & Warren, 1985b). Our cultural values for thinness put the early maturing girl on a life trajectory of concern about her body at an early age.

Some early maturing girls may also be at risk for adjustment difficulties. Early maturing girls who experience negative events at home and at school are more likely to report depressed affect than late maturing girls with similar events (Brooks-Gunn, Warren & Rosso, in press). Early maturing girls date earlier and are more popular than on-time and late girls (Simmons & Blyth, 1987). Such an advantage during early adolescence may have negative consequences later. Early maturing girls have been found to be involved in more norm-breaking behaviors (such as getting drunk and playing truant) than late maturing girls (Stattin & Magnusson, 1990) and problem behaviors (Caspi & Moffitt, in press). By adulthood, early maturing women have two to three years less education and lower prestige jobs. In particular, those early maturers who had older, working boyfriends were more likely to show these negative outcomes (Stattin & Magnussin, 1990). In considering the effects of puberty on adjustment, it is important to consider moderators of the effects. As discussed earlier, Caspi and Moffitt (in press) find pubertal timing effects on delinquent behaviors only for girls in mixed-sex schools.

In an upper middle class suburban sample as well as in a lower to middle class rural sample, we found that early maturing girls expected to marry earlier than on-time and late maturers (Bingham, Stemmler, Crockett & Petersen, 1991). Such expectations during adolescence may indirectly influence the student's school performance and educational plans. Late maturing girls have been found to being doing quite well in school (Dubas, Graber & Petersen, in press), perhaps compensating for a lack of popularity. Others have found that late maturation in girls may be a protective factor against depressed affect (Baydar, Brooks-Gunn & Warren, in press). The longer term effects of pubertal timing on transitions to adulthood, as well as achievement and educational outcomes, will soon be evaluated in our sample.

Questions surrounding the association between pubertal development and psychosocial functioning can no longer involve only direct effects questions; rather, the models must address questions such as under what circumstances puberty effects occur. Such models are currently receiving considerable attention.

SUMMARY

In this chapter, we have: (a) described the process of puberty in adolescent girls, presenting some data reviewing the relevant literature, and (b) reviewed the studies of psychosocial correlates of puberty. From the biological studies, we conclude that puberty is a developmental process, not a single event, and that developmental phenomena experienced by all normal girls in this process may be differentiated from changes which lead to variation among mature individuals. Furthermore, puberty involves many different characteristics whose development proceeds at different rates with different sequences for various characteristics among individuals.

In considering the effects of pubertal development on adjustment, it is important to keep in mind that effects for pubertal timing are small (Brooks-Gunn, 1988). Not all early maturing girls will exhibit problems or have poorer adult outcomes than their on-time or late maturing counterparts. The adolescent's social world is organized by her grade in school and the effects of grade in school are often stronger than those of pubertal timing (Petersen & Crockett, 1985). The results of Caspi et al. (in press) remind us of the role of context in enhancing or diminishing the effects of pubertal timing. Future research on puberty will continue to elucidate the mechanisms and contexts under which pubertal effects are found.

REFERENCES

Angsusingha, K., Kenny, F. M., Hankin, H. R., & Taylor, F. H. 1974. Unconjugated estrone, estradiol and FSH and LH in prepubertal and pubertal males and females. *Journal of Clinical Endocrin. Metab.*, 39:63-68.

Baydar, N., Brooks-Gunn, J., & Warren, M. P. (in press). Determinants of depressive symptoms in adolescent girls: A four year longitudinal study. *Developmental Psychology*.

Bayer, L. M. & Bayley, N. 1959. *Growth Diagnosis*. Chicago: University of Chicago Press.

Bingham, C. R., Stemmler, M., Crockett, L. J., & Petersen, A. C. 1991. Pubertal timing, socioeconomic status, and gender as predictors of adulthood transitions: A comparison of resource-rich and resource-poor communities. Paper presented at the XIth biennial meetings of the *International Society for the Study of Behavioral Development*, Minneapolis, MN.

Blyth, D., Simmons, R., & Zakin, D. 1985. Satisfaction with body image for early adolescent females: The impact of pubertal timing within different school environments. *Journal of Youth and Adolescence*, 14(3):207-225.

Bock, R. D., Wainer, H., Petersen, A., Thissen, D., Murray, J., & Roche, A. 1973. A parameterization for human growth curves. *Human Biology*, 45:63-80.

Brooks-Gunn, J. 1988. Antecedents and consequences of variations in girls' maturational timing. *Journal of Adolescent Health Care*, 9:365-373.

Brooks-Gunn, J., Petersen, A. C., & Eichorn, D. 1985. The study of maturational timing effects in adolescence. (Special Issue). *Journal of Youth and Adolescence*, 14 (3 & 4).

Brooks-Gunn, J. & Reiter, E. O. 1990. The role of pubertal processes. In S. S. Feldman & G. R. Elliot, Eds., *At the Threshold: The Developing Adolescent* (pp. 16-53). Cambridge, MA: Harvard University.

Brooks-Gunn, J. & Ruble, D. N. 1982. The development of menstrual-related beliefs and behaviors during adolescence. *Child Development*, 53:3-14.

Brooks-Gunn, J. & Warren, M. 1985a. Measuring physical status and timing in early adolescence: A developmental perspective. *Journal of Youth and Adolescence*, 14:163-189.

Brooks-Gunn, J. & Warren, M. 1985b. Effects of delayed menarche in different contexts: Dance and nondance students. *Journal of Youth and Adolescence*, 14:285-300.

Brooks-Gunn, J. & Warren, M. P. 1989. Biological and social contributions to negative affect in young adolescent girls. *Child Development*, 60:40-55.

Brooks-Gunn, J., Warren, M. P., & Rosso, J. T. (in press). The impact of pubertal and social events upon girls' problem behaviors. *Journal of Youth and Adolescence*.

Carey, S. & Diamond, R. 1980. Maturational determination of the developmental course of face encoding. In D. Caplan, Ed., *Biological Studies of Mental Processes* (pp. 60-73). Cambridge, MA: MIT Press.

Caspi, A., Lyman, D., Moffitt, T. E., & Silva, P. A. (1990). *Unraveling girls' delinquency: Biological, dispositional, and contextual contributions to adolescent misbehavior.* Manuscript submitted for publication.

Caspi, A. & Moffitt, T. E. (in press). Individual differences are accentuated during periods of social change: The sample case of girls at puberty. *Journal of Personality and Social Psychology*.

Conte, F., Grumbach, M. M., Kaplan, S., & Reiter, E. 1980. Correlation of leutinizing hormone-releasing factor-induced luteinizing hormone and follicle-stimulating hormone release from infancy to 19 years with the changing pattern of gonadotropin secretion in agonadal patients: Relation to the restraint of puberty. *Journal of Clinical Endocrinology and Metabolism*, 50:163-168.

Crockett, L. J. & Petersen, A. C. 1987. Pubertal status and psychosocial development: Findings from the Early Adolescence Study. In R. M. Foch & T. T. Foch (Eds.),

Biological-psychosocial Interactions in Early Adolescence: A Life Span Perspective (pp. 173-188). Hillsdale, NJ: Erlbaum.

Diamond, R., Carey, S., & Beck, K. J. 1983. Genetic influences on the development of spatial skills during early adolescence. *Cognition*, 13:167-185.

Dorn, L. D., Crockett, L. J., & Petersen, A. C. 1988. The relations of pubertal status to intrapersonal changes in young adolescents. *Journal of Early Adolescence*, 8:405-419.

Dubas, J. S. 1991. Cognitive abilities and physical maturation. In R. M. Lerner, A. C. Petersen, & J. Brooks-Gunn, Eds., *Encyclopedia of Adolescence* (pp. 133-138). New York: Garland.

Dubas, J. S., Crockett, L. J., & Petersen, A. C. 1990. *A longitudinal investigation of sex and individual differences in cognitive abilities during early adolescence: The role of personality and timing of puberty*. Manuscript submitted for publication.

Dubas, J. S., Graber, J. A., & Petersen, A. C. 1991. A longitudinal investigation of adolescents' changing perceptions of pubertal status. *Developmental Psychology*, 27:580-586.

Dubas, J. S., Graber, J. A., & Petersen, A. C. (1991). The effects of pubertal development on achievement. *American Journal of Education*, 99:444-460.

Duncan, P. D., Ritter, P. L., Dornbusch, S. M., et al. 1985. The effects of pubertal timing on body image, school behavior, and deviance. *Journal of Youth and Adolescence*, 14:227-235.

Eichorn, D. E. 1975. Asynchronies in adolescent development. In S. Dragastin & G. H. Elder, Jr., Eds., *Adolescence in the Life cycle: Psychological Change and the Social Context* (pp. 80-95). New York: Wiley.

Eveleth, P. B. & Tanner, J. M. 1990. *Worldwide Variation in Human Growth* (2nd Edition). Cambridge: Cambridge University Press.

Forest, M. G., Cathiard, A. M., & Bertrand, J. A. 1973. Total and unbound testosterone levels in newborn and in normal hypogonadal children: Use of sensitive radioimmunoassay for testosterone. *Journal of Clinical Endocrin. Metab.*, 36:1132-1142.

Grave, G. D. 1974. Introduction. In M. M. Grumbach, G. D. Grave, & F. E. Mayer, Eds., *The Control of the Onset of Puberty*. New York: Wiley.

Grumbach, M. M., Roth, J. C., Kaplan, S. L., & Kelch, R. P. 1974. Hypothalamic-pituitary regulation of puberty: Evidence and concepts from clinical research. In M. M. Grumbach, G. D. Grave & F. E., Mayer, Eds., *Control of the Onset of Puberty* (pp. 115-166). New York: Wiley.

Gunnar, M. A. & Collins, W. A. 1988. *Development During the Transitions in Adolescence: Minnesota Symposia on Child Psychology* (Vol. 21). Hillsdale, NJ: Erlbaum.

Gupta, D., Attanasio, A., & Raaf, S. 1975. Plasma estrogen and androgen concentrations in children during adolescence. *Journal of Clinical Endocrin. Metab.*, 40:636-643.

Hayes, A. & Johanson, A. 1972. Excretion of follicle stimulating hormone (FSH) and leuteinizing hormone (LH) in urine of pubertal girls. *Pediatric Research*, 6:18-25.

Hill, J., Holmbeck, G., Marlow, L., Green, T., & Lynch, M. 1985a. Pubertal status and parent-child relations in families of seventh-grade boys. *Journal of Early Adolescence*, 5:31-44.

Hill, J., Holmbeck, G., Marlow, L., Green, T., & Lynch, M. 1985b. Menarcheal status and parent-child relations in families of seventh-grade girls. *Journal of Youth and Adolescence*, 14:301-316.

Jones, M. C., Bayley, N., MacFarlane, J. W., & Honzik, M. P., Eds. 1971. *The Course of Human Development*. Waltham, MA: Xerox College Publishing.

Kagan, J. & Moss, H. A. 1962. *Birth to Maturity*. New York: Wiley.

Kulin, H. E., Grumbach, M. M., & Kaplan, S. L. 1969. Changing sensitivity of the pubertal gonadal hypothalamic feedback mechanism in man. *Science*, 166:1012-1013.

Linn, M. & Petersen, A. C. 1985. Gender differences and spatial ability: Emergence and characterization. *Child Development*, 56:1479-1498.

Lord, F. M. & Novick, M. R. 1968. *Statistical Theories of Mental Test Scores*. Reading, MA: Addison-Wesley.

MacMahon, B. 1973. *Age at Menarche: United States*, DHEW Publication No. (HRA) 74-1615, NHS Series 11, No. 133, National Center of Health Statistics, Rockville, MD.

Malina, R. M. 1990. Physical growth and performance during the transitional years. In R. Montemayor, G. R. Adams, & T. P. Gullotta, Eds., *From Childhood to Adolescence: A Transitional Period?* (pp. 41-62). Newbury Park, CA: Sage.

Malina, R. M., Bouchard, C., & Beunen, G. 1988. Human Growth: Selected aspects of current research on well-nourished children. *Annual Review of Anthropology*, 17:187-219.

Marshall, W. A. & Tanner, J. M. 1969. Variations in pattern of pubertal changes in girls. *Archives of Diseases in Childhood*, 14:291-303.

Marshall, W. A. & Tanner, J. M. 1986. Puberty. In F. Falkner & J. M. Tanner, Eds., *Human Growth: A Comprehensive Treatise*. Second Edition (pp. 171-209). New York: Plenum Press.

Newcombe, N. & Dubas, J. S. 1987. Individual differences in cognitive ability: Are they related to timing of puberty? In R. M. Lerner & T. Foch, Eds., *Biological-Psychosocial Interactions in Early Adolescence: A Life Span Perspective* (pp. 249-302). Hillsdale, NJ: Erlbaum.

Penny, R., Parlow, A. F., Olambwonnu, N. O., & Frasier, S. D. 1977. Evolution of the menstrual pattern of gonadotropins and sex steroid concentrations in serum. *Acta Endocrin.*, 84:729-732.

Petersen, A. C. 1973. *The relationship of androgenicity in males and females to spatial ability and fluent production*. Unpublished Ph.D. dissertation, The University of Chicago.

Petersen, A. C. 1976. Physical androgyny and cognitive functioning in adolescence. *Developmental Psychology*, 12:524-533.

Petersen, A. C. 1983. Menarche: Meaning of measures and measures of meaning. In S. Golub, Ed., *Menarche: The Transition from Girl to Woman* (pp. 63-76). Lexington, MA: Lexington Books.

Petersen, A. C. 1984. The early adolescence study: An overview. *Journal of Early Adolescence*, 4:103-106.

Petersen, A. C. 1988. Adolescent development. *Annual Review of Psychology*, 39:583-607.

Petersen, A. C. & Brooks-Gunn, J. 1988. Puberty and adolescence. In E. A. Blechman & K. D. Brownell, Eds., *Handbook of Behavioral Medicine for Women* (pp. 12-27). New York: Pergamon.

Petersen, A. C. & Crockett, L. J. 1985. Pubertal timing and grade effects on adjustment. *Journal of Youth and Adolescence*, 14:191-206.

Petersen, A. C. & Taylor, B. 1980. The biological approach to adolescence. In J. Adelson, Ed., *Handbook of Adolescent Psychology* (pp. 117-155). New York: Wiley.

Preece, M. A. & Heinrich, I. 1981. Mathematical modelling of individual growth curves. *British Medical Bulletin*, 37:247-252.

Rosenfield, R. L. 1972. Personal communication.

Simmons, R. G. & Blyth, D. A. 1987. *Moving into Adolescence: The Impact of Pubertal Change on School Context*. New York: Plenum.

Simmons, R. G., Blyth, D. A., Van Cleave, E. F., & Bush, D. M. 1979. Entry into adolescence: The impact of school structure, puberty, and early dating on self-esteem. *American Sociological Review*, 44:948-967.

Stattin, H. & Magnusson, D. 1990. *Paths through Life, Vol. 2: Pubertal Maturation in Female Development*. Hillsdale, NY: Erlbaum.

Steinberg, L. 1987. Impact of puberty on family relations: Effects of pubertal status and pubertal timing. *Developmental Psychology*, 23:451-460.

Steinberg, L. & Hill, J. 1978. Patterns of family interaction as a function of age, the onset of puberty, and formal thinking. *Developmental Psychology*, 14:683-684.

Tanner, J. M. 1962. *Growth at Adolescence* (2nd ed.). Oxford: Blackwell.

Tanner, J. M. 1969. Growth and endocrinology of the adolescent. In L. I. Gardner, Ed., *Endocrine and Genetic Diseases*. Philadelphia: W. B. Saunders.

Thissen, D., Bock, R. D., Wainer, H., & Roche, A. F. 1976. Individual growth in stature: A comparison of four growth studies in the U.S.A. *Annals of Human Biology*, 3:529-542.

Tobin-Richards, M. H., Boxer, A. M., & Petersen, A. C. 1983. The psychological significance of pubertal change: Sex differences in perceptions of self during early adolescence. In J. Brooks-Gunn & A. C. Petersen, Eds., *Girls at Puberty: Biological and Psychosocial Perspectives* (pp. 127-154). New York: Plenum.

Waber, D. P. 1976. Sex differences in cognition: A function of maturational rates. *Science*. 192:572-574.

Winter, J. S. P. & Faiman, C. 1973a. Pituitary-gonadal relations in female children and adolescents. *Pediatric Research*, 7:948-953.

Winter, J. S. P. & Faiman, C. 1973b. The development of cyclic pituitary-gonadal function in adolescent females. *Journal of Clinical Endocrin. Metab.*, 37:715-718.

Zacharias, L. & Rand, W. M. 1983. Adolescent growth in height and its relation to menarche in contemporary American girls. *Ann. Hum. Biol.*, 10:209-222.

2 Differential Cognitive Development and Achievement in Adolescent Girls

Judith Semon Dubas, Ph.D.
Anne C. Petersen, Ph.D.

The pervasive physical changes accompanying puberty transform the body of a girl into a woman and the body of the boy into a man. Accompanying these changes in physical development are changes in relationships with parents (Steinberg, 1990), an intensification of conformity to gender-role stereotypes (Hill & Lynch, 1983), increases in self-esteem (Petersen, 1988), and increases in the capacity for abstract thought (Keating, 1990). The physical differences between men and women are obvious and undisputed, yet sex differences on many behavioral dimensions, especially with regard to cognitive abilities, often result in considerable debate. The topic of controversy regarding gender differences in cognitive differences varies from discussion of the nature and importance of these differences to their causes and consequences.

In this chapter, we review the existing literature on sex-related differences in cognitive functioning at adolescence, as well as the literature discussing the development of these differences. Few investigators, except for those studying formal operational thought, have focused on cognitive functioning particular to adolescence as a stage of life. Rather, most of our information on cognition at adolescence is based on studies using adolescent subjects, usually without consideration of any stage-related qualitative changes in the cognitive traits being measured. While it was once believed that sex-related differences in cognition first appeared during adolescence (Maccoby & Jacklin, 1974), more recent reviews indicate that some differences exist prior to adolescence, others emerge

This chapter was supported in part by a grant from the National Institute of Mental Health, MH30252/38142 to Anne C. Petersen. A few portions of this paper appeared in the first edition of *Female Adolescent Development*, written by Anne C. Petersen with Michele Andrisin Wittig; the vast majority of this chapter, however, is new material.

during adolescence, while others simply do not exist. A comparison of studies published earlier versus later reveals that many sex differences have diminished in recent cohorts. Historical changes in the size of sex differences have implications for the role of various factors in understanding gender differences.

APPROACHES TO STUDYING COGNITIVE FUNCTIONING AND SEX DIFFERENCES

In the present chapter we distinguish between four approaches to the study of cognitive functioning: intelligence, cognitive development, cognitive abilities, and academic achievement. We discuss the study of gender differences in each of these domains, beginning with an historical overview of the approach to the study of gender differences. While most earlier reviews of gender differences consisted of either narrative reviews and/or vote counting (tallying the percentage of studies finding a significant difference favoring either males or females and concluding whether the percentage of significant effects warranted a conclusion of significant differences), later reviews used a statistical method called meta-analysis to quantify and combine evidence from different studies.

Meta-analysis provides not only a statistical answer to the question "do sex differences exist?" but also a statistic which characterizes the magnitude of the difference. The most common statistic computed from meta-analyses examining gender differences is the d statistic, which is computed as the difference between the male mean and the female mean, divided by the pooled within group standard deviation (Linn & Hyde, 1991). Hence, the d statistic indicates how far apart male and female means are in standard deviation units. For our discussion, positive values of d indicate that males show higher scores than females and negative values indicate that females show higher scores than males. A rule of thumb for interpreting effect size is that an absolute value of .20 is considered small, .50 is medium, and .80 is large (Cohen, 1969). Figure 2.1 shows the degree of overlap in the distribution of test scores for males and females that would result from small, medium, and large effect sizes. It should be noted from this figure that even when an average difference is considered large there is still considerable overlap between the scores of males and females. Therefore, using gender to predict cognitive functioning would not be very successful.

Intelligence

The first review of research on gender differences in intellectual skill was conducted by Helen Thompson Wooley in 1910. At that time, the early research

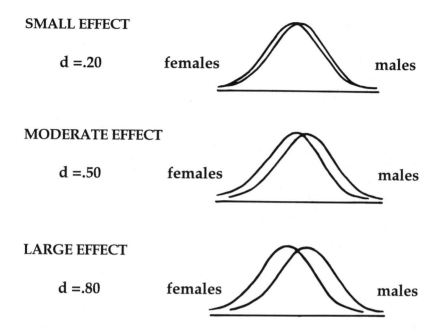

SMALL EFFECT

d =.20   females   males

MODERATE EFFECT

d =.50   females   males

LARGE EFFECT

d =.80   females   males

FIGURE 2.1. *Frequency distributions for male and female test scores exhibiting small, moderate, and large effect sizes for sex differences. (The figures depicted illustrate homogeneous variances.)*

included such skills as tapping a telegraph key, handwriting, and tests of association. Whereas the researchers at that time concluded that women were inferior to men in each of these domains, Wooley concluded from her review that the research was too methodologically flawed and biased to warrant such assertions. With the advent of the mental testing movement set in motion by the development of the intelligence test by Binet, research on gender differences in abilities burgeoned (Hyde, 1990). Originally published in France in 1905 and later expanded and published in America by Terman in 1916 (and called the Stanford Binet), Binet's intelligence test provided one general intelligence score called the IQ, or intelligence quotient. Both Terman and Binet believed that there was no gender difference in intelligence and therefore carfully constructed their test to yield no gender differences in IQ scores. Thus, most reviews of research on general intelligence have not found gender differences (e.g., Maccoby & Jacklin, 1974). Even though one might conclude that there are no sex differences in general intelligence, this finding is confounded by the fact that most IQ tests control for sex differences by deleting items or balancing for items which might differentially benefit one sex versus the other.

Cognitive Abilities

As psychologists' interest in the study of intelligence grew, competing theories concerning the nature of intelligence were developed. Whereas Binet, Terman, and Spearman suggested that a single factor—"g"—was the key to understanding intelligence, Thurstone (1938) proposed that seven factors, which he labeled the "Primary Mental Abilities," were the core of intelligence. The seven abilities believed to be at the core of intelligence were: verbal comprehension, word fluency, numerical computation, spatial visualization, memory, perceptual speed, and reasoning. This new conceptualization of intelligence, coupled with the ease of administering Thurstone's test (The PMA), laid the foundation for research on sex differences on specific cognitive abilities (Hyde, 1990). By the late 1960s, several reviews of research on sex-related cognitive differences were published (Anastasi, 1937; Maccoby, 1966; Tyler, 1947). (See Hyde, 1990 for a brief discussion of their conclusions.)

By the early 1970s, thousands of research papers had been published that examined sex differences in psychological functioning, including hundreds of studies on cognitive abilities. In their classic review of the literature on sex-related differences, Maccoby and Jacklin (1974), using the vote counting method, concluded that there are three cognitive abilities showing reliable sex differences: spatial ability, mathematical ability, and verbal ability. Males on the average score higher than females on tests of spatial ability and mathematical ability, whereas females on average score higher on tests of verbal ability. These differences were reported to first emerge during adolescence. Hyde (1981) reanalyzed Maccoby and Jacklin's review and computed values of d for the studies they reported. For spatial ability $d = .45$, for mathematical ability $d = .43$, and for verbal ability $d = -.24$. According to criteria suggested by Cohen (1969), these results suggest that for studies conducted prior to 1974, sex differences in spatial and mathematical ability are moderate while sex differences in verbal ability are small.

Recent meta-analyses have been conducted on studies published before and after 1974 reporting gender differences. These recent analyses have focused on specific subtypes of abilities within each domain, as well as testing for age and/ or historical changes in the magnitude of the effects.

Spatial ability.

Spatial ability is generally described as the ability to represent, transform, and recall symbolic nonlinguistic information (Linn & Petersen, 1985). In conducting their meta-analysis of studies of sex differences in spatial ability, Linn and

Petersen (1985) distinguished between three subtypes of ability: spatial perception, mental rotation, and spatial visualization. Spatial perception tasks require an individual to determine a spatial relationship among task components in spite of distracting information. Tests such as the rod-and-frame test or water-level task tap this ability. Mental rotation tasks require the ability to rapidly and accurately rotate a two-dimensional drawing of either two- or three-dimensional objects. Tests such as the PMA Spatial Relations test (Thurstone, 1938) or the Vandenburg test (Vandenburg & Kuse, 1978) measure this ability.

Spatial visualization tasks require multiple-step analytic processing of complex spatial stimuli. Tests that measure this dimension vary considerably and include the ETS Paper Folding test, the Wechsler Block Design test, and the Minnesota Paper Form Board Test. Linn and Petersen (1985) found a moderate advantage for boys on spatial perception tests ($d = .44$), a large male advantage on the rotation of three-dimensional representations ($d = .94$), a small male advantage for simple two-dimensional figures ($d = .26$), and no male advantage on spatial visualization tasks ($d = .13$). When analyzed for age differences in the magnitude of these effects, no age differences were found on mental rotation or spatial visualization tasks. For tasks involving spatial perception, sex differences existed at age seven, but were not significantly greater than zero until age 18. Sex differences in mental rotation were found as early as it has been measured. An examination of historical change in the magnitude of these effects reveals that sex differences in overall spatial ability are diminishing (Feingold, 1988; Linn & Hyde, 1991; Rosenthal & Rubin, 1982).

Mathematical ability.

Most studies of gender differences in mathematical ability have used data from large scale national assessments of mathematical achievement (Linn & Petersen, 1986). Whereas Hyde (1981) reported an average effect size of .43 for studies published prior to 1974, data from recent samples of the National Assessment of Educational Progress (NAEP) items, Differential Aptitude Test (DAT) scales, and preliminary Scholastic Aptitude Test (PSAT) indicate that the size of these differences has declined to less than or equal to .20 (Linn & Hyde, 1991). Gender differences in performance on the Scholastic Aptitude Test (SAT) have not declined, however ($d = .41$ for the 1983 voluntary sample). When tests were divided into two general subtypes, computation ability and problem-solving, girls were found to outperform boys on computation problems while boys outperformed girls on estimation and word problems that did not require a lot of computation (Dougherty, Herbert, Edenhurt-Pape & Small, 1980). Additional studies revealed that males are more apt than females at choosing the correct solution strategy and girls are more likely than boys to choose "I don't know" as an answer (See Linn & Petersen, 1986, for a review.)

The female advantage in computation ability exists as early as elementary school, but disappears by age 17. The male advantage on problem-solving is largest in older samples beginning at around age 14 and is consistent with enrollment patterns in more complex courses. Linn and Hyde (1991) report precalculus and calculus classes consisted of 36 percent females in 1978, 45 percent in 1982, and 39 percent in 1986. Thus, boys show an advantage in mathematical ability through late adolescence and this difference increases as students elect to enroll (or not to enroll) in more advanced courses.

Verbal ability.

Hyde and Linn (1988) conducted a meta-analysis of studies that examined gender differences in verbal ability. The overall d was $-.11$, indicating a small advantage for females. When partitioned into different types of verbal ability, their study revealed a small effect for speech production ($d = -.33$), a small male advantage on analogies ($d = .16$), and virtually no effect on vocabulary ($d = -.02$), reading comprehension ($d = -.03$), and essay writing ($d = -.09$). They found no systematic variation with age. When studies were combined to examine historical effects, they found that studies published prior to 1974 yielded an overall d of $-.23$ while studies published since 1974 had a combined d of $-.10$. Hyde and Linn (1988) concluded that gender differences in verbal ability have decreased over time and no longer exist. These results are consistent with the results of other investigators who have also examined time trends (Feingold, 1988; Rosenthal & Rubin, 1982).

Thus, it appears that many of the sex differences once believed to be large and pervasive now tend to be small in size and limited to a few very specific subtypes of ability (the primary exception being mental rotation). Moreover, most sex differences, when found, appear to exist as early as it can be measured rather than emerging at adolescence as claimed by Maccoby and Jacklin (1974). Many have argued that the decrease in sex differences that has occurred during the past 20 years has been faster than would be expected by any change due to biological factors (Linn & Hyde, 1991; Rosenthal & Rubin, 1982). Sex differences in achievement also reveal strong support for sociological factors in influencing sex-related differences in cognitive functioning.

Achievement

It is difficult to differentiate tests of cognitive abilities and aptitude from tests of achievement. Rather than focus on sex differences in achievement tests per se, we focus our attention on other quantifiable achievement outcomes: course grades, years of education completed, and occupational aspirations.

Girls receive higher grades than boys at all grade levels and in all academic areas (National Science Foundation, 1988). Over the last 20 years, women have made considerable gains in their education. In 1990, women earned 53 percent of the baccalaureate degrees, 52 percent of the master degrees, and 36 percent of the doctorates. However, many of the degrees were earned in areas tradition- ally earned by women. Only one-third as many women as men choose to major in the sciences and even fewer become employed in the sciences using their skills (Brush, 1991). In our research following an affluent sample of young adolescents into their senior year in college, we found that males and females were just as likely to be finishing college, but the women aspired to lower status jobs (Dubas & Graber, 1991). We also found that these young women plan to play a larger role in family responsibilities and have lower confidence in attaining their (already lower) work expectations (Camarena, Stemmler & Petersen, in press). Thus, despite no differences between males and females in college com- pletion, women are still not aspiring to be as successful as men in the world of work.

Cognitive Development

A rather different way of viewing cognitive functioning was introduced by Jean Piaget. He viewed cognition not as a set of abilities that increase quantita- tively with the development of the child but rather as a transformation of thinking through qualitatively different cognitive stages. During young adolescence, young people develop the capacity for formal operational thought, that is, the ability to think abstractly (Inhelder & Piaget, 1958). Many, though not all, tests of formal operations show dramatic sex-differences, with boys two to four times more likely than girls to show evidence of formal capacity (Dulit, 1972). Meehan (1984) conducted a meta-analysis of more recent studies of sex differences in formal operational thought. Studies were classified into three categories of scien- tific reasoning: propositional logic, combinatorial reasoning, and proportional reasoning.

Propositional reasoning tasks usually reflect the ability to identify variables and systematically formulate and test hypotheses. Examples of propositional reasoning tasks include the law of floating bodies and bending rods (Inhelder & Piaget, 1958). Combinatorial reasoning tasks require the individual to generate all possible combinations of a given set of elements. Tasks that Inhelder and Piaget (1958) describe as falling into this category include colorless chemicals and colored tokens. Proportional reasoning tasks primarily reflect the ability to conduct four transformations—identity, negation, reciprocity, and correla- tive—on binary operations. Examples of these tasks include equilibrium in a balance, and the projection-of-shadows test. Meehan (1984) reported that moder- ate, reliable sex differences on proportional reasoning tasks were found ($d = .48$), while sex differences on propositional logic and combinatorial reasoning were small ($d = .22$ for propositional logic and $d = .10$ for combinations) and unreliable. No differences were found between studies with younger (12- to 17-year-olds) and older (18+ year-olds) subjects, suggesting that the size of the effect is consistent across adolescence.

FACTORS INFLUENCING THE DEVELOPMENT OF SEX-RELATED DIFFERENCES IN COGNITIVE FUNCTIONING

There are several possible factors which might influence cognitive functioning: timing of puberty, hormones, socialization, and educational experiences, to name four. The earlier belief that gender differences in cognitive abilities emerged at adolescence (Maccoby & Jacklin, 1974) is no longer held. Much of the research following Maccoby and Jacklin's review focused on identifying factors relevant to the divergence between boys and girls. Because puberty is coincident with adolescence, many researchers believed the physical changes during this stage of life might play some role in the development of gender differences. The mechanism through which timing of puberty might influence cognitive abilities was through either brain organization, hormones, or socialization, or some combination of the three. We review the most current hypotheses for the development of sex-related differences in cognitive functioning and present the evidence for and against their support.

Timing of Puberty

Waber (1976, 1977) proposed that timing of puberty might affect profiles of cognitive ability, with early maturers showing higher verbal relative to spatial ability, while later maturers would show the opposite profile. She proposed that the mechanism through which timing affects cognition was through brain lateralization. At that time it was believed that brain lateralization continued until puberty, and more complete lateralization was associated with better spatial ability. Therefore, in early maturers, the brain would be less lateralized, resulting in higher verbal, relative to spatial, skills. Late maturers would be more lateralized, resulting in higher spatial, relative to verbal, skills. Because males on the average mature two years later than females, timing of puberty might explain sex differences in cognitive abilities.

Waber's data comparing early and late maturers supported her hypothesis about laterality, but only among her older subjects (13-year-old girls and 16-year-old boys), not the younger ones (10-year-old girls and 13-year-old boys). Late maturers, both younger and older, were better at spatial tasks than earlier maturing girls and boys, but no differences were found between the timing groups on a verbal fluency measure.

There is now controversy over whether brain lateralization develops maturationally (e.g., Kinsbourne & Hiscock, 1977). In addition, several attempts to replicate an association between lateralization and spatial ability have been inconsistent (e.g., Newcombe & Bandura, 1983; Newcombe, Dubas & Baenninger, 1989; see Newcombe, 1982, for a discussion of earlier work) and more specific localization of function and myelineation of the brain are currently being investigated (see Gibson & Petersen, 1991).

Moreover, in a recent meta-analysis examining the literature on studies of the association between timing of puberty and cognitive abilities, Newcombe and Dubas (1987) concluded that the relationship between timing of puberty and spatial ability is small and unreliable; no relationship between timing and verbal fluency was found. When spatial tests were classified using the criteria of Linn and Petersen (1985), the strongest association was found for spatial visualization tests, where no consistent sex differences are typically found. Thus, it seems unlikely that timing of puberty could explain gender differences.

Hormones

Given the clear influence of the gonadal hormones on somatic and other biological features differentiating males and females (Petersen & Taylor, 1978), researchers have begun to examine whether hormones are related to cognitive abilities.

Petersen (1976) found evidence that the gonadal hormones might be involved with the pattern of cognitive abilities showing sex differences. In her study, adolescent males and females with more androgynous somatic characteristics showed the typical "masculine" cognitive pattern of spatial superiority relative to verbal performance (as measured by fluent production). Both males and females, with somatic characteristics more stereotypic for their respective sexes, showed the usual "feminine" pattern of verbal superiority relative to spatial performance. In a study relating circulating levels of testosterone to spatial ability in men, Shute, Pellegrino, Hubert & Reynolds (1983) found that those with moderate levels of testosterone showed the highest spatial ability. This and other research with males suggests that hormonal environment may play some role. (See Petersen, 1978, and Newcombe & Baenninger, 1989, for reviews).

More recent research examining the role of hormones in influencing cognition is just beginning to be examined in adolescence. The mechanisms through which hormones may influence cognition need to be further specified and refined. Research on whether an association between hormone levels and cognition at adolescence or adulthood reflects activational or organizational effects needs to be conducted using prospective longitudinal studies. JoAnne Finnegan and colleagues measured prenatal amniotic hormone levels in a sample of Canadian youngsters and will be following these children into adolescence (Finnegan, Bartleman & Wong, 1987).

Socialization and Experience

As an alternative to biological explanations for sex differences in cognitive functioning, a variety of work has been conducted examining the effects of experiential and socialization processes on the development of individual differences in cognitive abilities. (Although each of these factors is discussed in isolation, it is very possible that they interact. For example, it is possible that activity preferences are related to prenatal hormone exposure.) Most of this work has focused on spatial and mathematical ability, with some work done on scientific reasoning and verbal ability. Nash (1978) has hypothesized that socialization influences cognitive performance first at the level of sex-typing of cognitive tasks; verbal capacity is considered feminine while mathematical proficiencies and spatial tasks are considered masculine. This sex-typing of intellectual domains interacts with the individual's gender identity to produce a particular kind of cognitive performance. For example, a femininely identified girl approaching a masculine task might feel cognitive dissonance and be unmotivated to perform well on the task. On the other hand, a masculine or androgenous girl might approach the task with high motivation and perform well. This hypothesis is supported by studies showing that labeling a task as sex-appropriate results in better performance by students of that sex than when it is labeled as sex inappropriate (Montemayor, 1974; Naditch, 1976). Newcombe, Bandura and Taylor (1983) found that many activities in daily life found to be related to spatial ability are often sex-typed as masculine. Moreover, Baenninger and Newcombe (1989) found participation in spatial activities to be related to spatial ability.

A variety of studies were conducted to examine whether the possession of sex role personality characteristics was related to specific cognitive abilities. Sex-role personality characteristics have been primarily divided into two dimensions—masculinity and femininity. Masculinity refers to the possession of personality traits characterized by independence, instrumentality, and competitiveness. Femininity refers to the possession of personality traits characterized by expressiveness, sensitivity to the needs of others, and emotionality. Signorella and Jamison (1986) conducted a meta-analysis of this literature and found no relationship between sex role identity and performance on verbal tasks, whereas complicated relationships for spatial and mathematical abilities were found.

Among spatial tasks, results differed by type of task. For mental rotation tasks, male and female adolescents and adults who described themselves as more masculine performed better than those who described themselves as less masculine. For spatial perception tasks, a more complex relationship was found. For adolescent and adult women, lower femininity was associated with higher ability. For adolescent males, higher femininity was associated with higher ability, although for adult males no relationship with femininity was found. For adult males, higher masculinity was associated with better performance. For spatial visualization tasks, higher masculinity was related to better performance for females only; no relationship was found for males.

Results for mathematical ability were similar to those for spatial perception tasks. For adolescent and adult females, higher masculinity and lower femininity were associated with higher mathematical ability. For adolescent males, better performance was associated with more feminine scores. For men, better performance was associated with more masculine scores. Dubas, Crockett, and Petersen (1990) examined whether sex differences in mental rotation ability would be removed statistically if sex-role personality traits were controlled. Even though there were large sex differences in masculinity and femininity, sex differences in mental rotation still remained after entering sex-role characteristics in a regression equation. These results cast doubt on the hypothesis that sex-role personality characteristics can explain gender differences in spatial ability.

The same sort of cognitive consistency principle may be applied to course taking. An androgenous or masculinely-identified girl may be comfortable taking courses labeled as male, whereas a femininely identified girl may find it cognitively dissonant to take such courses. Females are much less likely than males to enroll in advanced mathematics or science courses. The behavior of adolescent girls may be based more on fears of negative social consequences if they achieve. For example, Fox, Tobin, and Brody (1978) cite several studies in which adolescent girls express fear of negative peer pressure, particularly from boys, if they were to pursue advanced mathematics courses and do well. Moreover, in our affluent sample of youngsters followed during early adolescence, we found that there are some girls whose self-esteem is enhanced when their achievement declines (Roberts, Sarigiani, Petersen & Newman, 1990).

Further evidence of the importance of sex-role appropriateness to performance by early adolescents is reviewed by Nash (1978) and more recently supported by the work of Eccles and her colleagues (1983; Eccles, Adler & Meece, 1984) on math achievement and career choice. Nash (1978) cites evidence that the differential value attached by young people to performing sex-appropriate versus sex-inappropriate tasks is related to their actual performance on these tasks. In addition, the levels of performance considered satisfactory on these tasks are related to actual performance. Parsons, Ruble, Hodges, and Small (1976) cite three socialization mechanisms which might lead to performance affected by sex-role stereotypes. Parents and teachers convey expectations consistent with stereotypes. Similarly, these socializers respond differently to the achievements of boys and girls. Finally, males are more likely to attribute success to internal factors (e.g., ability, hard work) and failure to external factors (e.g., luck, task

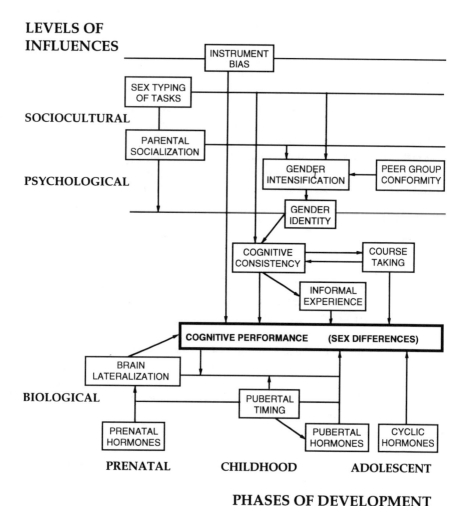

LEVELS OF INFLUENCES

SOCIOCULTURAL

PSYCHOLOGICAL

BIOLOGICAL

INSTRUMENT BIAS

SEX TYPING OF TASKS

PARENTAL SOCIALIZATION

GENDER INTENSIFICATION

PEER GROUP CONFORMITY

GENDER IDENTITY

COGNITIVE CONSISTENCY

COURSE TAKING

INFORMAL EXPERIENCE

COGNITIVE PERFORMANCE (SEX DIFFERENCES)

BRAIN LATERALIZATION

PUBERTAL TIMING

PRENATAL HORMONES

PUBERTAL HORMONES

CYCLIC HORMONES

PRENATAL   **CHILDHOOD**   **ADOLESCENT**

PHASES OF DEVELOPMENT

FIGURE 2.2. *A model for biopsychosocial influences on sex differences in cognition. (Adapted from Petersen, 1979.)*

difficulty), while females attribute success to external factors and failure to internal ones.

AN INTEGRATED HYPOTHESIS FOR THE DEVELOPMENT OF SEX-RELATED DIFFERENCES IN COGNITIVE FUNCTIONING

Figure 2.2 presents a model for the development of sex-related differences in cognitive functioning as proposed by Petersen (1979) in the first edition of this volume. Three levels of influence are specified: sociocultural, psychological, and biological. The weights of each of the factors are probably different for each particular cognitive outcome. Moreover, this model probably explains more within-sex variation than between-sex variation. It is possible that the important influence of gonadal hormones is prenatal. Prenatal hormones may organize the brain to become more strongly lateralized if the individual is male, or more bilateralized if the individual if female. Pubertal hormones may have an activation effect permitting the potentials organized earlier to become manifest.

At the same time, there are clear socialization and experiential factors influencing sex-related differences and individual differences in cognitive functioning. Gender identity may be more important at this time than during earlier stages because of the clear somatic appearance as a member of one sex versus the other. This effect would heighten the importance of gender identity in the cognitive consistency paradigm discussed earlier. Furthermore, because the major developmental task at adolescence is the formation of identity, gender identity may be closer to societal stereotypes during adolescence, becoming more flexible and individual in post-adolescent years.

CONCLUSIONS

Much of the evidence discussed in this chapter indicated that the size of sex-related differences in cognitive functioning has decreased considerably over the last few decades. There are no longer differences between males and females for verbal ability, spatial visualization, and mathematics computation. Males are found to have a large advantage over females on mental rotation tasks and on the math SAT. Smaller male advantages are also still found on spatial perception tasks and proportional reasoning. The model we present that could explain sex-related and individual differences in cognitive tasks takes an interactional approach between sociocultural, psychological, and biological factors. There is substantial overlap in the performance of males and females, far greater than the biological similarity of the sexes. Moreover, there is more within-sex variability than between-sex variablity.

Prior to adolescence, differential socialization pressures on girls focus mainly on personality variables such as dependence and activity. With adolescence, however, pressures related to sex roles and future roles such as child-rearing become more important, while educational success begins to recede in importance. Even today, girls get a strong message about what level of achievement is appropriate and in what areas. The media continue to portray women in stereotypic roles.

Even though many of the cognitive differences between boys and girls are decreasing, the gender differences in occupational prestige and wages have not kept pace with these declines. Moreover, women who do work must also bear the primary burden for household tasks and child care. Individuals concerned with the development of girls must also focus their attention on the development of boys who are willing to take a more egalitarian role in their own families.

REFERENCES

Anastasi, A. 1937. *Differential Psychology: Individual and Group Differences in Behavior.* New York: MacMillan.

Baenninger, M. & Newcombe, N. 1989. The role of experience in spatial test performance: A meta-analysis. *Sex Roles*, 20:327-344.

Brush, S. G. 1991. Women in science and engineering. *Amer. Scientist*, 79:404-419.

Camarena, P. M., Stemmler, M., & Petersen, A. C. (in press). The gender-differential significance of work and family: Developmental perspectives. In R. K. Silbereisen, Ed., *Adolescence in Context: The Interplay of Family, Peers, School, and Work.*

Cohen, J. 1969. *Statistical Power Analysis for the Behavioral Sciences.* New York: Academic.

Dougherty, K., Herbert, M., Edenhurt-Pape, M., & Small, A. 1980. *Sex-Related Differences in Several Aspects of Mathematics Achievement: Grades 2-5.* Manuscript. St. Louis: CERMEL.

Dubas, J. S., Crockett, L. J., & Petersen, A. C. 1990. *A longitudinal investigation of sex differences in cognitive abilities during early adolescence.* Manuscript submitted for publication.

Dubas, J. S. & Graber, J. A. 1991. Adolescent and concurrent predictors of young-adult career aspirations. Poster presented at the Biennial Meetings of the Society for Research in Child Development. Seattle, Washington.

Dulit, E. 1972. Adolescent thinking a la Piaget: The formal stage. *J. of Youth/Adol.*, 4:281-301.

Eccles, J., Adler, T. F., Futterman, R., Goff, S. B., Kaczala, C. M., Meece, J. L., & Midgley, C. 1983. Expectations, values and academic behaviors. In J. T. Spence, Ed., *Achievement and Achievement Motivation.* San Francisco: Freeman.

Eccles, J., Adler, T. F., & Meece, J. L. 1984. Sex differences in achievement: A test of alternate theories. *J. Person./Social Psych.*, 46:26-43.

Feingold, A. 1988. Cognitive gender differences are disappearing. *Am. Psychol.*, 43:95-103.

Finnegan, J., Bartleman, B., & Wong, P. Y. 1987, April. A window for the study of prenatal hormone influences on postnatal development. Paper presented at the biennial meetings of the Society for Research on Child Development, Baltimore, MD.

Fox, L. H., Tobin, D., & Brody, L. 1978. Sex role socialization and achievement in mathematics. In M. A. Wittig & A. C. Petersen, Eds., *Sex-related Differences in Cognitive Functioning: Developmental Issues.* New York: Academic.

Gibson, K. R. & Petersen, A. C., Eds. 1991. *Brain Maturation and Cognitive Development: Comparative and Cross-cultural Perspectives.* New York: Aldine de Gruyter.

Hill, J. P. & Lynch, M. E. 1983. The intensification of gender-related role expectations during early adolescence. In J. Brooks-Gunn & A. C. Petersen, Eds., *Girls at Puberty: Biological and Psychosocial Perspectives.* New York: Plenum.

Hyde, J. S. 1981. How large are cognitive gender differences? A meta-analysis using omega squared and *d. Amer. Psychol.*, 36:892-901.

Hyde, J. S. 1990. Meta-analysis and the psychology of gender differences. *Signs: J. Women Culture/Soc.*, 16:1-19.

Hyde, J. S. & Linn, M. C. 1988. Gender differences in verbal ability: A meta-analysis. *Psychol. Bull.*, 104:53-69.

Inhelder, B. & Piaget, J. 1958. *The Growth of Logical Thinking from Childhood to Adolescence.* New York: Basic.

Keating, D. P. 1990. Adolescent thinking. In S. S. Feldman & G. R. Elliott, Eds., *At the Threshold: The Developing Adolescent.* Cambridge, MA: Harvard.

Kinsbourne, M. & Hiscock, M. 1977. Does cerebral dominance develop? In S. J. Segalowitz & F. A. Guber, Eds., *Language Development and Neurological Theory.* New York: Academic.

Linn, M. C. & Hyde, J. S. 1991. Trends in cognitive and psychosocial gender differences. In R. M. Lerner, A. C. Petersen, & J. Brooks-Gunn, Eds., *Encyclopedia of Adolescence.* New York: Garland.

Linn, M. C. & Petersen, A. C. 1985. Emergence and characterization of sex differences in spatial ability. *Child Develop.*, 56:1479-1498.

Linn, M. C. & Petersen, A. C. 1986. A meta-analysis of gender differences in spatial ability: Implications for mathematics and science achievement. In J. S. Hyde & M. C. Linn, Eds., *The Psychology of Gender: Advances through Meta-analyses.* Baltimore: Johns Hopkins.

Maccoby, E. E. 1966. *The Development of Sex Differences.* Stanford, CA: Stanford.

Maccoby, E. E. & Jacklin, C. N. 1974. *The Psychology of Sex Differences.* Stanford: Stanford.

Meehan, A. 1984. A meta-analysis of sex differences in formal operational thought. *Child Develop.*, 55:1110-1124.

Montemayor, R. 1974. Children's performance in a game and their attraction to it as a function of sex-typed labels. *Child Develop.*, 45:152-156.

Naditch, S. F. 1976. Sex differences in field dependence: The role of social influence. Presented at the annual meeting of the American Psychological Association, Washington, DC.

Nash, S. C. 1978. Sex role as a mediator of intellectual functioning. In M. A. Wittig & A. C. Petersen, Eds., *Sex-related Differences in Cognitive Functioning: Developmental Issues.* New York: Academic.

National Science Foundation 1988. *Women and Minorities in Science and Engineering.* Washington, DC: National Science Foundation.

Newcombe, N. 1982. Sex-related differences in spatial ability: Problems and gaps in current approaches. In M. Potegal, Ed., *Spatial Abilities: Development and Physiological Foundations.* New York: Academic.

Newcombe, N. & Baenninger, M. A. 1989. Biological change and cognitive ability in adolescence. In G. Adams, R. Montemayor, & T. Gullota, Eds., *Biology of Adolescent Behavior and Development.* Beverly Hills, CA: Sage.

Newcombe, N. & Bandura, M. M. 1983. Effects of age at puberty on spatial ability in girls: A question of mechanism. *Develop. Psychol.*, 19:215-224.

Newcombe, N., Bandura, M. M., & Taylor, D. G. 1983. Sex differences in spatial ability and spatial activities. *Sex Roles*, 9:377-386.

Newcombe, N. & Dubas, J. S. 1987. Individual differences in cognitive ability: Are they related to timing of puberty? In R. M. Lerner & T. T. Foch, Eds., *Biological-psychosocial Interactions in Early Adolescence*. Hillsdale, NJ: Erlbaum.

Newcombe, N., Dubas, J. S., & Baenninger, M. A. 1989. Associations of timing of puberty, spatial ability, and lateralization in adult women. *Child Develop.*, 60:246-254.

Parsons, J. C., Ruble, D. N., Hodges, K. L., & Small, A. W. 1976. Cognitive developmental factors in emerging sex differences in achievement-related expectancies. *J. Social Issues*, 32:47-62.

Petersen, A. C. 1976. Physical androgyny and cognitive functioning in adolescence. *Develop. Psychol.*, 12:524-533.

Petersen, A. C. 1978. Hormones and cognitive functioning in normal development. In M. A. Wittig & A. C. Petersen, Eds., *Sex-related Differences in Cognitive Functioning: Developmental Issues*. New York: Academic.

Petersen, A. C. 1979. Differential cognitive development in adolescent girls. In M. Sugar, Ed., *Female Adolescent Development*. New York: Brunner/Mazel.

Petersen, A. C. 1988. Adolescent development. *Annual Rev. Psychol.*, 39:583-607.

Petersen, A. C. & Taylor, B. 1978. Puberty: Biological change and psychological adaptation. In J. Adelson, Ed., *Handbook of Adolescent Psychology*. New York: Wiley.

Roberts, L. R., Sarigiani, P. A., Petersen, A. C., & Newman, J. L. 1990. Gender differences in the relationship between achievement and self-image during early adolescence. *Journal of Early Adolescence*, 10:159-175.

Rosenthal, R. & Rubin, D. C. 1982. Further meta-analytic procedures for assessing cognitive gender differences. *J. Educat. Psychol.*, 74:708-712.

Shute, V. J., Pellegrino, J. W., Hubert, L., & Reynolds, R. W. 1983. The relationship between androgen levels and human spatial abilities. *Bull. Psychonomic Soc.*, 21:465-468.

Signorella, M. L. & Jamison, W. J. 1986. Masculinity, femininity, androgeny, and cognitive performance: A meta-analysis. *Psychol. Bull.*, 100:207-228.

Steinberg, L. 1990. Autonomy, conflict, and harmony in the family relationship. In S. S. Feldman & G. R. Elliott, Eds., *At the Threshold: The Developing Adolescent*. Cambridge, MA: Harvard.

Thurstone, L. L. 1938. *Primary Mental Abilities*. Chicago: Chicago.

Tyler, L. E. 1947. *The Psychology of Human Differences*. New York: Appleton-Century-Crofts.

Vandenberg, S. G. & Kuse, A. R. 1978. Mental rotations: A group test of three-dimensional spatial visualization. *Percept. Motor Skills*, 47:599-604.

Waber, D. P. 1976. Sex differences in cognition: A function of maturational rates. *Science*, 192:572-574.

Waber, D. P. 1977. Sex differences in mental abilities, hemispheric lateralization and rate of physical growth at adolescence. *Develop. Psychol.*, 13:29-38.

Wooley, H. T. 1910. A review of the recent literature on the psychology of sex. *Psychol. Bulletin*, 7:335-342.

PART II
PSYCHODYNAMICS

3 Female Adolescence: Toward a Separate Line of Female Development

Joan J. Zilbach, M.D.

INTRODUCTION

"I look at my face in the glass and see a halfborn woman." (Rich, 1978, p. 41)

"—a girl in the years of puberty becomes quiet within and begins to think about the wonders that are happening to her body.

"I experience that, too . . .

"I think that what is happening to me is so wonderful, not only what can be seen on my body, but all that is taking place inside.

"Each time I have a period—and that has only been three times—I have the feeling that in spite of all the pain, unpleasantness, and nastiness, I have a sweet secret, and that is why, although it is nothing but a nuisance to me in a way, I always long for the time that I shall feel that secret within me again" (Anne Frank, 14 yrs, 6 mos, pp. 117-119, In Dalsimer, 1986).

What does the young "halfborn" adolescent girl see in the glass? She "sees" in adolescence, as she does throughout her life, with her feminine mind and body.

The adolescent girl is "halfborn" at puberty. Adolescence occurs between her early childhood years, on the way to womanhood but not yet having arrived. Puberty ushers in early adolescence, and as late adolescence wanes, adulthood begins. Work, both outside and inside the home, job and career, and potentially motherhood loom ahead. In the second quotation, Anne Frank, at age 14 and six months, poignantly expresses her early adolescent experience: ". . . what is happening to me is so wonderful, not only what can be seen on my body, but all that is taking place inside." This chapter has a particular focus on the "wonderful . . . inside" happenings of feminine development in adolescence.

Turbulence, discontent, rebellion, and the problematic tortuous paths of adolescent identity formation have characterized the descriptions in the psychoanalytic literature on adolescence. One classic and oft repeated descriptive statement was made by Anna Freud (1958), who characterized adolescence as a period of craziness. Recent and still classical psychoanalytic formulations emphasize redoing earlier separation-individuation processes and the "second chance" or "second individuation process" (Blos, 1980) that is said to occur in adolescence. These concepts are based on classical psychoanalytic theory, which has changed, developed, and modified some aspects of basic theory and developmental formulations.

However, conceptions of female development have remained essentially unchanged for many decades. In contrast to an emphasis on troublesome difficulties, separation-individuation problems, and other female deficiencies, recent formulations of feminine development emphasize interdependence, mutuality, affiliation, connection, and a female "relational" self (Gilligan, 1982; Gilligan, Lyons & Hanmer, 1990; Miller, 1984; Jordan & Surrey, 1986). These theoretical formulations of feminine development are based on the concept of a separate line of development with unique female developmental characteristics. Other authors emphasize concepts of primary femininity, early gender identity development, and the ongoing influence of the mother-daughter relationship (Chodorow, 1978; Kaplan & Klein, 1985; Notman, Klein, Jordan & Zilbach, 1991; Notman, Zilbach, Miller & Nadelson, 1986; Stoller, 1976; Zilbach, 1987, 1990).

The widening psychosocial world of adolescents and their families has been characterized as "separation" or "breaking away" from family rather than as loosening, expansion, and differentiation of the goals of the adolescent. The oft heard identity question, "What will I become," is seen as a question of impending rupture with the family rather than differences from the family. Even future motherhood is considered as imposing restrictions and limitations for the adult female (Deutsch, 1945; Gleason, 1985; Herman & Lewis, 1986).

With ongoing psychological development of femininity in the center of our formulations, we will emphasize continuity, expansion, and loosening of ties in adolescence rather than separation, autonomy, and independence. This requires a major shift in our thinking. For example, in this chapter the vicissitudes of the mother-daughter relationship will be regarded as just as significant in adolescence as the daughter's increasing erotic attraction to, and relationship with, her father. This requires a consideration and integration of continuity and change in the girl's relationship to her mother as a major factor in adolescent development, rather than as a "breaking" of ties in the multifaceted and ongoing mother-daughter relationship.

The focus will remain on central processes of feminine development in adolescence as they are explicated throughout this chapter. The term "adolescent female" will be used throughout this chapter rather than "girl" or "young woman." The adolescent female is no longer a "girl," nor is she yet a "woman." No intermediate term is available, and so "adolescent female" seems the best choice at present. "Female" is a term used by many authors, specifically for the biological aspects of women. However, as used by this author, "adolescent female" is a term which goes beyond biology towards a broader biopsychosocial approach.

In order to discuss adolescence, we must lay a groundwork first defining basic concepts and then reviewing early female development. I will return to female adolescent development and discuss sexuality, identity formation, and the psychological importance of the development of a new and uniquely female organ, the breasts, and a unique event, menarche and the processes of menstruation. But now I will briefly review the classical Freudian view of early female development.

Classical Freudian Theory of Early Female Development

Early female development as presented in the following sections is significantly different from the classical Freudian view of female development. Since the latter can be found in many publications, only a brief summary will be presented.

S. Freud postulated that the first three years of psychic life were the same, i.e., "masculine," for both sexes:

> The third phase is that known as the phallic one, which is, as it were, a forerunner of the final form taken by sexual life and already much resembles it. It is to be noted that it is not the genitals of both sexes that play a part at this stage, but only the male ones (the phallus). The female genitals long remain unknown. . . . (Freud, 1938/40, p. 154)

Divergence occurs only with and after the discovery of anatomical differences. At that point, the little girl discovers her lack of penis and that discovery becomes a central organizer of subsequent female development. Her lack, or inferiority, becomes the bedrock of female psychosexual development. This conviction remained unchanged, as indicated in the quotation just cited from Freud's "Outline of Psychoanalysis," published posthumously (Freud, 1938, 1940).

SEPARATE LINES OF DEVELOPMENT

Everywoman is significantly different from everyman from conception to the end of the life course. An increasing recognition of these differences had led to the formulation of the concept of separate lines of development, which has permitted female psychological development to emerge from within a singular and primarily masculine delineation of psychoanalytic concepts of early development. (The latter part of the statement refers to classical "Freudian" psychoanalytic theory of development that has just been summarized.)

The "voice," character, and vicissitudes of female development are strikingly different from male development. These differences, as such, are not the subject of this chapter. Thus, masculine development will not be discussed, since the focus will be on female adolescent development.

In recent years, as psychoanalytic developmental research has focused on direct observation of infants and children, three developmental concepts have become particularly germane to the understanding and further delineation of separate paths of development. These concepts are primary femininity, gender identity, and core gender identity; they distinguish and define various components of the sense of being female (and male). In addition, as development proceeds, they are useful for the description not only of behavior but also of inner states of being feminine. From here on, I will not continue to say "female and male." As mentioned earlier, my focus is on being female, and aspects that are also relevant to being male are beyond the scope of this chapter.

Primary Femininity and "Active Engulfment"

The concept of primary femininity refers to the early unconflicted sense of being female and contains several elements: primitive female body awareness, early imitation and identification with mother, and a cognitive component of "knowing what goes with being a girl." This is a definition originally used by Stoller (1976) to fill in the missing gap, the "empty space" in female development in the early months and years before the occurrence of the so-called "Oedipal complex." However, as used in this chapter, consideration of the development of primary femininity goes beyond the original statement and makes the concept relevant to all phases of female development. The psychological manifestations of primary femininity begin in the earliest postnatal moments, if not before, and continue throughout female development undergoing manifold changes, expansions, and diminutions.

This aspect of female selfhood, or primary femininity, has a central component based on the early inner psychological existence of female body awareness. Early awareness of vaginal secretions and of the uterus as a container contributes to this sense of a female body (Kestenberg, 1968). By the middle of the second year female body awareness in primitive body representations has become distinct. Infant researchers report, with general agreement, that between 18 months and three years, the little girl consolidates an irreversible sense of female self (Kestenberg, 1968; Parens, 1990; Parens, Stern, & Kramer, 1976; Roiphe & Galenson, 1981; Stoller, 1976, 1980; Tyson & Tyson, 1990).

The concept of primary femininity defines a central aspect of femininity and the feminine self. However, the term primary femininity as a descriptor is rather bland and nondescript. The term "active engulfment" has been used by this author to describe and denote primary or core femininity and central female life focus. "Active engulfment" describes a center of female psychological activity. In its earliest form and continuing throughout life, "active engulfment" is a center of pro-creativity which will take many forms in the course of being tamed and civilized (Zilbach, 1987, 1990). The earliest biological form is the engulfing of the sperm by the egg at the moment of fertilization. The sperm does not penetrate; rather the egg surrounds the sperm (Johnson, 1985).*

Core Gender Identity and Gender Identity

Two additional concepts of recent origin will be defined to assist in following the vicissitudes of female psychological development and primary femininity. These additional concepts are core gender identity and gender identity.

The term "gender" itself refers to psychosocial elements as distinct from biological and genetic characteristics. Gender identity is the mixture of masculine and feminine psychological attributes found in every individual, including the membership in a particular biological class, i.e., sex, male or female. It is the inner knowledge of the gender of a particular individual. Core gender identity is the earliest phase of gender identity (Money & Erhardt, 1972; Stoller, 1976). Core gender identity is the first stage of gender identity and becomes the central nexus around which femininity and masculinity, or gender identity, gradually accrue. Core gender identity is the most primitive, conscious sense of belonging to one sex and not to the other (Tyson, 1982). Core gender identity begins at birth (if not before), with designation or gender assignment:

> Observation of children leaves no doubt that as soon as the infant is given a female name she is bombarded with verbal and nonverbal messages which convey a sense of femaleness, as defined in the family. (Kleeman, 1976, p. 13).

The process of gender assignment may begin before birth with the designation of sex of the fetus by prenatal procedures such as amniocentesis. However, the intricacies of prenatal development are beyond the scope of this chapter. For our purposes, we will consider gender designation to begin at the moment of birth, and as the beginning of the development of core gender identity. From the outset, the "messages" of gender assignment include an admixture of psychological, social, and biological attributes.

---

*Female active sexual receptivity in humans appears to be somewhat similar in primates. With primates, active sexual solicitation and receptivity are dependent on the female's age, the dominant female in the cohort, as well as the age and position of the male in the group (Rosenblum, 1990, p. 65). This seems to support the active engulfment concept proposed here.—Editor

Early Development

This review of early development is selective rather than comprehensive, emphasizing two aspects of feminine development: first, the development of femininity, primary femininity, and active engulfment: second, the development of the mother-daughter relationship.

Femininity (at birth or before) develops under the influence of factors that are external to the infant and others that originate within the infant: (1) the effect of hormones and other biological factors within the infant, (2) gender designation/assignment and parental attitudes about gender assignment that are reflected onto the infant, (3) caretaking patterns of handling the infant, and (4) the female infant's developing body awareness.

(1) Hormones and biological factors.

The first group of factors influencing femininity, hormones and other biological influences on femininity, are beyond the scope of this chapter. The second, third, and fourth factors will be discussed below.

(2) Gender designation at birth or before.

Gender designation is particularly important in the formation of the earliest stages of development of primary femininity within the female infant, the earliest sense of being a female (Stoller, 1976).

(3) External/parental caretaking influences.

Gender designation/assignment is followed immediately by ongoing parental attitudes and caretaking patterns. There is a large body of literature on parental attitudes and interactions or caretaking patterns with their infants in the earliest postnatal days and months of infant life. There are striking differences in maternal behavior and attitudes towards their female and male children beginning immediately at birth and continuing in the subsequent months.

Mothers respond initially more to male infants who are more irritable at birth and in the early postnatal period than female infants. Male infants are permitted longer periods of unfettered crying, accompanied by large muscle movements. Female infants are more constrained and contained by their caretaking mothers and others. Female infants are perceived as significantly softer, finer-featured, smaller, and more inattentive than male infants. These observations were studied in one-day-old interactions where these differences were not objectively present (Rubin, Provenzano & Luria, 1974). In another study (Will, Self & Datan, 1976) using the same six-month-old baby, when the infant was designated as a girl, "she" was handed a doll more frequently than when she was said to be a boy. A toy train was offered to "him" more frequently than a doll. These differences are maintained and increased over the subsequent months.

(4) Female infants' developing body awareness.

Although the female infant's internal experience is unknown, we can speculate about the internal effect of the external influences just discussed. Touching, holding, smiling, vocalizing, and eye-to-eye contact are of critical importance in early bonding with attachment. The attunement of the mother to her female infant is to another who is fundamentally like her. Thus, the beginning of primary femininity is stimulated within the infant as an early inner psychological resonance within her body. There can be little doubt that the female infant responds to these external factors, particularly to the mother's attitudes and caretaking behaviors, although we can only speculate about the characteristics of this response. This resonance is the beginning of the gradually increasing female force of "active engulfment" that will develop over time into the tamed adult female characteristics of affiliation, connection, nurturance, and other aspects of the "caretaking" female self in adulthood.

From the beginning, the mother-female infant interaction is characterized by the processes of "reciprocal identification." The attunement of the mother to her female infant is based on mother's identification with her own mother and with her own infant daughter. The female infant receives these identifications and responds with the development of her side of the "reciprocal identification." This process of primitive reciprocal identificatory interactions is central to the development of primary femininity. The importance of this process is not limited to the early years; rather it is ongoing throughout the life cycle and will be emphasized in the later discussion of adolescence in this chapter. (Details of this process throughout female development will be found in other publications [Zilbach & Notman, in press].)

Core gender identity, beginning at birth and developing under the influence of primary femininity, can be observed in considerable detail and with distinct characteristics within the second year of life. This can be observed in many activities of the two-year-old girl in which she imitates her mother. Little girls preen and doll play increases, along with genital stimulation.

The expression of a wish for a baby becomes evident and has been carefully studied as part of primary femininity (Kleeman, 1976; Parens, 1990; Roiphe & Galenson, 1981). Thus, core gender identity and primary femininity, the early consolidated sense of being female, develop primarily within the continuing dyadic relationship with mother, though other caretakers, including father, contribute to this development.

Core gender identity can be observed clearly by the time a child is walking; it may be irreversible by the age of 18 months. Gender identity becomes secure and with manifold manifestations by the age of four or five.

Early Childhood/First Genital or So-Called "Oedipal" Phase

After the initial establishment and early development of primary femininity, in the next phase there is a surge of genital interest and other manifestations of an upsurge of childhood sexuality. A general increase in the manifestations of sexuality can be observed in the increasing frequency of masturbation and, with less frequency, direct vaginal exploration that occur throughout this period (Clower, 1975; Kestenberg, 1968).

At this period of female development, the term "Oedipal phase" is a serious misnomer. The story of Oedipus is a male myth about the boy's love of his mother and rivalry with his father. In contrast, in this period of female development, the young girl increases her expressions of interest in her father, along with a desire to have her father's baby. The desire to have a baby, like mother, has been established in the previous period of early development and now adds the additional element of the desire to have father's baby. Formulations have focused on the girl's interest in or "turning toward" father, but her increasing identification with mother is as important as her interest in her father.

The "turning towards the father" is assisted by the receptivity of the mother to this development and the little girl's increasing identification with her mother. The manifestations of this identification include all the varied and myriad aspects of being "like mother," along with identifying with mother's relationship with father. It is noteworthy that the wish for the baby is not a substitute for a wish for a penis, but develops from the girl's increasing identification with mother. Envy and turning away from mother occur during this period, assisted by encouragement and love from both parents, as well as by acceptance of her angry and aggressive wishes, primarily directed towards the mother.

In this period, the little girl becomes more exhibitionistic and thus demonstrates her developing femininity as she practices her expanding conception of feminine gender identity and gender roles. Elaboration of a feminine ego ideal is an important aspect of psychic development in this period. The little girl certainly notices and at times envies mother's breasts. The developing female ego ideal includes many aspects of mother, not only mother's breasts but also her intelligence, activity, and general sexuality (Blum, 1976).

The complexity and outcome of this phase will be influenced by many forces, including temperament, cognitive development, and real environmental circumstances of her life. Mother continues to be the little girl's rival for father, while there is also a similarity and coincidence of interest between them. The oft noted female characteristics of affiliation, connection, and cooperation will be present in a nascent form in this developmental period. It will be observed in the growing and continuing identification in the mother-daughter relationship (Gilligan, 1982, 1990; Miller, 1984; Notman, Klein, Jordan & Zilbach, 1991).

Classical psychoanalytic formulations of the "resolution" of this period have emphasized the "shock" of the discovery of the anatomical differences between the sexes and the subsequent development of penis envy as the "potent" factor in the resolution of this period and entry into "latency." The formulation just presented does not rely on this deficit-phallocentric model of female development. Discovery of anatomical difference certainly occurs much earlier, and may or may not produce penis envy (Roiphe & Galenson, 1981).

The resolution of the "triadic" period depends on both parental poles, maternal and paternal. The girl's identification with her mother is as important as her attraction and turning towards her father. This is part of her growing positive feminine identity and what she has inside as part of her female body image rather than representing a deficit-phallic model (Parens, 1990; Tyson, 1982).

Middle Childhood/"Latency"

The next developmental stage, the so-called "latency" period, is not a period of quiescence or "latency," as it was originally designated (Freud, 1905), but rather the overt evidence of sexuality is not as turbulent as it was in the preceding period or will be in adolescence. The ongoing influence of primary femininity/active engulfment produces considerable elaboration and consolidation of gender identity.

The middle childhood girl develops a further array of feminine gender roles which she will carry into and elaborate on in adolescence, and again in adulthood. Same-sex friendships flower during this period, while relationships with important adults, both male and female, will contribute to the structure and content of the developing feminine ego ideal. Sexuality continues, with masturbation and other genital sensations increasingly evident throughout this period (Clower, 1975, 1979).

The importance of the clitoris as a female organ of pleasure becomes more prominent than in earlier periods (Kulish, 1991). Childhood games such as riding horseback on father's knee produce clitoral sexual stimulation. In this period, more active and independent games, such as jumprope and other girls' games, may provide stimulation of the clitoris, at times to orgastic proportions. At the same time, the development of the superego disguises, forbids, or obscures the sexual meaning of these activities (Tyson & Tyson, 1990).

Significant elaboration of the psychological structures of femininity occurs in latency. The body image and female body awareness are of particular importance and contribute significantly to developments in adolescence which we will discuss in the next section.

FEMALE ADOLESCENT DEVELOPMENT

There is no doubt, even to the casual observer, of the upsurge of sexuality with its myriad biopsychological manifestations in adolescence. Other central aspects include major changes in identity formation and consolidation by late adolescence. The continuing expansion into the larger world, which is accompanied by loosening and expansion of ties to families and others, a process which has started much earlier, has received considerable attention in the adolescent literature (Blos, 1980; A. Freud, 1958; Offer, 1969).

It is to be noted that the adolescent literature is based primarily on studies and data of adolescent males. Gilligan, et al. (1990) noted, ''As the *1980 Handbook of Adolescent Psychology* wryly observed: 'Adolescent girls have simply not been much studied' '' (Gilligan, et al., 1990, p. 1). Recently there have been studies of adolescent females that contribute considerably to our understanding (Gilligan, Lyons & Hanmer, 1990).

Though adolescent development contains more than sex, the so-called sexuality of adolescence is complex, including the adolescent version of primary femininity/ active engulfment and also the adolescent modifications of gender identity. Underlying female adolescent sexual activity is her desire to ''take in'' as an adolescent version of ''active engulfment.'' This surrounding, containing, and taking-in is in distinct contrast to the adolescent male's phallic desires and expressions of thrusting and penetration.

Adolescent female surrounding and taking-in is active and forceful and becomes more sexually focused than in earlier developmental periods. She is not merely a passive partner for the ''sexual scoring'' of the adolescent male. The active desire to take in and surround describes adolescent female sexuality more adequately than the usual description of being ''penetrated.'' Painful and wounding aspects of adolescent female sexuality are often emphasized. However, the central feminine characteristics of the expression of adolescent active engulfment are not adequately characterized by such a painful emphasis or by being penetrated. Penetration is, of course, part of female experience of intercourse; but by itself such a description has a strong and primarily phallic component. This is in contrast to describing the female experience as taking-in and containing or ''actively engulfing'' the penis. The entire genital apparatus and female body, including breasts, not only the vagina, is part of, and participates actively in, female adolescent sexuality.

Breasts

Sometimes, when I lie in bed at night, I have a terrible desire to feel my breasts and to listen to the quiet, rhythmic beat of my heart. I already had these kinds of feelings subconsciously before I came here, because I remember that once when I slept with a girlfriend, I had a strong desire to kiss her, and that I did so. I could not help being terribly inquisitive over her body, for she always kept it hidden from me. I asked whether, as proof of our friendship, we should feel one another's breasts, but she refused. I go into ecstasies when I see the naked figure of a woman, such as Venus, for example. It strikes me as so wonderful and exquisite, that I have difficulty in stopping the tears rolling down my cheeks . . ." (Anne Frank, quoted in Dalsimer, 1986, pp. 116-117)

The exquisite wonder of the changes in the young girl's body as she develops breasts is a striking and oft-neglected aspect of her feminine adolescent development. In early adolescence, primed by earlier pubertal changes, sexual stirrings are stimulated by the early budding of breast development. These are new! Girls eagerly await the full flowering of their breasts and watch each other's breast development very carefully. The existence of these new organs is marked by the female rite of the acquisition of the first bra. The girl whose development lags behind her peer group anxiously desires to join them. Comparisons with mother and others are made frequently. As her breasts grow larger, they become part of the girl's female self and contain an estimate of her own attractiveness.

This female development of breasts is quite different from the pubertal male penile and testicular changes. These male organs have been present throughout life, though certainly the adolescent changes are important. The girl, in her earlier development, has seen and experienced her mother's breasts but has had none of her own. As mentioned, the acquisition of her first bra is an important "rîte du passage" to be noted as unique in marking the recognition of breasts in female development.

One of the classical psychoanalytic concepts of adolescence that is frequently used as explanatory is the "second chance" or second individuation process (Blos, 1980). Though perhaps relevant to other aspects of development, this concept is noted here in order to emphasize and differentiate the unique aspects of feminine adolescent development. Breast development, menarche, and subsequent menstruation are not "second chances"—these are firsts!

The direct nurturing function of breasts as an organ will become more active in adulthood, when motherhood is achieved. In recent studies of adolescents, there is some data to indicate that attractiveness is more important to adolescent girls than to boys. This may be a manifestation of the importance of the development of this new organ, along with other factors (American Association of University Women, 1991). Adolescents, both male and female, are intrigued by the physical attributes of the same and other sex. As captured in essence by one author, "Adolescent girls visually undress boys routinely, just as the reverse happens, but girls keep this a secret among themselves" (Sugar, 1990, p. 3).

Menarche and Menses

The menarche, or first menstrual period, is another unique female event which does not have any previous versions in female development—it is also a significant first. The onset of menses contributes to the ongoing development of primary femininity and in particular marks the presence of a female organ, the uterus/womb. The beautiful description by Anne Frank deserves our attention:

> What is happening to me is so wonderful, and not only what can be seen on my body, but all that is taking place inside. I never discuss myself with anybody: that is why I have to talk to myself about them.
>
> Each time I have a period—and that has only been three times—I have the feeling that in spite of all the pain, unpleasantness, and nastiness, I have a sweet secret, and that is why, although it is nothing but a nuisance to me, I always long for the time that I shall feel that secret within me again. (Dalsimer, 1986, p. 117)

Anne Frank, in this passage, refers to her "sweet secret . . . within" along with the references to what can be seen on her body. She is likely referring to her awareness of earlier body changes, including newly curved hips, breasts, and pubic hair. For many years, the popular expressions used to denote menstruation, such as "the curse" and "monthly sickness," reflected a predominantly negative view of menstruation. Anne Frank's "sweet secret within" and the term "I have my friend" have been added to the vocabulary of young girls as cultural and other attitudes towards menstruation have changed in a positive direction.

The female center of procreativity has been defined earlier as primary femininity fueled by active engulfment. Menstruation as a biopsychosociological process adds significantly to the adolescent development of primary femininity. Though the little girl has had some awareness of female inner organs, menses focuses upon and enhances the adolescent's awareness of her uterus and the other associated reproductive organs.

In addition, menarche and the menstrual process create a new phase in the girl's identification with her mother. In many instances it is mother's instructions about menarche which have induced the attitudes with which menarche is received by the girl. However, it is not only the information but the underlying reflection of mother's feminine self-image that is important in the mother-daughter interaction around menstruation.

Menstruation also marks the establishment of reproduction as a real possibility for girls. Procreativity and reproductive potential are usually emphasized in discussions of menstruation. The emphasis in this chapter is on the changes in feminine body image and feminine expansion of the ego ideal to include the reproductive potential. This is further enlarged, particularly in late adolescence and, of course, in adulthood, if motherhood is attained.

Other Aspects of Adolescence

Adolescence is a developmental period of further expansion of relationships outside the family and into the broader arenas of society. These have been characterized as separation or "breaking away" from family, including particularly from mother and other significant family members. Rather than separation and "breaking away," the terms "loosening" and "expansion" are more relevant descriptive terms for female adolescents. Though rebellion and turbulence may characterize adolescence, recent studies do indicate that there are other available pathways for adolescents (Offer, 1969). These include a rather steady and relatively calm progression through these years in which expansion can occur.

The obvious and sometimes abrasive differences in values and customs in teenagers from their parents and even older siblings are evident for both males and females. However, they may be seen as "different" rather than total rejection of parental values. The differing from, and battling with, adults is certainly important. However, an ongoing feeling of acceptance for the girl, particularly by her mother, is most important. The differences and comparisons that female adolescents make often contain an implicit ongoing identification with the mother. For example, adolescent girls will borrow jewelry, makeup, and other items simultaneously with their apparent rejection of mother's appearance, makeup, and values.

As adolescence proceeds into late adolescence, the manifold expressions will include more obvious inclusion of mother's and other family figures' values and behaviors. This may be accompanied by verbal rejection, but if we look below the surface we see that late adolescent female identity development contains many aspects of her family, and particularly of her mother. The following clinical example has been chosen to illustrate particularly some vicissitudes of mother-daughter relationships:

An angry late-adolescent woman complained about her mother: "When I started high school, she was so strict she did not let me wear nylons or lipstick. All my friends were wearing makeup and even dating. She was not interested in what my friends were doing, she had so many rules." These are familiar complaints of many young women who seem to be filled with desire to rebel against mother's rules. However, as the tirade continued, other complaints began to emerge. The young woman asked, "Where was my mother? She was not around. She was only in the kitchen, she was not with me." She elaborated on this comment and indicated that as her world widened well beyond her home, she really missed her mother's influence.

Gradually, material emerged that indicated how much she missed her mother as adolescence proceeded. She said that her mother had delivered rules in the present but not recipes that she could take with her into the wider world. She realized that a lot of emotional distance had developed between herself and her mother. Her complaints became, "She did not teach me how to be a teenager and then a woman.'' Her lack of connection and amplification of identification in adolescence with her mother was an impediment in the development of her femininity, particularly in late adolescence and early womanhood.

This young woman had a warm, positive relationship with her father. He encouraged her in the pursuit of schoolwork and future career. However, he was not interested in the attributes of her changing adolescent femininity. She wished for particular maternal support and interest from her mother, with such things as hairstyles and prom dresses.

This brief example indicates the importance of the ongoing and continuing enlargement of the full range of feminine identifications in the course of adolescence. In this case, the girl experienced increasing distance and nonresolution of maternal identifications in late adolescence. We may say that although her core gender identity and primary femininity were developed and sufficient through latency, in adolescence there was a significant lack, or inadequate development, of the adolescent phase of primary femininity and adolescent female gender identity.

CONCLUSIONS

In this chapter, female adolescent development has been characterized by the expansion of primary femininity and gender identity in adolescence. Breast development and menarche occurring in early adolescence have been discussed as new and unique female events. This is in distinction to reworking in the ''second individuation'' process, which is often used as the primary explanatory developmental concept for adolescence.

A separate line of development, starting at birth, for females has been discussed. Emphasis has been placed on primary femininity/active engulfment, core gender identity, and gender identity development. The differentiation from, and simultaneous interdependence with, mother in particular and others in adolescence are most important aspects of the female adolescent's development. A focus on the mother-daughter relationship based on ''reciprocal identification'' has been discussed. The development of autonomy and independence, as emphasized by Erikson (1964) and others, is not adequate for understanding female adolescence. The female characteristics of procreativity, connectedness, and interdependence have been emphasized. The general nurturing qualities of, and caretaking of others by, adult women have their origin in the female body, the female body image, the adolescent development of breasts, and identification with mother. The effects of menarche and menses, unique female psychological events, provide for new additions to primary femininity in adolescence. The adolescent impetus in the development of primary femininity adds substantially to the active female life force of active engulfment.

In this chapter, pursuit of a separate line of female development into and through adolescence has provided a base for a significant reformulation for a psychoanalytic understanding of adolescent female development.

REFERENCES

American Association of University Women. 1991. Report: *Shortchanging Girls, Shortchanging Women*. Washington, DC: American Association of University Women.

Bernay, T. & Cantor, D., Eds. 1986. *The Psychology of Today's Woman: New Psychoanalytic Visions*. New Jersey: Analytic Press.

Blos, P. 1980. Modifications in the traditional psychoanalytic theory of female adolescent development. *Adolescent Psychiatry*, 8:8-24.

Blum, H. 1976. Masochism, the ego ideal and the psychology of women. *J. Am. Psychoanal. Assoc. (Supplement)*. 24:157-191.

Chodorow, N. 1978. *The Reproduction of Mothering*. Berkeley, CA: University of California.

Clower, V. 1975. Significance of masturbation in female sexual development and function. In I. Marcus & J. Francis, Eds., *Masturbation: From Infancy to Senescence*. New York: International Universities Press.

Clower, V. 1979. Theoretical implications in current views of masturbation in latency girls. In H. Blum, Ed., *Female Psychology*. New York: International Universities Press.

Dalsimer, K. 1986. *Female Adolescence: Psychoanalytic Reflections on Literature*. New Haven, CT: Yale University.

Deutsch, H. 1945. *The Psychology of Women*, Vols. 1 and 2. New York: Grune and Stratton.

Erikson, E. 1964. Inner and outer space: Reflections on womanhood. *Daedalus*, 93:582-606.

Frank, A. 1947. *The Diary of a Young Girl*. New York: Pocket Books.

Freud, A. 1958. Adolescence. *Psychoanal. Study of the Child*, 16:255-278.

Freud, S. 1905/1959. Three essays on the theory of sexuality. In *The Standard Edition*, Vol. VII. (pp. 135-243). London: Hogarth.

Freud, S. 1925/1961. Some psychical consequences of the anatomical distinction between the sexes. In *The Standard Edition*, Vol. XIX. London: Hogarth.

Freud, S. 1931/1961. Female sexuality. In *The Standard Edition*, Vol. XXI. (pp.225-243). London: Hogarth.

Freud, S. 1933. On Femininity. Lecture XXXIII. In *The Standard Edition*, Vol. XXII. (pp. 112-136). London: Hogarth.

Freud, S. 1938/1940. An Outline of Psycho-Analysis. In *The Standard Edition*, Vol. XXIII. London: Hogarth.

Gilligan, C. 1982. *In a Different Voice: Psychological Theory and Women's Development*. Cambridge, MA: Harvard University Press.

Gilligan, C., Lyons, N. P., & Hanmer, J. J. 1990. *Making Connections: The Relationship Worlds of Adolescent Girls at Emma Willard School*. Cambridge, MA: Harvard University Press.

Gleason, M. 1985. *Daughters and Mothers: College Women Look at Their Relationships.* (Work in Progress #17), Wellesley, MA: Stone Center for Developmental Services and Studies.

Herman, J. L. & Lewis, H. B. 1986. Anger in the mother-daughter relationship. In T. Bernay & D. Cantor, Eds., *The Psychology of Today's Woman.* New Jersey: Analytic Press.

Johnson, L. 1985. Personal communication.

Jordan, J. & Surrey, J. 1986. The self-in-relation: Empathy and the mother-daughter relationship. In T. Bernay & D. Cantor, Eds., *The Psychology of Today's Woman.* New Jersey: Analytic Press.

Kaplan, A. & Klein, R. 1985. *Self Development in Late Adolescence* (Work in Progress #17), Wellesley, MA: Stone Center for Developmental Services and Studies.

Kestenberg, J. 1968. Outside and inside, male and female. *J. Am. Psychoanal. Assoc.,* 16:457-520.

Kleeman, J. 1976. Freud's views on early female sexuality in the light of direct child observation. *J. Am. Psychoanal. Assoc. (Supplement).* 24:3-27.

Kulish, N. M. 1991. The mental representation of the clitoris. (unpublished manuscript).

Miller, J. B. 1984. *The Development of Women's Sense of Self* (Work in Progress #12), Wellesley, MA: Stone Center for Developmental Services and Studies.

Money, J. & Ehrhardt, A. A. 1972. *Man and Woman, Boy and Girl: The Differentiation and Dimorphism of Gender Identity from Conception to Maturity.* Baltimore, MD: Johns Hopkins University Press.

Nadelson C., Notman, M., Miller, J. B., & Zilbach, J. J. 1982. Aggression in women: Conceptual issues and clinical implications. In M. Notman & C. Nadelson, Eds., *The Woman Patient,* Vol. 3. New York: Plenum.

Notman, M., Klein, R., Jordan, J., & Zilbach J. 1991. Women's unique developmental issues across the life cycle. In A. Tasman & S. Goldfinger, Eds., *Review of Psychiatry,* Vol. 10. Washington, DC: American Psychiatric Association.

Notman, M., Zilbach, J. J., Miller, J. B., & Nadelson, C. 1986. Themes in psychoanalytic understanding of women: Some reconsiderations of autonomy and affiliation. *J. Amer. Acad. of Psychoanalysis,* 14:241-253.

Offer, D. 1969. *The Psychological World of the Teen-Ager.* New York: Basic Books.

Parens, H. 1990. On the girl's psychosexual development: Reconsiderations suggested from direct observation. *J. Amer. Psy. Assoc.,* 38:743-772.

Parens, H., Stern, J., & Kramer, S. 1976. On the girl's entry into the Oedipus complex. *J. Amer. Psychoanal. Assoc.,* 24(suppl.):79-107.

Rich, A. 1978. *The Dream of a Common Language: Poems 1974-1977.* New York: Norton, p. 41.

Roiphe, H. & Galenson, E. 1981. *Infantile Origins of Sexual Identity.* New York: International Universities Press.

Rosenblum, L. A. 1990. A comparative primate perspective in adolescence. In J. Bancroft & J. M. Reinisch, Eds., *Adolescence and Puberty.* New York: Oxford.

Rubin, J., Provenzano, T., & Luria, Z. 1974. The ego of the beholder: Views on sex of newborns. *American Journal of Orthopsychiatry,* 44, 4:512-519.

Stoller, R. J. 1976. Primary femininity. *J. Amer. Psychoanal. Assoc.,* Supplement. 24:59-78.

Stoller, R. J. 1980. Femininity. In M. Kirkpatrick, Ed., *Women's Sexual Development: Exploration of Innerspace*. New York: Plenum.

Sugar, M. 1990. The atypical adolescent and sexuality: An overview. In M. Sugar, Ed., *Atypical Adolescence and Sexuality*. New York: Norton.

Tyson, P. 1982. A developmental line of gender identity, gender role, and choice of love object. *J. Amer. Psychoanal. Assoc.*, 30:61-86.

Tyson, P. & Tyson, T. 1990. *The Psychoanalytic Theory of Development: An Integration*. New Haven, CT: Yale University Press.

Will, J., Self, P., & Datan, N. 1976. Maternal behavior and the perceived sex of infant. *Amer. J. Orthopsychiat.*, 46:1, 135-139.

Zilbach, J. J. 1987. *In the "I" of the Beholder: Toward a Separate Path of Development of Women*. Slavson Lecture, American Group Psychotherapy Association: New Orleans.

Zilbach, J. J. 1990. *Adam's Rib: Early Development of Women*. Presentation at First *Psychoanalytic Forum*: Boston College, Boston.

Zilbach, J. J., & Notman, M. (in press). *The dark continent: Psychoanalytical psychology of women*. New Haven, CT: Yale University Press.

4 The Changing Body Image of the Adolescent Girl

Maj-Britt Rosenbaum, M.D.

"Our bodies ourselves" is a poignant theme during adolescence. The dramatic bodily changes of puberty set in motion an important stage in self-development: the integration of sexual maturity into the totality of self-experience. The changing body provides powerful stimuli to self and others. Many new perceptions, new thoughts, and new feelings about the body have to be confronted, mastered, and integrated with the unfolding sense of self during adolescence. In this chapter, I plan to discuss how concrete physical changes were experienced by a group of adolescent girls. Hopefully, this will enable us to better understand the ongoing interplay of body growth and ego growth.

I am repeatedly struck by the prominent role of concerns about the body in the psychotherapy of adolescent girls. The body is experienced as a reflection of the self; it is often devalued and denigrated; it can be a source of conflict, shame, and inadequacy, as well as of pride and pleasure. How the body is perceived by others, often with painfully acute self-consciousness, is an area of considerable concern and speculation for many adolescent girls. I was curious to find out how skewed a picture I had been getting through the looking glass of my psychiatric office and decided to compare my impressions from treating adolescent female patients with the experiences of apparently normal healthy adolescent girls. The present discussion is based on anecdotal material obtained in interviews with 30 "normal" adolescent girls.

I shall discuss: 1. the changing body image during adolescence, with an emphasis on how the girl attempts to integrate the sexual and reproductive aspects of her maturing body into the changing psychic concept of her body; 2. the role the changing body image plays in relation to the developmental tasks of adolescence—how a biologically triggered turning point sets into motion a psychological state of crisis, a growth crisis necessitating change; 3. how the body image and self-image are interrelated and influenced by the ongoing interaction with the social environment and the miniculture of the family and peer group, as well as with the larger social environment and our culture that has tended to devalue women, to overemphasize their external attributes, and to see them more as objects than subjects.

BODY IMAGE

Body image, "the picture of our own body which we form in our mind" (Schilder, 1935), is a plastic, constantly changing concept, continuously modified by bodily growth, trauma, or decline, and significantly influenced by the ever-changing interaction with the social environment. We expect an individual entering puberty to have a fairly intact, integrated sense of the body as separate from others, a sense of gender—of being male or female, a sense of mastery or of control over the body, and a sense of inhabiting or "owning" the body, as well as a relatively positive attitude towards one's own body.

I like to think in terms of a "core body image," a sense of body self that stretches from early childhood, continuously modified by life circumstances as certain body parts are highlighted by illness, pain, pleasure, or attention. A latency age child tends to accept the body with statements like: "I don't think much about my body—it works for me." The changes at puberty bring about a change in this cohesive sense of body self.

Two aspects related to the body image stand out at this time. First, bodily changes during adolescence bring in their wake a sense of fragmentation in the body image. There is an upsurge in sexual energy, with an abundance of libido that is invested in the own body (Freud, A. 1962). However, this does not occur in a uniform manner; various parts of the body seem to occupy inordinate amounts of psychic space and attention—there is many a proverbial sore thumb. The gestalt of the body image at the onset of puberty has to undergo several revisions over the next few years. New gestalts are repeatedly created to replace the outgrown ones. There is a movement from an initial sense of fragmentation towards an increasingly more cohesive image of the own body, paralleling the changing self-image during this transition period.

It appears to take longer for girls than for boys to sort out the parts and the whole of their anatomy, perhaps because girls lack the organizing quality of the insistent genital sexuality of the adolescent boy (Sarrel & Sarrel, 1979). Except for the vulva, female genitalia are not available for external perception, and there is little discernible motility involving them. The girl has to rely more on diffuse proprioceptive messages, as well as on intellectual learning, than her male peers. The proprioceptive learning will involve some painful stimuli from menstrual cramps, as well as becoming familiar with the ebb and flow of the cyclical inner climate regulated by the hormones. Female genitalia are not only hidden from the self, but also from others, and therefore not available for comparison and consensual validation. Thus, the body parts that are visible to the self as well as to others, the breasts, come to occupy an inordinate amount of psychic space.

The formation of a more mature image of the body also involves the integration of the dual nature of female sexual physiology—the acceptance of the body as both sexually active and potentially childbearing.

The second major aspect focuses on adolescence as the time for an increasing differentiation between the genders, as the biological sex differences become increasingly visible. The internal struggle to consolidate a sense of sexual identity is often mirrored in the way clothing and body adornments are used to either accentuate or obliterate biological sex differences. The girls may vacillate between wearing "conforming" uniforms that cloak all in neutral sameness and dressing in revealing "sexy" outfits.

ADOLESCENT EGO DEVELOPMENT

"The ego is first and foremost a bodily ego," stated Sigmund Freud (1962, p. 26), referring to the developing ego during the early years of life. This certainly also holds true for the developing self during the adolescent period. Body growth can lead the way to ego growth—bodily change can be a powerful stimulus resulting in a disequilibrium necessitating reappraisal and psychic change. One 15-year-old girl illustrates how body growth can point the way, waiting for ego growth to follow, in her statement: "My body is too big for me—too old—too mature—too voluptuous. I don't fit it yet."

Adolescent development has until recently been conceptualized predominantly according to the male model of separation-individuation, as a journey towards an increasingly autonomous self. We have lately come to better appreciate the somewhat different experience of growing up female; how the maturing self is organized around an ability to make and maintain connections with others, how loss of a relationship is experienced as loss of self, and how self is defined not by reflection but by interdependence and interaction with others (Gilligan, 1982; Miller, 1976). In this construction, the "premise of separation yields to the depiction of the self in connection, and the concept of autonomy is changed. The seeming paradox 'taking charge of yourself by looking at others around you' conveys the relational dimension in this self-initiated action" (Gilligan, 1988, p. 7). "The central metaphor for the identity formation of adolescent girls becomes dialogue rather than mirroring; the self is defined by gaining voice and perspective and known in the experience of engagement with others" (Gilligan, 1988, p. 17).

Attanucci's (1988, pp. 201-224) discussion of the various relationships between self and role, between the experience of "I and me," are relevant in terms of the changing body image. She sees the experience of self as an ongoing interaction of self and role, between the first person and third person perspectives on self in relationship. ''Congruity between self and role, often termed adaptation, contributes to personal and social stability. On the other hand incongruity between self and role creates conflict'' (p. 202). Thus, experience of the body and the self is an ongoing interaction between the subjective and the objective perspective and dependent on which perspective is used for self-descriptive statements. Gilligan (1982) has shown that females show a greater propensity for defining themselves in connected terms, and males show a greater tendency to use separate terms when describing themselves in relation to others.

In this study, I attempt to explore not only how the girls themselves experienced their changing bodies, but how they experienced their girlfriends', boyfriends', mothers', and fathers' reactions to their changing bodies.

The developmental line of increasing autonomy is conceptualized by Blos (1967) as the four developmental challenges of adolescence: adolescent individuation and separation, ego-continuity, coping with residual trauma, and sexual identity. When used as a counterpoint to the changing interpersonal context, they provide a useful framework within which to discuss the experience of the changing body.

Individuation-Separation

This stage is based on Mahler's (1963) concept of the first separation-individuation phase during ''the first two years of life, at which time the child gradually emerges, that is to say 'hatches' from the symbiotic membrane with the mother.'' Mahler considered the demarcation of the body image of the self from the image of the object, the mother, as the core of the process of forming an identity. Blos (1967) has extended and adapted this concept to adolescence, when there is an ''urgency for changes in psychic structure in consonance with the maturational forward surge'' (p. 163). There is no doubt that the perception and awareness of one's own body taking on adult contours are powerful stimuli in the separation-individuation process. This is most clearly illustrated in cases of faulty separation, such as the anorexic girl who literally starves herself back into childhood to avoid confronting this developmental separation.

When the body very concretely takes on the contours of a more mature woman, the girl confronts the changing relationship with her mother. Her identification with, her dependency on and her need to separate from mother all need to be confronted in this new light. Many of the separation struggles with mother are related to the body. The question of who has the final say, who ''owns'' this body, comes up around many issues of hygiene, choice and care of clothes, diet, hairstyle, etc.

The fact that the body is increasingly becoming a source of pleasure and the realization that it is now capable of childbearing are stimuli to the separation-individuation process, as well as to a more mature identification with mother as an adult woman. It is of note that adolescence brings into awareness the genitals as organs for relating to others. How issues of sexual activity, contraception, and pregnancy are handled can be poignant illustrations in this regard.

The quest for separateness from mother can be seen in attempts at dressing as differently as possible and in denigrating mother's looks and dress in favor of the peer group's style. At other times, there is also a strong pull toward adopting mother's ways and seeking her continued advice, criticism, and reassurance. Separation from, and change in the relationship to, father has many ramifications in terms of the body. With both fathers and daughters aware of the sexually stimulating effect of the changing body and knowing that sexual relatedness is now concretely possible, incestuous conflicts are reawakened. How to handle body contact and how to comment on or react to changing looks and dress are often sensitive areas for father and daughter alike.

Ego Continuity and Residual Trauma

The disorganizing effect of rapid body growth can be sensed in terms of a disconnected body image. Body parts can be disassociated, reacted to as if they were not parts of self—in girls the breasts especially may at times seem to be disconnected appendages. The body can seem so different, so changed, that it appears totally "new." Yet body continuity—a sense that this is the same body, albeit altered by growth—is an essential aspect of ego continuity. The adolescent girls who are interrupted in their development by a physical illness, trauma, or disability can constitute painful illustrations in this regard (Cash & Pruzinsky, 1990, Chapters 6 & 7; Fisher & Apfel, 1988; Orr, Reznikoff & Smith, 1989).

Just as psychic trauma is inevitable in the growing-up process, so is bodily trauma, either concretely or in terms of the many unavoidable disappointments and discrepancies when one's own body is compared with an "ideal" body. To confront, accept, and integrate—in a sense to "master" these bodily imperfections and flaws—is one of the major tasks in the formation of a realistic and positive body image and self-image.

Sexual Identity

The consolidation of sexual identity enters a new phase in adolescence. It builds on the differentiation of gender identity that occurs in the first years of life and is generally more stable in girls than in boys, presumably due to the primary identification with mother (Stoller, 1973). The elaborations during adolescence involve integrating mature sexual functioning into the sense of being female—with the realization that mature functioning involves both direct sexual expression and reproductive potential. As Blos (1977) stated: "Sexual activity per se is, obviously, no indication of adolescent closure, and offers no assurance that sexual identity has been achieved." Obviously, neither is the experience of a pregnancy or an abortion an indication of sexual maturity. Sexual identity involves integrating mature sexuality, the capacity to form mature object relationships, to relinquish infantile self- and object-idealizations in favor of more realistic and "adult" ones. It also involves "the transmutation of the infantile, narcissistic ego-ideal into the adult abstracted and desexualized ego-ideal" (Blos, 1977).

The concrete illustrations of this process are often expressed in terms of the increasing acceptance of, and comfort with, one's own body, such as it is. The road, however, is paved with difficulties in acknowledging sexual feelings as part of the self, as emanating from the inside, not the outside. It involves coming to terms with reawakened feelings of shame and resultant inhibitions as the girl confronts new developmental milestones, such as menarche, masturbation, first sexual experiences, and loss of virginity. It involves the complexities in learning to relate sexually to a partner. How these developments are handled will affect sexual identity.

SOCIAL ENVIRONMENT

Despite some recent changes, our culture still raises girls and boys differently in terms of the importance of physical attractiveness. Our society, reflecting a conglomerate of individual psychodynamics and attitudes, views physical beauty as a more important factor in the evaluation of women than in the evaluation of men (Bar-Tal & Saxe, 1976; Fallon, 1990). Not only is physical attractiveness in our culture more important for women than for men, but there are fewer ways open for women to compensate for a lack of beauty (Wilson & Nias, 1976). Thus, it is not surprising that self-esteem and self-confidence, as well as level of anxiety, which fluctuate with the state of our body image, tend to do so more in women than in men (Davies & Furnham, 1986; Fisher, 1974; Freedman, 1984; Secord & Jourard, 1953). One way of influencing body image and self esteem is through plastic surgery. Data from plastic surgery offer interesting information about how surgical correction of a distressing body part improves overall self-esteem (Burk, Zelen & Terino, 1985; Hollyman, Lacey, Whitfield & Wilson, 1986).

We often do not consciously admit to ourselves how much importance we do attribute to attractiveness in our relations with others—and that we almost automatically see beauty as being more than skin deep (Fallon, 1990). During adolescence, the evaluation of self and other is especially dependent on these "superficial" clues; there is an acute awareness of how attractive each individual is in relation to others. One national survey in 1964 of nearly 2000 girls ages 11 to 18 showed that over 50 percent of them worried about their looks (Sherman, 1971). Adolescence, the time "when thinking becomes self-consciously interpretive, is also the time when the interpretive schemes of the culture, including the system of social norms, values, and roles, impinge more directly on perception and judgment, defining within a given society what is 'the right way' to see and feel and think, the way 'we' think" (Gilligan, 1988, p. xxiii). In the context of body image, I would like to add: and the "right way" to *look*.

An interesting illustration of the interplay between culture and body image comes from a study comparing the body satisfaction of 71 homosexual and 71 heterosexual men. The homosexual men showed more body dissatisfaction, more fluctuation of self-esteem with fluctuations of weight, and more eating disorders than the heterosexual men, reflecting the values of a subculture that places a heightened emphasis on appearance (Silberstein, Mishkind, Striegel-Moore, Timko & Rodin, 1989).

INTERVIEWS WITH ADOLESCENT GIRLS

Many of my female patients express anxiety and conflict in terms of concerns about their bodies (Rosenbaum, 1977). There is the preoccupation with various body parts and with asynchronous growth; there are many questions about normalcy and the innumerable concerns that come under the guise of weight control. There is the girl who hides her sexuality behind a chubby facade, "so she will not be raped when she travels . . ." There is the girl who squashes her breasts in a desperate attempt to arrest their growth, as well as the one who adds socks to her empty bra, stating mockingly, "What God has forgotten, we fill in with cotton." There are the girls obsessed with their next haircut or with the possibility of having a "nose-job" or breast-reduction surgery. There is the girl who "plucks the weeds from the jungle of her eyebrows" every morning until she bleeds—as well as the many disadvantaged, ill, or handicapped girls, with their "broken" bodies, who sometimes have insurmountable obstacles in their way to healthy ego growth. The organism in distress can highlight aspects we cannot usually see when development progresses smoothly with a harmonious interplay of various factors.

Curious to learn more about how "normal" adolescent girls felt about their bodies, I decided to ask them directly. Using a semistructured psychiatric interview, I turned to a group of adolescent girls easily available to me at the time (1978): the friends of my children, the children of my friends and of their friends. It is a small sample, a biopsy of the "normal" population in the same predominantly white, suburban, upper-middle-class area that I draw my patient sample from.

The 30 girls ranged in age from 11 to 17 years, covering early and mid-adolescence. All of them appeared to function well in school and within their social environment; none of them had been in treatment. Five of them were premenstrual and five had had intercourse.

There has been a trend to nonvirginity among teen-age women over the past couple of decades. Among metropolitan-area teenagers, 15 to 19 years of age, premarital coitus moved from 30 percent in 1971 to 43 percent in 1976 and to 50 percent in 1979, as reported by Zelnik and Kantner (1980). The most recent data, reported by Reiss & Reiss (1990, p. 244) indicate that there has been only a modest increase in nonvirginity during the 1980s—53 percent of 15-19 year old women were nonvirginal in 1988.

Some of my questions were inspired by the crude rating scales that the adolescents sometimes devise for themselves as they ruthlessly and openly categorize each other, occasionally with mathematical precision, as a miserable 4 or 5—or an exceptional 9 or 10—usually with an acute awareness of where they themselves stand in the hierarchy of the current scale in use. I asked the girls to rate their attractiveness, from their own point of view, as well as from that of their female and male peers. The ratings tended to be internally consistent—the girls saw themselves as others saw them. (The prepubertal girls had difficulty with the question—it is as if they had not yet turned an observing eye to their own body.) The ratings tended to fall within a rather narrow range. Most of the girls rated themselves very close to average, with only minor, cautious deviations from the mean.

Whenever there was a discrepancy between the ratings, the harshest critic turned out to be the self—with a third of the girls seeing themselves as less attractive than they thought their peers considered them. Generally, they saw their girlfriends as more positive in their assessment than were the boys. The exceptions were two girls who realized that the boys found them attractive because of their generous breast endowment.

The fact that these adolescent girls had started turning more to peers than to parents for "evaluation" reflects their separation from the family. This was also evidenced in their feelings that the least critical judges were the parents, especially mothers, whose opinions were generally discounted: "She thinks I'm gorgeous—that I have a perfect figure—but that is a lie! That's what all mothers say." Yet mother's influence was still there, although in a more subtle way, reflecting the basic primitive identification with her. There was a definite indication that the girls who estimated that their mothers felt good about their own looks felt better about themselves.

What specifically did the girls like about their bodies? In general, it was difficult for most of the girls to think of something positive about their bodies. They often looked perplexed and troubled and voiced statements related to their not standing out from the crowd. They liked being of average height and weight and often mentioned the absence of a particular flaw, such as: "I don't have pimples, I don't have freckles, I'm not fat." Being well-proportioned and "fitting in" with her peer group were highly valued (Freedman, 1990, p. 291).

The one part of the body that most girls mentioned was their hair. Two-thirds of them mentioned that their hair was one of their best features, citing its length, color, thickness, degree of curliness or straightness, and especially the fact that they could "do something with it." This is interesting, especially in view of the fact that the hair is one of the most disassociated parts of the body physiologically.

This may represent an attempt at externalizing conflict, moving it as far out from the center as possible. It may also represent an outward symbolic expression of the inner anatomy, which defies attempts at management, in contrast to the manageable hair. The hair was certainly the one part of their body they had some influence over: they could cut it, shape it, improve its color, body, shine, and degree of curliness. It is also of note that the hair tends to be one of the ongoing battlegrounds where the conflict of control, as well as separation-individuation, is fought between mothers and daughters. During adolescence, a girl tends to move into autonomous ownership of this body part.

The next most frequently mentioned body parts were the eyes; half the girls were pleased with theirs. Otherwise the results were meager—one or two mentioned their complexion, their mouth, their smile, or their small feet. Compare these results with an answer from a 14-year-old boy who, when asked what he liked about his body, stated, "It's alive, it's smart, it moves; I can talk, I can see, I have all my senses." Both genders have a tendency to depersonalize, to objectify the body—girls in the direction of being observed, boys in the direction of action, of the body as machine, in keeping with our cultural stereotypes.

When asked to describe what they didn't like about their bodies, the girls' answers came more easily, reflecting the difficulty in accepting their bodies and changing selves, so that the flaws tended to tumble out. The leading concerns were related to weight—in full conformity with our cultural norms and ideals (Cash & Pruzinsky, 1990, p. 288). Even the slimmest of the girls would point to specific areas that they saw as too big: thighs, hips, a potbelly, or a pudgy, round face. The ones who mentioned that they were too thin would, on further questioning, reveal that their real concern was not weight, but the feeling that they had not developed enough and the fear that they would never develop any further. The concerns about weight certainly reflect our cultural preoccupation with this aspect of the body. It is also a reflection of relating the "curves" of a mature female body to "fat," mirroring the conflict of the wish and the fear to mature (perhaps even the wish and fear to become pregnant).

Other concerns were more specific and individual. Many girls disliked their complexions and the problem they had with acne; others would have liked a smaller nose or preferred ears that did not "stick out"; in addition to these being beauty flaws, one could speculate on the possible phallic implications of these concerns. Generally the tendency was in the direction of wanting certain body parts to be smaller and less obtrusive. The only exception were the breasts, which consistently were the only body parts considered too small. Reflecting the need to consolidate a female sexual identity, one noteworthy concern was having too much body hair. It was seen as "messy, too dark, not feminine, something boys were supposed to have."

I gave the girls three magic wishes—asking them what they would like to change about their bodies. The most common wish: to lose weight and keep it off. Other wishes included blonder hair and bluer eyes, a clear complexion and a perfect figure, getting rid of glasses or straightening out noses—all drawing the girl closer to our society's stereotypes of ideal female beauty as portrayed by Miss America and the models in the women's magazines, which the girls frequently consulted for guidelines.

All the girls had at one time or another entertained the wish to be a boy, many of them fervently so during a tomboy period "when they were little." All of them had come to value being female, stating that "It's better to be a girl, because I know what it is like," or "It's fun to care about looks, make-up and clothes," and "Femininity is very special. It is easier to be more feeling." Our society is more tolerant of gender-role deviant behavior in girls than in boys; girls can and do act as tomboys with full societal sanction and even praise, whereas an effeminate boy invites ridicule and the risk of being ostracized (Green, 1974). There is also some evidence that sex-role preference is stronger among girls than among boys (Silvern, 1977). It is of note that the onset of menstruation frequently brings about a rather rapid swing from the tomboy role, as it did in these girls. It is as if the experience of menstruation fortifies the feelings of feminine identity (Jacobson, 1964).

Following the lead of our cultural stereotypes, these girls felt that boys and girls do feel differently about their bodies: "Boys brag about their muscles and being strong—girls worry about how they look." "Boys don't worry so much about their bodies; girls compare more." "Girls are more critical and more selfconscious." Seen through the girls' eyes, boys take their bodies more for granted and worry more about height and strength, muscles and sexual prowess, whereas girls were more particular about the details of their appearance and worried about having a nice figure and looking good. Some of the older girls, however, stated: "I don't think there is much of a difference—it depends on the person."

Movement plays an important part in forming a body image. Sports tend to be a significant aspect of the growing up experiences of boys in our culture; active and successful participation in athletic activities seemingly go hand in hand with healthy ego development. The hypothesis, based on my clinical experience, was that this also applies to girls. Therefore, I also explored the role played by physical activity in the body image of these 30 girls. There was a definite trend: The girls who were active in sports or who danced regularly generally felt better about their bodies—"They worked for them." One girl, not physically active, stated: "I wish I were more athletic, I think I'd feel better about myself, more at home with my body."

The onset of menstruation is one of the most dramatic events during the adolescent period; it is a significant marker in both biological and psychological development. The positive effects of menarche as an organizer and cornerstone of feminine identification have been discussed by Kestenberg (1961) and Blos (1967). Menarche has been seen as a nidus around which a clearer, better-defined body image is built, leading to reorganization of the ego (Hart & Sarnoff, 1971).

The girls I interviewed generally dealt with menstruation in a matter-of-fact, at times almost resigned, manner. They all felt well prepared for it intellectually and often took a somewhat removed emotional stand to their periods. However, they often mentioned the reaction of others whom they had told about it initially. Menarche was clearly perceived as interpersonal, as a social rite of passage as much as a private milestone. The general impression was: "I used to worry more about it beforehand." This was especially so if they were late compared to their peers. Once they had crossed this biological threshold, it became an accepted or, perhaps more accurately, a tolerated fact of life. Inserting the first tampon became the next obstacle to negotiate, evoking considerable anxiety in some girls. Some had never tried; others had tried a couple of times and given up, postponing it to a later age. The ones who used tampons—some of whom had inserted them easily and on their first attempt, others (this was the rule) who had struggled—generally had a feeling of relief, of accomplishment, of having mastered a task (Shopper, 1979).

One 16-year-old girl summarized: "I had a realistic view of menstruation. I felt breast development was more important. If my period is late, I worry that something is wrong. No specific worries, like being pregnant. More that I may not know something, that something may be happening that I'm supposed to know about. I don't worry about things I know. When I finally got my period, I felt that now I am stuck with it for a long time. All of a sudden I felt it could have waited a bit longer. I expected it. I wasn't excited, nor worried. The main feeling: Now I don't have to worry about it any longer. Sometimes I worry that the Tampax will get stuck in there, or lost—into the uterus probably. But I don't let myself imagine too far. It is as if I have a dialogue with myself. I tell myself that it has to be there, I try to quiet the fears down." She expresses the feelings of many girls, who have not yet assimilated and integrated intellectual knowledge with body experience and with the irrational part of their minds. There was a common theme of worrying more about potential change, about development yet to come, than about the road already traveled. Once the milestones had been passed, these girls easily integrated the change. It was looking at the uncharted road ahead that held anxiety.

Breast development tends to be a sensitive and emotionally laden aspect of body change for most girls. It is of note that with breast growth a new body part is added, going well beyond merely enlarging upon an existing structure. No wonder the breasts are often disassociated from the rest of the body for quite some time, experienced as "not-me," as appendages that don't quite belong—yet. The breasts most clearly represent sexuality, an overt signal to self and others that the body is maturing. Thus, they often become the focus for conflict related to sexual feelings, as well as to phallic or exhibitionistic concerns. Since the breasts also represent mothering and symbolize nurturing, they are experienced as a concrete expression of the dual nature of a woman's sexuality.

Most of the active concerns of the girls I interviewed centered around their breasts. All of them mentioned that they would like to change some aspect of their breasts, usually size. Only one girl was somewhat uncomfortable because her breasts were too large, stating: "My breasts are a little too big for my age (14), but I'll grow into them." Bigger was generally—within some limits—seen as better. Breasts were usually commented on in the interpersonal context. Bigger was better, not so much for the self, but because of the value big breasts were perceived to have for the boys: "I worry about if my breasts are appealing to boys." Large breasts were sometimes ambivalently perceived. They were more voluptuous, sexier, but also "more of a bother."

The first bra was seen as another rite of passage, an event they remembered in terms of their own as well as others' reactions. Most of the girls preferred to wear a bra, feeling that "it looked better." They felt that going braless was at times more comfortable, but many regarded it as too "loose" and sexy. There were concerns about normalcy of nipples, breasts being too "pointy" or too low, how tight a sweater could be, how low-cut a neckline. The sharpest discomfort was felt by the girls who developed earlier or later than their peers, and they could vividly recall the teasing and the embarrassment. The pain for the flat-chested girl was different but equally acute. Her fear was that she would always be that way and she "just couldn't believe" that anyone would complain that their breasts were too big.

All of the girls had thought about breast-feeding, again an illustration of reacting to the interpersonal context of the breasts, even though far in the future. One girl will not breast-feed, "because the whole idea sickens me." Another prefers bottles, because it is easier. About half of the girls plan to breast-feed, because it is "healthier," "more natural," or "because that's why they are there." One girl even stated that she would like to, but feared that she wouldn't be able to—just like her mother. The identification with mother was strong and concretely direct: All of the girls who planned to breast-feed had themselves been breast-fed, and vice versa.

The early adolescents tended to see their breasts as their most important "sexual organ"—the visible badge of their femininity. At 16 and 17, they became less preoccupied with breast size: "He should like me for what I am." They also tended to become more comfortable going braless, stating that they felt less self-conscious. Yet they were often acutely aware of the reaction of others, feeling that going braless made people around them uncomfortable—reflecting both reality-orientation and projection. Thus, the breasts were perceived as the most consciously sexualized body parts, concrete symbols of the maturing sexuality of the girl.

This became evident when I asked the girls to name their most important sexual organs. All the younger girls spontaneously mentioned the breasts, and usually also their vaginas. As they grew older, other body parts were added to the list: The uterus, the fallopian tubes, and the ovaries were occasionally mentioned, the mouth several times, the skin a couple of times. Significantly, the clitoris was mentioned only by two girls, including one who listed all the organs as if responding to a test, but who had no idea what they were. When I would mention parts of their sexual anatomy that they had not brought up—hymen, clitoris, uterus, etc.—the girls had usually heard the terms, but many had only a vague and confused picture of the anatomy. We can speculate whether the confusion is due to repression because of the psychically charged nature of these parts of the anatomy or is a result of lack of learning (reflecting more accurately society's inhibitions than the inner reluctance of the growing girl). Most likely, it is a combination of both.

I also asked the girls to estimate the size of their internal organs. Interestingly they were often compared to fruits: Many uteri were seen as grapefruits, cantaloupes or large oranges; there was even a banana thrown in. Ovaries were compared to lemons, plums and apples—as well as eggs and fists—but often the terms remained words, with only an intellectual definition attached to them. The younger girls—and, in fact, all the girls in retrospect, remembering their younger days—thought of the vagina as "everything down there" or "the vagina is where the urine comes out," actively subscribing to the "cloacal theory."

In fact the label "vagina" usually seemed to refer to the vulvar area. Significantly, the vulva, the only part of the female genitalia available to external perception, had usually not been included in the "sex education" of these girls. The focus had been on the inner organs. Several of the girls had examined themselves with a mirror, usually not knowing what to look for, and coming away more confused than enlightened. There were many concerns about normalcy as well as a wish to sort out the parts. For instance, one girl was concerned because of the surprising length of her inner lips; another one feared that the dark greenish coloration of her inner lips was caused by buildup of "ground-in dirt."

The gulf between intellectually "knowing," including the use of sophisticated scientific terminology, and "bodily knowing" the sexual body parts was only occasionally bridged by some of the older girls. In the words of one of the 17-year-olds: "I know scientifically pretty much what happens, how the lining of the uterus sloughs off and all that. I was always curious. I can sort of picture what's happening, like seeing it projected on a screen. In my mind the uterus seems fairly large—about football size I would guess. But it has to fit inside of me—it's hard to picture a football fitting. I guess I know generally—I have dissected a cat—I could draw you a picture—but I don't know about *me*." She estimated her ovaries to be fist-sized, but when asked how she would answer if asked on a biology test, she forced herself to cut the measurements down to more realistic size. About her vagina she mentioned: "I can't remember exploring it—but when I put in a tampax it was no surprise." None of these girls reported consciously or bodily having known that they had a vagina when "they were little," yet a comment such as the one above indicates an awareness of its existence on a less conscious level (Greenacre, 1952; Horney, 1933).

The possibility of future pregnancy was an important aspect of the changing definition of self. All the girls had "rehearsed" being pregnant in their fantasies; they had all thought about being pregnant and had imagined what it might feel like, that it may be "a heavy burden." Most of them also expressed some fears, usually of pain, often mentioning that they had seen a film on TV that "looked like it hurt." There were fears of the baby being abnormal, not having all the arms and legs, being retarded. There were fantasies about delivery: the excitement of giving life, the wish to be "awake and the first one to see my kid." Around the age of 15 the concerns became more realistic: the fear of becoming pregnant before they wished to; thoughts about deciding whether to have an abortion or not.

In exploring the conscious awareness of sexuality, I also asked the girls if they had ever been sexually excited or "horny." The younger girls thought of that as something that applies to boys, or being perverted or "gross." After having had some experience with kissing or petting, the girls would usually affirm that they were occasionally "horny." The answers to how and where they felt it were interesting. They often used vague terms like: "It feels funny," or "It's an indescribable feeling—my head feels full, my heart beats, my hands get sweaty," or "It's a feeling of wanting to touch someone." Sometimes it was more cognitive: "I think of my boyfriend—of wanting to see him, of being with him."

Only the girls who had had genital sexual experiences would even mention any genital sensations, usually only upon direct questioning, stating, "It's a lustful feeling. I guess most girls don't feel much and are not aware of any feelings down there." One sexually active girl stated, "I have a general increased feeling of desire. I want some kind of physical contact—it's a vague feeling. Guys are more direct." The general impression was one of slowly learning about their sexuality, about how their bodies felt when sexually excited, reflecting again both our cultural repression of female sexuality and the rather inaccessible, less visible genital anatomy of the woman. For these girls, the experience of sexuality coalesced slowly as it unfolded within an interpersonal context.

Masturbation is phase specific for adolescence (Frances, 1968). It has been described as an "indispensable part of healthy adolescence," especially in relation to the formation of a body image that includes sexual functioning, and as a means of encouraging ego development (Laufer, 1968). The literature, in keeping with the times, expressed its predominantly male focus on development in the past. It is of relevance that adolescent girls generally masturbate considerably less than boys and only about 15 percent practice it twice a week or more (Gagnon & Simon, 1973). The data from Kinsey, Pomeroy, Martin and Gebhard (1953) show that 12 percent of 12-year-old girls, 20 percent of 15-year-old girls, and 33 percent of 20-year-old females had masturbated to orgasm. The incidence has increased markedly over the past decade so that 80-90 percent of female adolescents masturbate (Sarrel & Sarrel, 1990). Only four of the girls in this group said that they masturbated—although many more guessed that they probably used to do it as a child.

Even the ones who masturbated did so only occasionally. The general feeling, except for the older girls, was: "Masturbation is something boys do. I've heard that girls do it too, so I guess they do, but I really don't believe it."

Crossing the threshold that leads to loss of virginity can be seen as another developmental crisis, as well as an occasion for organizing previously confusing experiences, feelings, and fantasies. The consensus on virginity was that, although "it was an old-fashioned thing," it was still personally important. Several of the girls felt that they would not go to bed with someone unless they married him. The virgins considered losing their virginity an important step, both personally and interpersonally. Not only was it seen as changing the relationship with the boy, but the feeling was that it would change their perception of themselves. There was a curiosity about "being devirginized" and it was seen as an important rite of passage that would organize experiences and feelings.

One girl described her first sexual experience: "I enjoyed the petting, the fact that he was interested in me, all my own expectations. It was almost too dreamlike, too much like fantasy to be real—I enjoyed all the trimmings—and especially I enjoyed breaking a wall, doing it." And another one: "It is as if I have a new definition of myself as female. It's different now—it's for real. I feel I'm different; I feel everyone can tell I'm different. I move differently on the dance floor, sexier. I feel I project a totally new image." This girl had accentuated her change by cutting her hair.

And a 16-year-old girl contemplated the future: "I think being a non-virgin will change me. I think I'll learn more about myself. It implies being more of a woman—no longer a teenager. I hope I will feel better, more whole. I hope it will organize something. You don't know what to expect—even as much as you read. Having sex would get me in touch with another, unexplored part of myself—I'd be more totally me."

CONCLUSIONS

Interview material from 30 young women in early and middle adolescence is used to illustrate the effect of the biological changes of puberty on body image, as it is reflected in the changing sense of self moving through the developmental tasks of adolescence. The importance of the self in the context of relationships is seen as a crucial factor in the transformation of the girl's body image and self-concept during adolescence. Physical change becomes a nidus for psychological growth, a nidus around which to organize the experience of self, both as subject and object, both as I and me.

The core body image of a girl entering puberty undergoes repeated revisions during the next few years. Fragmentation and disassociation of various parts give way to an ever-increasing sense of cohesiveness and consolidation of the body image as the sexual aspects of the maturing body become integrated. This includes genital sexuality as well as reproductive potential, significantly experienced in its interpersonal dimension. Menarche, breast development, experiences with petting, masturbation, loss of virginity, the rehearsal in fantasy of future role as sexual partner and mother are all important threads in the final fabric of a cohesive body image.

Gender differences in body image become consolidated during adolescence. Gone are the tomboy fantasies, to be replaced by an ever-increasing acceptance, comfort and pride in being a physically mature woman. There is a consistent movement from more superficial concerns about weight distribution, hair growth, and degree of breast development to a more complex, flexible acceptance of self as maturing woman.

Body growth provides a stimulus for ego development and a transformation of the sense of self in relation to others. The changing relationship with mother is reflected in the changing body image. Mothers tend to be discarded as authorities on appearance and dress, to be replaced by peers and cultural images of perfection. Separation issues are fought on many fronts, with hair often becoming a convenient focus. As the girl's body takes on the unmistakable contours of an adult woman, the pull of the primitive mother-identification surfaces again, necessitating a change in the relationship. The resolution involves both a differentiation from mother and an acceptance of similarities, e.g., seeing oneself as a mother in one's own right, yet breast-feeding according to a "program" laid down by mother.

Acute awareness of the many inevitable discrepancies between one's own body and the ideal embodiment of female beauty has ramifications in terms of body image, self-esteem, level of anxiety, realistic self-perception, and self-acceptance. The younger girls seemed more concerned with minor flaws and imperfections; the older ones became increasingly aware of the total gestalt and more realistically accepting of their body-selves.

Because of the inaccessible anatomy, limited, if any, sexual experience, as well as the yet unrealized potential to bear children, it is difficult for adolescent girls to paint an accurate, detailed picture of their sexual anatomy. There are many gaps in information, much confusion and misinformation and a gulf between intellectual knowing and "body-knowing."

Culturally stereotyped gender differences are alive and well, at least in this group of girls from a socioeconomically and intellectually advantaged background. It would be of interest to compare this experience with other groups. These girls were all selfconsciously concerned about their looks, well aware of the value their society places on attractiveness for women. Most of the girls tended to devalue themselves, seeing themselves as less attractive than others saw them. Even very attractive girls underestimated their level of attractiveness. The norm was to see the self as "average," with a considerable number of specific flaws. Of note was that the girls who were physically active tended to feel better about their bodies. They also had higher levels of self-esteem, which consistently fluctuated with how positively the body was valued.

Talking to these girls provided many concrete and personal illustrations of how the subjective experience of body-change was also experienced as an ongoing change in the relationships with others, setting in motion a transformation of the sense of self in the social context. The girls tended to be very sensitive to the reaction and evaluation of others. The majority of them admitted to being very self-conscious about their bodies, although most of the girls also liked and accepted their bodies, such as they were. They were continually revising their body image as they reacted to, learned about, accepted, and integrated bodily change. This was reflected in increased comfort with, and growing mastery of, their bodies, in the lessening of the discrepancy between their experience of I and me, between the subjective and the objective sense of self, in their increasing autonomy as individuals, and in their more complex and mature sexual identity. The girls came to increasingly integrate the various aspects of their body images and self-images, answering the inner questions of: 1. how she was like all other girls; 2. how she was like some other girls; and 3. how she was like no other girl (Attanucci, 1988).

SUMMARY

This chapter has attempted to provide some concrete examples of the ways in which girls develop a coherent sense of their bodies. Body change and ego growth are intimately connected with, and significantly influenced by, the ever-changing relationships within the social matrix. The evolving body image and self-transformation of the adolescent girl hinge on change in self-perception within the context of relationships.

REFERENCES

Attanucci, J. 1988. In whose terms: A new perspective on self, role, and relationship. In C. Gilligan, J. V. Ward, & J. M. Taylor, Eds., *Mapping the Moral Domain*. Cambridge, MA: Harvard University Press, pp. 3-19.

Bar-Tal, D. & Saxe, L. 1976. Physical attractiveness and its relationship to sex-role stereotyping. *Sex Roles*,2:123-133.

Blos, P. 1967. The second individuation process of adolescence. *Psychoanal. Study Child*, 22:162-186.

Blos, P. 1977. When and how does adolescence end: Structural criteria for adolescent closure. *Adol. Psychiat.*, 5:5-17.

Burk, J., Zelen, S. L., & Terino, E. O. 1985. More than skin deep: A selfconsistency approach to the psychology of cosmetic surgery. *Plast. Reconstr. Surg.*, 76:270-280.

Cash, T. F. & Pruzinsky, T., Eds., 1990. *Body Images: Development, Deviance, and Change*. New York, London: The Guilford Press.

Davies, E. & Furnham, A. 1986. Body satisfaction in adolescent girls. *Brit. J. Med. Psychol.*, 59:279-287.

Fallon, A. 1990. Culture in the mirror: Sociocultural determinants of body image. In T. F. Cash & T. Pruzinsky, Eds., *Body Images: Development, Deviance, and Change*. New York, London: The Guilford Press. pp. 80-109.

Fisher, S. 1974. *Body Consciousness*. New York: Jason Aronson, p. 50.

Fisher, S. M. & Apfel, R. J. 1988. Female psychosexual development: Mothers, daughters, and inner organs. *Adol. Psychiat.*, 15:5-29.

Frances, J. J. 1968. Masturbation—panel report. *J. Amer. Psychoanal. Assoc.*, 16:95-112.

Freedman, R. J. 1984. Reflections on beauty as it relates to health in adolescent females. *Women and Health*, 9:29-45.

Freedman, R. 1990. Cognitive-behavioral perspectives on body-image change. In T. F. Cash & T. Pruzinsky, Eds., *Body Images: Development, Deviance, and Change*. New York: London: The Guilford Press.

Freud, A. 1962. *The Ego and the Mechanisms of Defense*. (First published 1946) New York: International Universities Press, p. 166.

Freud, S. 1962. *The Ego and the Id*. (First published 1923.) Standard Edition, Vol. 19. London: The Hogarth Press, p. 26.

Gagnon, J. & Simon, W. 1973. *Sexual Conduct*. Chicago: Aldine, pp. 54-67.

Gilligan, C. 1982. *In a Different Voice: Psychological Theory and Women's Development*. Cambridge, MA; and London, England: Harvard University Press.

Gilligan, C. 1988. Remapping the moral domain: New images of self in relationship. In C. Gilligan, J. V. Ward, & J. M. Taylor, Eds., *Mapping the Moral Domain*. Cambridge, MA: Harvard University Press. pp. 3-19.

Green, R. 1974. *Sexual Identity Conflict in Children and Adults*. New York: Basic Books.

Greenacre, P. 1952. *Trauma, Growth and Personality*. New York: Norton & Co.

Hart, M. & Sarnoff, C. A. 1971. The impact of menarche. A study of two stages of organization. *J. Amer. Acad. Child Psychiat.*, 10:257-271.

Hollyman, J. A., Lacey, J. H., Whitfield, P. J., & Wilson, J. S. 1986. Surgery for the psyche: A longitudinal study of women undergoing reduction mammoplasty. *Brit. J. Plastic Surgery*, 39:222-224.

Horney, K. 1933. The denial of the vagina. *Int. J. Psychoanal.*, 14:57-70.

Jacobson, E. 1964. *The Self and the Object World*. New York: International Universities Press.

Kestenberg, J. 1961. Menarche. In S. Lorand & Schneer, Eds., *Adolescents: Psychoanalytic Approach to Problems and Therapy*. New York: Hoeber, pp. 19-50.

Kinsey, A., Pomeroy, W. B., Martin, C. E., & Gebhard, P. H. 1953. *Sexual Behavior in the Human Female*. Philadelphia: W. B. Saunders Co., p. 173.

Laufer, M. 1968. The body image, the function of masturbation, and adolescence: Problems of ownership of the body. *Psychoanal. Study Child*, 23:114-137.

Mahler, M. S. 1963. Thoughts about development and individuation. *Psychoanal. Study Child*, 18:307-324.

Miller, J. B. 1976. *Towards a New Psychology of Women*. Boston: Beacon Press.

Orr, D. A., Reznikoff, M., & Smith, G. M. 1989. Body image, self-esteem and depression in burn-injured adolescents. *J. Burn Care and Rehab.*, 10:454-61.

Reiss, I. L. 1976. Adolescent sexuality. In W. W. Oaks, G. A. Melchiode, & I. Ficher, Eds., *Sex and the Lifecycle*. New York: Grune & Stratton, p.49.

Reiss, I. L. & Reiss, H. M. 1990. *An End to Shame: Shaping Our Next Sexual Revolution*. Buffalo, New York: Prometheus Books.

Rosenbaum, M-B. 1977. Gender-specific therapy problems in female youths. *Amer. J. Psychoanal.*, 37:215-221.

Rosenbaum, M-B. (1979). The changing body image of the adolescent girl. In M. Sugar, Ed., *Female Adolescent Development*. New York: Brunner/Mazel, pp. 234-252.

Sarrel, L. J. & Sarrel, P. M. 1979. *Sexual Unfolding: Sexual Development and Sex Therapies in Late Adolescence*. Boston: Little, Brown and Company, pp. 22-50.

Sarrel, L. J. & Sarrel, P. M. 1990. Sexual unfolding in adolescents. In M. Sugar, Ed., *Atypical Adolescence and Sexuality*. New York: Norton.

Schilder, P. 1935. *The Image and Appearance of the Human Body*. London: Kegan, Paul, Trench, Trubner & Co.

Secord, P. & Jourard, S. 1953. The appraisal of body-cathexis; body-cathexis and the self. *J. Consultive Psychol.*, 17:343-347.

Sherman, J. A. 1971. *On the Psychology of Women*. Springfield: Charles C Thomas, pp. 111-112.

Shopper, M. 1979. The (re)discovery of the vagina and the importance of the menstrual tampon. In M. Sugar, Ed., *Female Adolescent Development*. New York: Brunner/Mazel.

Silberstein, L. R., Mishkind, M. E., Striegel-Moore, R. H., Timko, C., & Rodin, J. 1989. Men and their bodies: A comparison of homosexual and heterosexual men. *Psychosomatic Medicine*, 51(3):345-349.

Silvern, L. E. 1977. Children's sex-role preferences: Stronger among girls than boys. *Sex Roles*, 3:159-171.

Stoller, R. J. 1973. The "bedrock" of masculinity and femininity: Bisexuality. In J. B. Miller, Ed., *Psychoanalysis of Women*. New York: Brunner/Mazel.

Wilson, G. & Nias, D. 1976. *The Mystery of Love*. New York: Quadrangle, pp. 1-14.

Zelnik, M. & Kantner, J. F. 1980. Sexual activity, contraceptive use and pregnancy among metropolitan-area teenagers:1971-1979. *Family Planning Perspectives*, 12:230-237.

5 The Superego in the Adolescent Female

Hyman L. Muslin, M.D.
Jonathan D. Lewis, M.D.

The superego is a construct of great importance in the psychoanalytic model of the mind. It is conceived of as an intrapsychic system that comprises both contents and functions. The contents, internalized from infancy, serve as prohibitions against, or inhibitors of, instinctual derivatives, i.e., moral codes. Additionally, the superego embodies a set of aspirations and ideals representing standards to be lived up to. These two sets of contents, known as the *conscience* and the *ego-ideal*, are conceptualized as major components of the system superego.

The superego is also conceptualized as having a set of functions acting intersystemically with the ego and id to promote repression or other ego defenses in alliance with the ego, and to stand in opposition, in the main, to the egress of instinctual derivatives from the id. Other functions of the mature or autonomous superego are: to release signals of anxiety, shame or guilt, which influence ego mechanisms to action in order to alleviate or prevent the experience of guilt if the conscience is being transgressed; or to spur the ego to act to alleviate shame if some ideal is not attained.

In order to place in perspective the constructs elaborated in this chapter, a review of the early and recent literature on the superego in females will be reviewed. Following this, the process and content features of the superego in the adolescent female will be developed.

REVIEW OF LITERATURE

In a previous paper on the "Superego in Women" (Muslin, 1974), the thesis was advanced that there is no specificity attached to the masculine or feminine superego in terms of the functions that are enacted by the superego. The superego, once consolidated in the adult form, functions to assist in the binding, neutralizing, and discharging of drives by holding out moral and ideal standards and emitting signals to which specialized aspects of the ego respond in appropriate ways.

The superego in women does have specific contents determined by membership in a group (so defined by the particular culture) and by individual experience. Thus, what becomes internalized to serve as conscience and ego-ideal is peculiar to women's special instinctual needs and development, particularly to the cultural values held out and internalized. (These superego contents frame the conscience and ideal standards for individual women and constitute the measure by which the self experiences failure versus victory, or shame and guilt versus well-being.) Women, like men, may typically experience symptoms, inhibitions, and anxiety, as well as guilt with loss of esteem. Additionally, the capacity for seeking truth and fighting for justice can be manifest or absent in women equally as in men. In sum, superegos are superegos, without sexual differentiation in terms of function. Finally, the distortion and value judgments about the lack of stability of the conscience in women have resulted from a confusion between the *process* and the *contents* of the superego in women.

In the literature on the female psyche and superego preceding the modern era of psychoanalysis, there is general agreement as to the major points that Freud (1924, 1925) posited in relation to the female Oedipus complex and its resolution or lack of resolution leading to the formation of the superego. Although several authors amplified the nature and importance of the preoedipal period (Brunswick, 1940; Deutsch, 1944; Lampl-de Groot, 1927), others disagreed with the importance of penis envy as a motivating force in the entry into the positive Oedipus complex (Horney, 1953; Jones, 1913), while still others placed the Oedipus complex at an earlier time in the developing child (Klein, 1928; Jones, 1913).

It would seem that the major features of the theory elaborated by Freud have been accepted, to wit: the lack of "destruction" in the fantasies of the Oedipus complex in females, since castration anxiety is not an impetus; and the length of time (oftentimes permanently) women may remain involved in the fantasies of the Oedipus complex (i.e., continues to seek for the male parent to complete her defective anatomy while still needing a female parent to render nurturance).*

In his early work, Freud had assumed that there was a complete parallel in the sexual life of girls and boys. This line of reasoning continued in his two seminal papers on female psychology (1924, 1925). Here Freud described the biphasic development of the Oedipus complex, including the girl's preoedipal phase as a love relationship with mother as object. This relationship ends with the girl's awareness of her castration, which begins the search for penis and child through the fantasied bond with the father—the positive Oedipus complex. The actual resolution of the oedipal struggle in females is not definitive and

---

*But not by all—see Chapter 3 by Zilbach.—Editor.

is often incomplete, so that the girl's search for the penis-baby is often not consummated. A stable, crystallized system of introjects operating as a major restraint against instinctual derivatives could not obtain in the system.

Of the modern writers, Greenacre (1952) stressed that the superego in the girl is imbued with feelings of wrongdoing emanating from past masturbation and the already present punishment of castration. This accounts for the aimless conscientiousness and worrying in females to be contrasted with the firmer, more condensed conscience in the male.

Jacobson's (1954) comments about the development of the superego in women revealed a disagreement with Freud about the female superego being defective; she believed that it is different in nature from the male superego. In her view, the girl develops a nucleus of a true maternal ego-ideal earlier than the boy, which is due to the early onset of the castration conflict in girls. Directly, as a result of the castration conflict, the girl suffers from intense castration fears but eventually her preoedipal disappointment and devaluation of her mother's and her own deficient genitals lead to a rejection of her mother as a sexual love object in favor of the phallic father. This sometimes eventuates in the premature disenchantment with all genital activities and results in the early establishment of the maternal ego-ideal: the ideal of an unaggressive, clean, neat little girl, determined to renounce sexuality. In Jacobson's view, the female ego-ideal absorbs and forever replaces the "illusory penis" fantasy. These are the females who deny penis envy but unconsciously have as representation of their "inner penis" an uncommon pride in their inner values and their moral integrity.

Hartmann and Loewenstein (1962) limited the term superego to the system that comes into being upon the resolution of the conflict of the oedipal phase. It comprises the following three functions: 1) the conscience, 2) self-criticism, 3) holding up ideals. Their comments on the female superego point up that it does have particular characteristics. Its origin is less climactic than is the case with boys, and its formation extends over a longer period. However they stated that in the girl the ego-ideal tends to set in earlier, that is, at a time when integration and objectivation and their autonomous functions are, comparatively speaking, less developed.

The supposition that women have superegos that are defective, either because of the contents or the structure, has been challenged recently in several quarters (Blum, 1976; Schafer, 1974). As a result of direct child observation, several psychoanalytic researchers have described the onset of femininity as a phenomenon occurring earlier than Freud had anticipated and due (in larger measures than he had posited) to influences such as object relationships and cognitive functions (Kleeman, 1977; Galenson & Roiphe, 1977). As Kleeman has stated: "Cognitive functions, learning experiences and language are believed to be more important than Freud stressed and penis envy and problems of inferiority are relegated to a less universal and less necessary place in the onset of femininity" (1977, p. 23).

In an interesting study of an analysis of a three-year-old girl, Glenn (1977) described clinical material that demonstrated that maternal identification did lead to femininity prior to the establishment of the Oedipus complex. The patient fantasied she possessed a penis and therefore feared castration once she developed the Oedipus complex. Finally, as Glenn (1977) stated, "When the analysis ended she appeared on her way to resolving her Oedipus complex and developing a superego" (p. 159).

"THE MORAL DOMAIN"

In the nearly 15 years since the publication of the first edition of this volume, a specific aspect of female superego development has been elaborated. Often referred to as a study of "the moral domain," this research focuses on the cognitive aspects of superego development, identifying the particular characteristics of the female superego, as they differ from that of the male. To place this recent work in context, it is necessary to review concepts of moral development espoused by Freud and Piaget, for the modern study of female moral values arose in part as a reaction to a view of moral development that had taken the male as its model.

Freud identified morality with the superego, stating that the superego "represents the claims of morality, and we realize all at once that our moral sense of guilt is the expression of the tension between the ego and the superego" (1933, p. 61). It was Freud's notion that the superego in women, and hence their sense of morality, did not attain the "strength" and "independence" it did in men (1933, p. 129).

For Freud (1925), the construction of morality and conscience in the male arose as a consequence of the abandonment of Oedipal wishes in the face of castration fears. Thus, according to Freud, the little girl, unthreatened by castration, had not the same impetus to develop a strict ethical system. In perhaps the best known or, in the case of the modernist/feminist critics, the most infamous statement of this position, Freud says, "[Women's] superego is never so inexorable, so impersonal, so independent of its emotional origins as we require it to be in men" (1925, p. 275). Freud goes on to say that this psychological situation accounts for the observation that women are more often influenced in their judgments by emotionality and show "less sense of justice than men."

Piaget also associated morality with the concept of justice, identifying "three great periods in the development of the sense of justice in the child" (1932, p. 314). Briefly stated, the first stage was one in which justice was defined by adult authority. In the second stage, notions of equality or "fairness" supplanted the reign of authority. By the age of 11-12, concomitant with the development of the capacity for formal thought, the child elaborates a third stage in which strict interpretations of justice, defined as equality, are tempered by considerations of context, relativity, equity, and reciprocity.

Piaget adds that the development of the sense of justice depends upon the development of autonomy in the child. "Authority as such cannot be the source of justice . . . For, resting as it does on equality and reciprocity, justice can only come into being by free consent" (1932, p. 318). However, it is important to note that Piaget emphasized that, in addition to autonomy, "cooperation and mutual respect" were also prerequisites to the development of a mature moral sense (ibid., p. 319).

The importance of this last statement lies in the fact that the recent descriptions of the differences between the male and female sense of morality attribute a central position to concepts of justice and autonomy in the moral life of the male, while connectedness, cooperation, and care are central to the female's sense of morality. Piaget clearly indicates that *both* autonomy and cooperation (mutuality) are requirements of a completely developed morality. Taking up where Piaget left off, Kohlberg, Levine and Hewer (1983) studied the development of morality in children, adolescents, and adults in an extensive series of studies that asked its subjects to respond to a set of hypothetical moral dilemmas. These studies began with Kohlberg's dissertation in 1958, which utilized a cross-section of young adolescent males. Further studies led to an extensive bibliography and culminated in a theory of moral development.

Kohlberg's theory, like Piaget's and Freud's is a structural theory, which in essence holds that there is a sequence of stages in the development of moral reasoning from childhood to maturity; that while not all people reach the highest stages of moral reasoning it is nonetheless an invariable sequence in that none of the lower stages can be skipped over in the attainment of maturity; and that central to moral reasoning are concepts of justice. Thus, Kohlberg, following Freud and Piaget, equates concepts of justice with the moral domain.

While denying that he ever directly states that males have a more developed sense of justice than females, as Freud did, Kohlberg does suggest that females, up until recently, have had less opportunity than men to engage in the more complex societal institutions and occupational functions that lay the foundation for the development of the higher stages of justice reasoning (1983).

It is the exclusive identification of morality with concepts of justice that has come under scrutiny and criticism recently as defining the moral domain in too narrow a fashion. Female analyst/critics urge a broadening of the concept of the moral domain by including in its purview concerns that they state are more allied with female psychology and with feminine values and ideals.

This idea was broached by Jean Baker Miller (1976) when she suggested that the ego and superego of women were not weaker than men's, as Freud had asserted, but rather different in nature. The formation of a woman's psyche was mediated by a more complex relation to reality. A woman was required to modify her drives, not just in response to the reality principle but in the service of the needs of others. This led to a self-system that was less autonomous because it was bound up by concerns for the needs of others as an organizing principle.

This notion has been elaborated upon extensively by Carol Gilligan and her colleagues (1982, 1988). Simply stated, Gilligan, et al. argue for an expansion of the limits of the moral domain to include concepts of care as a distinct line of moral development, separate from the development of concepts of justice. Gilligan and Wiggins (1988) view the development of morality as a function of the young child's experience of attachment, relatedness, and dependency, through which the child experiences both care and inequity; "The different dynamics of early childhood inequality and attachment lay the groundwork for two moral visions —one of justice and one of care" (Gilligan & Wiggins, 1988, p. 115).

While eschewing overly simple generalizations, they nonetheless assert a sexual difference in the focus of moral development: "observations of sex differences in moral understanding and moral behavior reflect a tendency for these problems to be differentially salient or differently organized in male and female development" (1988, p. 116). Gilligan (1982) states, "The moral imperative that emerges repeatedly in interviews with women is an injunction to care, a responsibility to discern and alleviate the 'real and recognizable trouble' of this world. For men, the moral imperative appears rather as an injunction to respect the rights of others and thus to protect from interference the rights to life and self-fulfillment" (p. 100).

Ultimately, Kohlberg, et al. acknowledge that Gilligan's contribution "usefully enlarges the moral domain" (1983, p. 123) and assert that their hypothetical sixth and final stage, or moral maturity, represents "an integration of justice and care which forms a single moral principle" (1983, p. 126). In response to this assertion, Gilligan and Wiggins (1988) reply that while Kohlberg's theory laid claim to an integration of the dual constructs of justice and care, "He never described how caring develops or how one knows what constitutes care" (p. 133).

Thus, the debate about what constitutes the moral domain, and how these constituents differ between males and females continues. Interestingly, Gilligan argues, with Freud, for the existence of a distinction between male and female superegos. For Freud, these psychological differences ultimately arose from the anatomical differences between the sexes; for Gilligan it is a matter of a difference in the socialization and enculturation processes between boys and girls which leads to the psychical distinctions.

As stated at the outset of this chapter, we are in agreement with the proposition that the *contents* of the superegos vary between males and females. The superego is above all the internalized representation of the values and ideals held up for emulation by a particular society. Because the cultural ideals for men and women differ, so the contents of the superego will differ in a very general fashion between men and women. However, superego functions and processes are the same for all individuals, varying individually along a continuum from less to more developed, and from the less healthy to the more healthy.

THE FEMALE ADOLESCENT SUPEREGO

The focus of this chapter is primarily on the psychological experiences of the female through adolescence, especially on how these experiences change the superego system. The endpoint of the psychological change in the superego in adolescence is alteration of the moral codes and the ideal standards sufficiently so that the young adult can now adapt to the invitations and challenges of adulthood. Specifically, one of the adolescent developmental achievements is to be able to experience formerly repressed drives and to master the environment with the egress of these neutralized drives. Another intrapsychic mutation consists of the assumption of realistic aspirations that can be followed and, therefore, provide a source of esteem. Additionally, there is a continual development of a conscience in which new contents are internalized, new injunctions established, while injunctions from previous developmental eras continue to serve as a censor, barring the outflow of unneutralized drives.

The endpoint of adolescence from the superego point of view consists in the addition of drive regulating contents and modifications in the ego-ideal, standards sufficiently cathected so as to establish or reestablish intrapsychic peace. These accomplishments must be enacted, while, at the same time, certain previously internalized moral values barring egress of instinct from infancy and childhood must be maintained for continuing adaptation.

Adolescence does begin with disequilibrium. The process could be viewed as superego disequilibrium since the balance between the repressed intrapsychic contents and that part of the repressing force within the superego is altered and new superego structure has to be accreted for equilibrium to be reestablished. The superego that is effective in latency is not adequate for the psyche in the years following the onset of puberty. The great accomplishments in childhood in the superego serve well to maintain repression over the childhood drives, but clearly cannot tame or deny the outpouring of drives once pubertal energies achieve psychic representation as the ''new'' version of sexual and aggressive drives.

In the view of many authors, the so-called adolescent turmoil here described as superego disequilibrium is inextricably bound up with the reemergence of the Oedipal complex; in fact, the central task of adolescence is to master this conflict and thus to separate permanently from parents as love objects, i.e., to effect a permanent de-cathexis of mother and father as love and hate objects. As Blos (1974) stated, "It is an accepted tenet in psychoanalytic theory that the Oedipus complex is reactivated during adolescence." He further related, "It is my contention that adolescence not only is faced with the revival of the Oedipal conflict as it was resolved or abandoned at its first decline, but that definitive resolution of the complex is the inherent task of adolescence." Deutsch (1944) observed that: "Young people of both sexes are tormented by a feeling of insecurity, uncertainty and inner restlessness throughout adolescence. The straight line of development and the effort of the ego to adjust itself and master reality are over and over again interrupted by the rising tides of sexuality" (p. 129).

Freud's (1905, p. 207) comments on adolescence dealt with the description of puberty as the time when three changes occurred that completed the development of the sexual life: 1) subordination of the erotogenic zones to genital primacy; 2) establishment of new sexual aims; and 3) seeking of new sexual objects. While Freud did not in that paper specifically relate adolescence to disequilibrium or to the reemergence of Oedipal conflict, he did speak of the pain of giving up of incestuous fantasies during puberty: "At the same time as these plainly incestuous phantasies are overcome and repudiated, one of the most significant but also one of the most painful psychical achievements of the pubertal period is completed: detachment from parental authority, a process that alone makes possible the opposition, which is so important for the progress of civilization, between the new generation and the old" (p. 227).

In actuality, Jones (1922, p. 399) was among the first to speak of adolescence recapitulating infancy. While other analytic observers contributed to the study of the development of the adolescent (Bernfeld, 1938; Hoffer, 1946), the next major study in this area was that of A. Freud (1936), who attributed the anxiety of adolescence to an increase in libido that energized a return of the repressed incest fantasy of childhood; however, soon adolescents become anxious in a global manner and fear the "quantity not the quality of their instincts" (p. 168). She also spoke of the inevitable turning away from anxiety as a modal feature of adolescence, and of the superego being treated as an incestuous object. In 1958, Anna Freud wrote that adolescence was an "interruption of peaceful growth" and that "the upholding of a steady equilibrium during the adolescent process is in itself abnormal."

Jacobson's (1964) work included her view of adolescent development and the changes in ego and superego during this time, which involve a "transitory partial collapse of the superego and the repressive barriers" as a result of the "overpowering instinctual strivings" (p. 178). She, too, spoke of the "temporary revival of preoedipal and oedipal strivings" (p. 170) during adolescence that must be relinquished permanently, she further stated: "In adolescence, the superego must once more enforce the incest taboo, yet at the same time it must open the barriers of repression and lift the burden of countercathexes" (p. 173).

It would seem that a consensus has been arrived at by most analytic observers of adolescent development regarding the finding (arrived at by observation of adolescents in analysis or retrospectively through adult analysis) that adolescents must undergo a stage of unrest, turmoil, or disequilibrium since there is at least a quantitative increase in instinctual urges and there may be a specific qualitative increase in urges from the reactivated Oedipal conflict. As Anna Freud (1958) stated in relation to the preadolescent character, "it has to be abandoned" (p. 264).

It is interesting in this connection to note observations from another vantage point, the findings of Offer (1969) and Masterson (1967) derived from interview and clinical data, self-assessment questionnaires, and projective examinations. Their findings pertaining to the notion of adolescent disequilibrium are capsulized by Masterson's comment: "It appears then that the theory of adolescent turmoil derived presumably from the study of neurotics (although this is not spelled out either) has been inconsiderately generalized to all adolescents" (p. 160). Their findings, in sum, although derived from a different data base, are that one must be mindful of speaking of adolescent turmoil in a global fashion, especially since the analytic theories are based upon data from adolescents in treatment. These authors stressed that in family situations with warmth, empathy, and continuity, a gradual detachment from parents takes place with little disequilibrium. Offer (1973) stated: "We cannot say that because we expect turmoil, find it and cherish it, it is a defining characteristic of the healthy adolescent" (p. 17). His remarks refer only to "normal" males.

These findings, while of serious interest, need to be appreciated as deriving from methods that are at a distance from the data gained through introspection and empathy in transference analysis. Although the behavior of all of Offer's male adolescents (1969) did not reveal turmoil or crisis, it does *not* indicate the presence or absence of intrapsychic crisis, which is made manifest only at times through transference analysis. On the other hand, the finding is well taken that one cannot define early adolescence in terms of the so-called ubiquitous behavior of crisis or tumoil studied in analyses of adolescent patients. It is interesting in this regard to note that Anna Freud (1958) was quite clear that crisis states do not affect only adolescents: "Adolescence of course is not the only time in life when alterations of a physiologic nature cause disturbances of mental equilibrium. The same happens in later years in the climacterum . . ." (p. 267).

Thus far, we have gathered together the pertinent remarks on the entry into adolescence and the necessary disequilibrium that eventuates intrapsychically, regardless of the manifest behavior, which may or may not reflect the inner process of changes that must take place for eventual equilibrium and growth. Further, this early adolescent phase has been described without special reference to sexual identity; seemingly, boys and girls undergo the same superego disequilibrium.

We believe it more accurate to say that the entry into enhancement of sexuality and aggressivity has resulted from physiologic changes and from a milieu that now invites more libido and aggression from the adolescent.

The adolescent experiences and manifests an overall increase in all drives, so that taming of the drives is a major issue and, as has been noted, provides for the intrapsychic disequilibrium. As A. Freud noted (1936): "As I have already remarked, adolescents are not so much concerned with the gratification or frustration of specific instinctual wishes as with instinctual gratification or frustration as such" (p. 168).

The entry into adolescence and the disequilibrium have apparently been observed and understood by most authors as revealing no significant differences between the sexes. However, Freud (1905) remarked that puberty ushered in a "wave of repression in which it is precisely clitoridal sexuality that is affected" (p. 220). As will be remembered, these remarks were part of his theories of eventual transfer of libido to the vagina as part of the nature of sexuality in women.

The intrapsychic or structural disarray thus requires new structure to reestablish intrapsychic peace. In the superego other changes are required; the childhood conscience, so well adapted to automatic censorship of specific drives, must now acquire new codes by internalization, while maintaining the previously established morality against ancient drives. The other area of the superego, the ego-ideal, which is usually adopted as a set of standards to live by and serves as a source of esteem in childhood (the good, clean, quiet girl), must now acquire a new set of aspirations that are in accord with the cultural role of the woman in our society. Many authors define the end of adolescence as the time when the ego-ideal becomes firmly cathected (Blos, 1974; Hammerman, 1965; Kohut, 1971; Ritvo, 1971).

The conscience and ideals are altered in adolescence by a process in which the superego disarray ushers in a phase of seeking for identifications, i.e., those moral codes and standards that will become internalized as the new voices of the conscience. These new moral codes and values must, over the long period of adolescence, enable the girl and boy to experience certain object-directed instinctual strivings without absolute restriction. To be sure, the restrictions against a variety of primitive drives retain their integrity. Thus, while the *conscience* barriers against incest and parricide maintain their cathexis, the barrier (moral code) against all heterosexuality is altered.

The structural changes in the superego are readily seen in the acquisition of internalized standards, i.e., ego-ideal contents. New moral codes are not internalized in the sense of identifying with new injunctions or censorship against drives. Rather, the ancient automatic censors against drives must be attenuated by the accommodation of the self to the newly acquired ego-ideal contents. Thus, in each mental act that involves the egress of instinctual derivations, the superego component will consist of a component of conscience tension (guilt signal) and ideal tension (shame signal). As Jacobson (1964) succinctly stated, "You are permitted to enjoy sexual and emotional freedom and freedom of thoughts and actions to the extent which you renounce your infantile desires, loosen your childhood attachments and accept adult ethical standards and responsibilities" (p. 176).

The process by which the internalization of new standards takes place results from the crisis of intrapsychic disequilibrium, which initiates the movement towards the quest for external objects to serve as idealized imagos. Thus, the breakdown of superego structure, in this view, precipitates the emergence of the method of resecuring esteem from childhood and the externalizing of self-libido onto parents and parent-substitutes. This process, as described by Kohut (1971), is terminated by the internalization of the idealized standards of one's leaders to serve as sources of esteem. Kohut (1971) has described the phase of psychic development in which the psyche of the child invests the parent with self-libido (narcissism) and then internalizes (transmuting internalization) the narcissistic aspects of the relationship with the parents, along with the object-cathected aspects of the parental imago, which forms the so-called idealized superego: "The internalization of the object-cathected aspects of the parental imago transmutes the latter into the contents and functions of the superego; the internalization of the narcissistic aspects accounts for the exalted position which these contents and functions have" (p. 41).

Especially important for the considerations in this chapter is another statement by Kohut (1971): "Once the nuclear psychological structures have been established (largely at the end of the oedipal period; but an important firming and buttressing of the psychic apparatus, especially in the area of the establishment of reliable *ideals*, takes place during latency and puberty, with a *decisive final step in late adolescence*), object loss, be it ever so crushing, will not leave the personality incomplete" (p. 43, emphasis added).

Thus, Kohut differentiated two sets of contents that are internalized and become the components of the superego system: those prohibitions emanating from the parental injunctions, which become conscience; and the idealized qualities of parents that become internalized to form our ideals. Kohut (1966) differentiated between the contents of the ego-ideal (standards, values, and ideals) and the idealizing (the narcissistic aspects) of the superego in general: "If the ego's instinctual investment of the superego remains insufficiently desexualized (or becomes resexualized) moral masochism is the result" (p. 251).

This process is thus not specific for the crisis of adolescence, but perhaps serves as one of the methods for resolution of intrapsychic conflict during those times when the psyche enters into disequilibrium due to increases in instinctual tension, i.e., during those periods when the superego is temporarily in disarray.

Now, at the stage of disarray when impulses are not adequately bound and are thus experienced in an intense manner, it is clear that, for the most part, these strivings preclude the reinvestment onto the parents of idealizing libido. The objects to be idealized, whose conduct and standards will ultimately be internalized for narcissistic sustenance, will ofttimes be peers or neutralized authority figures, but not necessarily. Whether a parent can serve as the idealized figure during this period of imbalance will depend on a variety of considerations, including: the pregenital and Oedipal parent-child interactions; the acceptability of the parent's values in adolescence; and the intensity and nature of the emerging impulses.

These considerations call into question the somewhat narrow understanding of what has been referred to as the ubiquitous process of adolescent structure building, or the loss of the parents as objects for identification. There is a process-content confusion here; the process that is constant is that the disequilibrium results in a quest for newly internalized objects. The rejection of the parents may or may not be an important feature. Thus, each adolescent's pathway must be appreciated without stereotyping.

Those aspects of the internalized and idealized objects that become components of the girl's ego-ideal are, of course, bound by the choices which exist in a particular society. In reviewing the literature in this area, one must be mindful of the contrast between the identification, i.e., the contents of the ideal in the adolescent girl, as differentiated from the process of internalizing. From this point of view, the ego-ideal in a woman will reflect what has been internalized. An interesting contrast in view of the destiny and ideals of women can be offered when one examines the notions of various authors over time, e.g., Deutsch (1944): "Only exceptionally talented girls can carry a surplus of intellect without injuring their affective lives, for woman's intellect, her capacity for objectively understanding life, thrives at the expense of her subjective emotional qualities" (p. 143). And again: "The sequence constituted by 1) greater proneness to identification, 2) strong fantasy, 3) subjectivity, 4) inner perception and, 5) intuition leads us back to the common origin of all these traits, feminine passivity" (p. 139).

Another statement that carries forward into adolescent psychology the notion that the girl's superego structure is defective comes from Blos (1974): "Remnants of a reattachment of the ego ideal to an outside person remains to some degree, the sine qua non of the female ego ideal" (p. 55). This statement is a carryover of the argument that the girl ofttimes does not resolve her Oedipus complex, but indeed continues to search outside for the penis to complete her psyche.

It would seem that there is at times confusion between the process of interiorization and the contents of the superego; the contents internalized (the identifications) are being taken as biological givens. Thus, Deutsch's comments clearly pertain to the values for women in 1944. An interesting study in specialty choices in medicine highlights the notion of changes in women as a reflection of the choices for identification within a given culture. McGrath and Zinet (1977, p. 290) reported that in a period of six years female specialty choices went from pediatrics and psychiatry to family practice, pediatrics, internal medicine, psychiatry, and surgery in that order.

The shape of the ego-ideal in female adolescents will reflect the internalized contents (identifications), and thus be a composite of those objects for identification that are held out to her as valued in her particular society and era in history. That many generations of women have continued to identify with those attributes of the maternal person in their self and in their ideal is only an indication of the narrowness of choices held out for women. Thus, it has come about that in speaking of the adolescent woman and her ideals, many authors in previous times accepted the mother role as the major standard and set of qualities to be internalized by the female, and, in fact, conceived of this learned role as a biological given. In 1977, Benedek spoke of the "new" marriage in which the man must recognize the independence and equality of his wife, and of the wife who ". . . is not free from the psychobiological desire for a strong man as a husband."

Thus, the cultural fallacy continues that the woman, during adolescence, will merge with an idealized imago (parent or otherwise) that exhibits "mothering" qualities, and once the transmuting internalizations have taken place, the adolescent girl will become another mothering woman. Her ideal, crystallized at the late adolescent phase, will now hold out to her narcissistic sustenance once she exhibits effective mothering. It seems clear that these notions reflect a view of a continuing destiny for women, similar to the "anatomy is destiny" notion, that requires correction—to wit, that the shape of the adolescent's ideal at the termination of adolescence will reflect the special contents which that particular woman has internalized, and that there is *no* destiny at which the woman will arrive that is preordained by genetics or endocrinology. These contents will reflect the psychosocial milieu of the individual woman.

Clearly, the traditional version of the woman is being altered in many societies, so that what any particular woman will hold up to be her ideals in future times is not clear. The changes in the acceptance of women in so many arenas—economic, professional, political—make it clear that we are approaching a more egalitarian society from the viewpoint of men and women. This is best demonstrated in some of our societal institutions, e.g., in the career choices of young women, in the types of bonds between men and women, and in the frequent childless marriages.

SUMMARY

The thesis has been presented that the adolescent woman undergoes personality changes that occur without regard to sex as a result of the ordinary upsurge of physiologic and psychic changes that create disequilibrium in the adolescent psyche. These intrapsychic changes involve all the psychic forces, which will then undergo modification so as to affect a new equilibrium. This chapter has focused on the superego changes, mindful that the self-system, in liaison with the superego, will develop new identifications that will also affect the intersystemic interactions (Wolf, Gedo & Terman, 1972).

This chapter is an attempt to clarify and correct a view of the psyche in women that has often identified the manifest personality traits of the woman in a particular society with the destiny of the woman. Specifically, the adolescent woman undergoes intrapsychic change as part of the superego disequilibrium, which then results in changes in the conscience and ideal facets of the superego. This process has been described as a generic reaction to intrapsychic disequilibrium in which superego restraints are not adequate to master instinctual tension, resulting in the transient periods of searching for idealized imagos. These states of regression are terminated when merger between self and the self object of the idealized imagos takes place, adding to the ideals within the superego so that the personality is now once again in a state of peace with its self.

These happenings have been described in a simplified and schematic manner deliberately to stress the system aspects, and not the contents or the ideals of the superego. What is internalized as the superego contents is, of course, a measure of the current role model for women and never to be confused with psychologic destiny. Thus, in one society, women are permanently to be imprisoned since their mana must be controlled, while in another society and at another time, women are to be adulated since their magic is life-giving and life-sustaining. At this moment there are a variety of forms and styles in our pool of role models for adolescent women to idealize and internalize, including the businesswoman, doctor, model, politician, scholar-athlete, TV-movie star, as well as the more traditional wife and mother. This situation is much different from the narrowness which was modal at the time of World War II and in previous times and places.

However, in the literature on the personality of women, there are descriptions of the ultimate identification with the so-called maternal ideal, the eternal feminine, or the mothering core. This accentuates once again the notion that there is a passive, nurturing genetic code for women that is not influenced by the psychologic process of internalized value systems formed by identifications. Perhaps the belief in the magna mater principle represents still another mythic bedrock that we must all relinquish, i.e., the omnipresent belief in the Great Mother who will emerge in crises to defeat our enemies (e.g., The Apocryphal Legend of

Judith vanquishing Holofernes [Muslin, 1977]). The myth of the Great Mother who will be everpresent for our salvation is a wish that, while understandable, must be (alas!) recognized as the ubiquitous childhood fantasy and not held out to women as the central trait to internalize as the core of the feminine ego-ideal.

REFERENCES

Benedek, T. 1977. Ambivalence, passion and love. *J. Amer. Psychoanal. Assn.*, 25:53-87.

Bernfeld, S. 1938. Types of adolescence. *Psychoanal. Quart.*, 7:243-253.

Blos, P. 1974. Genealogy of the ego ideal. *Psychoanal. Study Child*, 29:43-88.

Blum, H. P. 1976. Masochism, the ego ideal, and the psychology of women. *J. Amer. Psychoanal. Assn.* (Supplement), 24:157-191.

Brunswick, R. M. 1940. The preoedipal phase of the libido development. In R. Fliess, Ed., *The Psychoanalytic Reader*, Vol. I. New York: International Universities Press, 1950, pp. 231-253.

Deutsch, H. 1944. *Psychology of Women*, Vol. I. New York: Grune & Stratton.

Freud, A. 1936. *The Ego and the Mechanisms of Defense*. New York: International Universities Press.

Freud, A. 1958. Adolescence. *Psychoanal. Study Child*, 13:255-278.

Freud, S. 1905. Three essays on the theory of sexuality. *The Standard Edition*, 7:135-245. London: The Hogarth Press, 1953.

Freud, S. 1924. The dissolution of the Oedipus complex. *The Standard Edition*, 19:173-183. London: The Hogarth Press, 1961.

Freud, S. 1925. Some psychical consequences of the anatomical distinction between the sexes. *The Standard Edition*. 19:245-258. London: The Hogarth Press, 1961.

Freud, S. 1933. *New Introductory Lectures, The Standard Edition*, 22. London: The Hogarth Press, 1964.

Galenson, E., & Roiphe, H. 1977. Some suggested revisions concerning early female development. In H. P. Blum, Ed., *Female Psychology, Contemporary Psychoanalytic Views*. New York: International Universities Press.

Gilligan, C. 1982. *In a Different Voice*. Cambridge: Harvard University Press.

Gilligan, C. & Wiggins, G. 1988. The Origins of Morality in Early Childhood Relationships. In C. Gilligan, J. V. Ward, & J. M. Taylor, Eds., *Mapping the Moral Domain*. Center for the Study of Gender, Education and Human Development, Cambridge: Harvard University Press.

Glenn, J. 1977. Psychoanalysis of a constipated girl. *J. Amer. Psychoanal. Assn.*, 25:141-163.

Greenacre, P. 1952. Anatomical structure and superego. In *Trauma, Growth and Personality*. New York: Norton.

Hammerman, S. 1965. Conceptions of superego development. *J. Amer. Psychoanal. Assn.*, 13:320-355.

Hartman, H. & Loewenstein, R. M. 1962. Notes on the superego. *Psychoanal. Study Child.*, 17:42-81.

Hoffer, W. 1946. Diaries of adolescent schizophrenia. *Psychoanal. Study Child.*, 2:293-312.

Horney, K. 1953. On the genesis of the castration complex in women. *Internat. J. Psycho-Anal.*, 5:50-65.

Jacobson, E. 1954. The self and the object world. *Psychoanal. Study Child*, 9:75-127.

Jacobson, E. 1964. *The Self and the Object World*. New York: International Universities Press.

Jones, E. 1913. The phantasy of the reversal of generations. *Papers on Psychoanalysis*. Baltimore: Williams and Wilkins, 1948.

Jones, E. 1922. Some problems of adolescence. *Papers on Psychoanalysis*, Fifth Edition. London: Bailliere, Tindall & Cox, 1948.

Kleeman, J. 1977. Freud's views on early female sexuality in the light of direct child observation. In H. P. Blum, Ed., *Female Psychology, Contemporary Psychoanalytic Views*. New York: International Universities Press.

Klein, M. 1928. Early stages of the Oedipus conflict. *Internat. J. Anal.*, 9:167:180.

Kohlberg, L., Levine, C., & Hewer, A. 1983. *Moral Stages: A Current Formulation and a Response to Critics*. Basel: Karger.

Kohut, L. 1966. Forms and transformations of narcissism. *J. Amer. Psychoanal. Assn.*, 14:243-273.

Kohut, H. 1971. *Analysis of the Self*. New York: International Universities Press.

Lampl-de Groot, J. 1927. The evolution of the Oedipus in women. In R. Fliess, Ed., *The Psychoanalytic Reader*. New York: International Universities Press, 1933, p. 180-197.

Masterson, J. F. 1967. *The Psychiatric Dilemma of Adolescence*. New York: Little, Brown & Co.

McGrath, E. & Zinet, C. 1977. Female and male medical students: Differences in specialty choice selection and personality. *J. Med. Educ.*, 52:290-299.

Miller, J. B. 1976. *Toward a New Psychology of Women*. Boston: Beacon Press.

Muslin, H. 1974. Superego in women. In S. C. Post, Ed., *Moral Values and the Superego in Psychoanalysis*. New York: International Universities Press.

Muslin, H. 1977. *Judith and Esther, A study in the Old Testament heroines* (Unpublished).

Offer, D. 1969. *The Psychological World of the Teen-ager*. New York: Basic Books.

Offer, D. 1973. Normal adolescence in perspective. In J. C. Schoolar, Ed., *Current Issues in Adolescent Psychiatry*. New York: Brunner/Mazel.

Piaget, J. (originally published in French in 1932). *The Moral Judgement of the Child*, Trans. by Marjorie Gabain. Glencoe: The Free Press.

Ritvo, S. 1971. Late adolescence. *Psychoanal. Study Child*, 26:241-263.

Schafer, R. 1974. Problems in Freud's psychology of women. *J. Amer. Psychoanal. Assn.*, 22:259-285.

Wolf, E., Gedo, J., & Terman, D. 1972. On the adolescent process as a transformation of the self. *J. Youth Adol.*, 1:157-173.

6 Alterations in the Ego-Ideal in Girls in Mid-Adolescence

Vann Spruiell, M.D.

INTRODUCTION

Humans change, not only nicely, slowly, progressively, but at times extremely rapidly and perhaps not so nicely. At these times growth is not so much a matter of development as it is of maturation; it is not the mere altering of old structure—or, better, system—but the building of a new system on top of the old, supraordinate to it but still in relationship to the older, simpler one. Thus, a new system comes into being and in the process the older one's functions also become altered (Spruiell, 1990).

In relative health, these spasms of inner revolutionary change (one thinks of the moves from lap and knee baby to toddler, the initiation of latency, pubescence, parturition, menopause) are times of great opportunity and great risk. More or less ordinary people—more or less psychoneurotic people—negotiate the periods of rapid reorganization and new structure-building relatively well; they mature inwardly and outwardly in expectable ways. More disturbed people often come to grief during these times, fail to develop expectably, fall back on older and safer ways of being—however grossly inappropriate these ways of being might be for the external requirements of a particular age.

In this chapter, I will rely upon analytic experiences with adults and adolescents, as well as upon experiences with adolescents who were not patients to demonstrate the changes in the ego-ideal in girls that are a part—a crucial part, but only a part—of the maturational changes between early and late adolescence. At that time, in a reasonably healthy boy or girl, relationships with idealized persons or sets of ideas in the external world of the early adolescent are replaced by an *internal* relationship with a new ego-ideal, epigenetically built upon older versions of the ego-ideal. Concomitantly, the prohibitory functions of the superego become less weighty, more flexible and reasonable, and less childish. If this

97

reorganization is successful, the new system of regulators plays a central role in the young person's *beginning* to feel, think, and act like an adult.

THE REVOLUTION BETWEEN EARLY AND LATE ADOLESCENCE

Previous papers (Spruiell, 1972, 1975a, 1975b) were devoted to systemic transitions between early and late adolescence in both sexes, a consideration of three separate developmental lines of narcissism, and the alterations of these developmental lines in adolescent boys. In passing, the alterations of the ego-ideal were discussed in each. The ideas put forward in the previous papers will be summarized below. After this summary, the primary attention will be to the ego-ideal, but the other developmental "lines" will be taken up in passing, reversing the emphasis in the earlier papers. It would be a distortion to consider one without the others, inasmuch as they are usually so intertwined as to be inseparable. The ego-ideal is an aspect of narcissism, a felicitous development of a part of narcissism.

But what is meant by "ego-ideal"? What is meant by "narcissism"? This is not the place to become involved with abstract theoretical or historical discussions, valuable as they might be (see Blos, 1962, 1974; Laufer, 1964). In "experience-near" terms, the ego-ideal—part of the superego—is that part of the mind that concerns the versions of ourselves we aspire to be—our own collective ideals, the very best versions possible of ourselves. The closer to being like these versions, the higher is self-regard; the greater the distance, the more we are inclined to despair, shame, a sense of emptiness or worthlessness. This system of ideals, which may be largely unconscious, comes about in part as a series of inventions—layered replacements of the infantile states of grandeur and safety which reality progressively forces a person to doubt. In part, also, the ego-ideal comes about as a set of *external* "givens" served up to the persons at various developmental stages by parents and others—*their* idealized versions of us which we come to build into our own minds.

Theoretical abstractions concerning narcissism are even more treacherous (or merely windy) than those about the ego-ideal. In an effort to analyze developmental alterations in clinical, experience-near terms, I suggested (1975a) that narcissism be approached from the drive-controlling and drive-modulating aspects of the psyche, the ego-superego, particularly during transitions from one stage of development to another. These most often can be understood only in retrospect. To attempt to study these transitions in *status praesens* is like trying to understand a tropical squall without weather reports. We usually know about change after the fact, not anticipating it in advance or predicting its outcome. Except in retrospect, we are rarely able to understand even that the storm is a part of development or some aberration of it.

The transition between early and late adolescence is such a stormy period (Spruiell, 1972). My experience does not allow me to distinguish four separate phases of adolescence clinically as Blos (1962) theoretically does, nor three undefined separate phases—early, middle, and late—as other authors do. Rather, my experience suggests that a clinically and theoretically *definable* early adolescence is systemically different from an equally definable late adolescence. Early and late adolescent phases are as different as the difference between the oedipal period and latency. The reason both are called "adolescent" is a result of a semantic accident perpetuated in ordinary usage in a highly specialized modern society that requires many, if not most, of its 16-year-olds to begin years of preparation for specialized work. In much simpler societies, there is only what we call early adolescence. After it young people marry, go to work, have children, and take the roles of adulthood without going through the long period we call "late adolescence."

In our culture, the transition to what we call late adolescence can be marked in both sexes by the indications of great changes biologically, psychologically, and sociologically, that overlap and interact together.

The biological signifiers are the achievement of adult stature and the full capacity for procreation. Primary and secondary sexual organs have become mature. Young people—boys more than girls—become erotically ardent. The skeletomuscular system reaches adult form with the closure of the epiphyses. Sexually and muscularly, the young person has become not only the equal of his elders but their superior in terms of raw capacities. Perhaps, as Piaget (1936) thought, there is an actual maturation of the neurophysiological system to parallel the new formal operational thought.

These changes are often not well understood by the young person. Something dramatic occurs with relative suddenness; the whole process takes place within a few months or a year. Being "grown up" is usually acknowledged shyly or sometimes embraced obnoxiously. These biological changes and the conscious and unconscious perceptions of external physical parity with adults, signified by the mysterious and largely unconscious perceptions of inner bodily changes, act as *organizers* for the leap from early to late adolescence. The process is like the acquisition of walking for the toddler, as the first deciduous tooth may function for the latency child, as the growth spurt and new sexual capacities do for the pubescent child; as the alterations of parturition and delivery do for the mother; as menopause and other matters of decline do later.

Psychologically, besides the acquisition of new cognitive capacities, there are, in ordinary young people: 1) changes in the *drive organization* (with increased capacities to regulate, control, and *gratify* the drives in relatively non-narcissistic and relatively nonincestuous ways). In particular, there is a coming together, in normal and psychoneurotic people, a melding, of the three developmental lines of narcissism; 2) changes in the nature of compromises of conflict (Brenner,

1982) in the direction of an altered sense of time, a longer range of organization of goals, the relative "fixing" of specific neurotic or characterological patterns, the achievement of new levels of object relations that complement the melding of the strands of narcissism, the integration in action of lustful and tender feelings—all associated with the organization and elaboration of a new, *adult* body image; 3) adaptations to a world "outside" as a result of the perception of changed expectations and rewards—new levels of competition, new worlds of sexuality.

The young person *must* come to react to a psychic and bodily ego/self that is familiar, yet radically different, and to a world that is the same, yet radically new. The young person either masters the challenges or freezes them neurotically and characterologically—or retreats into more serious psychopathology. A structural transition *must* occur in the superego, its prohibitory functions altered to allow appropriate sexual exchanges with partners seen as peers, and facilitating processes in the form of a new ego-ideal that organizes the world of adult sexuality, work, and community. This late adolescent ego-ideal is more than the sum of its previous parts. It is a new structure, built upon the old. It offers more and more autonomous directions into maturity.

JOAN: HER PASSAGE THROUGH ADOLESCENCE

Years ago, I worked regularly with a girl named Joan, between the ages of 14 and 17. After that I saw her intermittently for four more years. And for years after her last visit, she has written occasionally from the distant city where she lives now with her husband and her own family. She has done well so far in her life, and for that reason her experiences can serve as a clinical baseline for a description of the normal and psychoneurotic alterations of the ego-ideal during adolescence. I shall discuss the work in a sketch initially; in the more general section following, more clinical material will be added.

When I first saw her, Joan was a somewhat angular, boyish gum-chewing, wise-cracking girl, always on the edge of a smile, never far from a laugh. But her spirits were mercurial; in a flash she could be in black despair. Her cheerfulness was infectious rather than irritating. And to empathize with her despair meant to experience distinct pain. She was very open about what she liked and did not like. Much of her life revolved around horses. She was a fanatic about them. She adored her own horse, showed him expertly, thought about him incessantly. Her symptoms—rebelliousness to the point of outright defiance with her mother, angry arguments related to competitiveness, school difficulties—seemed related to the continuation of struggles having to do with the separation of her parents two years before. She was violently jealous of her father's love for another woman ("That bitch! That *whore!*"), and had recently drifted away from him. She no longer was his hunting companion, his "best friend," his dirty-joke-telling, horseback-riding, scampish, laughing, cursing replacement for the boy he never had and always wanted.

It should be mentioned that the mother's character traits were very similar to Joan's. As sharply ambivalent as their relationship was, showing itself in unending alternations of combat and reconciliation, the identifications were deep. It seemed that the father was seeking more than a son in Joan; he was seeking a smaller copy of his wife, a phallic female—safer because more controllable.

Ironically, later work showed us that Joan also frequently took the *opposite* role. She took her father's part with the mother; in disguised ways she interacted with the mother just as he had done. It is to be emphasized, however, that at no time did these "split" oedipal derivatives, positive and negative, play more than parts in a psychoneurotic organization in this girl and woman; there were never indications of important preoedipal or highly narcissistic pathological organizations.

I would have liked to have worked psychoanalytically on a four or five times a week basis with this girl, who at first did not appear to conceal anything, and who was so intelligent, verbal, and well motivated. Unfortunately, it was not possible because she lived in a distant city, and because of limitations on the parental options. Most of the time, I saw her on a twice a week basis, occasionally more often.

Joan quickly settled into an intense relationship. She was still in the earlier phase of an adolescence rendered turbulent not only by the psychoneurotic conflicts, but also by the mother's collusions in engaging in dramatic verbal battles. The external problems were later ameliorated in part after the mother was referred to a psychiatrist.

The details of the first period of work, which lasted about a year, will not be discussed here except to say that Joan seemed to respond successfully but deceptively. The transference that grew had an idealized quality that I took to be mostly paternal in nature. While I did not interpret the idealized qualities, I did interpret the resistances to the transference and as much as I could of the transference itself. However, in that period of our work, Joan "stonewalled" any discussion of sexuality, beyond saying that she was a virgin and intended to remain one. It is impossible now for me to assess how much her usually eager acceptance of the work—excluding talk about sex—represented playful intellectualization and how much it represented work in deeper ways. That *some* of it was valid seems certain to me.

But it was incomplete, as would have been obvious to any experienced clinician. We discovered after a year and a half that her progress and her relationship with me during that time had also served to screen deeper internal conflicts. The discovery came about in this way: Because she had seemed so improved, and because considerable sacrifices were entailed by having to travel for sessions from the other city, we agreed that she could take a "vacation" from therapy. Joan was enthusiastic about this interruption and promised to return after some months.

It took only weeks for it to become clear that the rationalizations in favor of a vacation represented a flight into health on her part and a misjudgment of her psychoneurosis on mine. Not long after the "vacation" began, she became extremely depressed, was tearful at home, and had suicidal thoughts. But instead of recontacting me, she first sought "help" as she had more times than I had realized before, in a relationship with Mrs. M., an older woman, the ex-wife of a man (as came out later) strongly identified with me. Joan (as came out later) secretly hoped to reconcile Mr. and Mrs. M. Of course she failed. The importance of the relationship with Mrs. M. as a "split" in the transference had been underestimated. A "transference cure" had taken place, only to be demolished when the interruption came. Although it represented a protection against dangerous fantasies about me, it also represented another symbolic loss of her father. We rescheduled her appointments.

After resuming, she settled into another period of relative calm. But within months, she began to become more anxious, lost interest in her horse, had several minor automobile accidents, and received so many traffic tickets she almost lost her license. She also quickly acquired a reputation for being "fast" and a "drinker" for no other reason, as far as I know, than she acted as if these things were true.

With me she became more aggressively provocative. Repeated interpretations were made (in language understandable by her) that she seemed to be looking for punishment because of an inner sense of guilt and that she was repeating with me some of the problems with her parents. Joan apparently accepted these ideas, but they remained just that—ideas. Nothing much happened. It was also apparent—though not apparent enough to be interpreted—that erotic impulses toward me were either at a conscious or a near-conscious level.

Joan became very concerned with her body. Out of a fear (and wish) that she might be overweight, she alternately went on crash diets and eating binges. Her weight fluctuations were, however, not great. More seriously, she began to experiment with marijuana and various other drugs of uncertain nature. Her psychic processes seemed easily disrupted by the drugs, and each use was followed by intense guilt, anxiety, the surreptitious use of her mother's tranquilizers, "confession" to me, the resolve to stay away from the group using drugs, and then a "slip back," going through the sequence again.

In a deliberate departure from my usual stance, I took a firm position against her using any drugs *ever*. But it seemed to me questionable that she could control the acting out. I had strong feelings about this turn of events, but could not understand the dynamic issues. With an ineffectual mixture of anger, guilt, and fear, I felt that my patient might be becoming impossibly worse. She claimed helplessness. I claimed, "Can't means won't." Privately I considered hospitalization.

A break came soon afterwards, however, when she rushed into my office one day and said, "Oh my God, 'Sprue' " (as she called me), "I've done something *terrible!*" And she had done something that was, if not terrible, at least damaging to herself and several other people. It was *meant* to be damaging to me—and, at the same time, it was meant to be an act of love.

Her older friend, the divorced Mrs. M., had confided in Joan that she was having great problems in a love relationship. Mrs. M.'s friend had become depressed and vacillating, mostly secluding himself in a hotel room. Joan decided to go herself to "straighten out" the man in his room. She used "psychoanalytic knowledge" to interpret his problems to him; she was "sincere" to a fault; she "confessed" her own problems with boys—to show how *she* solved things. Although she claimed not to have been aware of it when she was alternately "telling him off" and "telling him exactly what Mrs. M. thinks," she was so seductive that the bewildered man made some sort of fumbling sexual advance. This she indignantly refused and she rushed home to tell Mrs. M. about it.

All this effectively destroyed not only Mrs. M.'s love affair, but also Joan's relationship with the older woman. She became deeply remorseful, but was able to settle into work again—but much more intensely and in much more an adult fashion. What emerged were guilt fantasies that she had destroyed the parent's marriage, rageful (and essentially castrating) feelings toward her father for his defensive attempts to make a boy out of her when she had intimations of his erotic interests, hostile competitiveness with Mrs. M., a need to destroy her father's love affair, a guilty need to "bring the roof down by just destroying everything," and finally, most importantly, parallel feelings and fantasies about me. Among other things, she had all along been waiting for me in actuality to "make a pass" at her.

This rush of work, particularly the rawness of the aggression coming out in the transference, aroused strong feelings in both of us. She was angry and disillusioned. She complained of my being "fake and phoney," making her worse, and incidentally ruining her life. Her stated judgment was that she should be in jail or a hospital, and that I should be in some other line of work. I believe that my holding to a stance that by this time had become definitely an analytic one allowed her to come to a less magical view of me. It also allowed me to stop taking parental functions with her surreptitiously. I became something else to her.

It was clear that the episode of acting out and its analysis had had the effect of crystallizing conflicts, making me more utilizable as a person in a new way (Winnicott, 1969). Aggression against me neither destroyed me as an effective person in her life nor led to overwhelming aggression from me. In Winnicott's sense, I became a less subjective and more objective object for her. I could be utilized as an available and more *autonomous* object. She could then analyze and recognize her wishes, resistances, fears, guilt, and anger in new ways. There was no more question of "play therapy" masquerading as therapeutic work. The remainder of the work became much more like expectable work with an adult. Among other things, she was able to relate preoccupations about getting fat, counterphobic risk-taking, and needs to provoke policemen and other authorities to fantasies of making up for her sense of castration on the one hand, and on the other hand to fantasies of its magical repetition. She could also understand that she sought punishment for the increasing intensity of the incestuous feelings manifested in the transference.

Ultimately, we could partially analyze some other important issues. The original "split oedipal" constellation, which helped facilitate a "split" in the transference, was related to very intense primal scene experiences. Her efforts ostensibly to put the family together again were related to an intense unconscious belief that her own evil impulses had caused the separation. The relative lack of resolution of either positive or negative oedipal constellations had left her prey to severe but unreliable and unrealistic superego strictures and failures. The ego-ideal, such as it was in early adolescence, became regressive and even more magical in nature.

During the next few months—Joan by then was 17—a number of external changes took place: Almost overnight she became pretty; she found her first serious boyfriend and was able to both experience and to place limits on strong erotic feelings. She came to accept her father's woman friend in spite of the mother's violent opposition. And she became quite a moralist about drug use among teenagers in spite of one or two "slip-ups." Gradually, she began to construct a new life for herself, in a different school, with different young people, and with different relationships. She also began to take pleasure in the use of her mind; the school problems disappeared.

The crucial happening had to do with breaking the relationship with the older woman and the concomitant (relative) undoing of the "split" transference. Its analysis allowed the separation from *one* aspect of the relationship with me. She rather quickly became disillusioned in that she no longer saw me as some species of superman; on the other hand, she was able to hold her respect and liking in other ways. In other words, she had previously seen in me the father (and, more deeply, the mother) to whom long ago she had ascribed lost childish narcissistic perfections. I became the carrier of the resultant expectations as the perfect and noble man whose deepest preoccupations had to do only with her welfare and her future.

It seems clear that this relationship had to become unstable because of two groups of phenomena. One had to do with adolescent maturational movements already mentioned. The other had to do with the "confrontations"—her own confrontation of herself in regard to Mrs. M. and the later confrontations with me. We came into interpersonal conflict (in contrast to intrapsychic conflict [Spruiell, 1988]) first over the issue of drug use and then over the analysis of strong erotic and destructive wishes in the transference.

The instability was partly resolved by internalizing the narcissistic aspects of the relationships, the previously external idealization of relations with adults who were important to her. She could continue patterns inwardly that previously occurred externally. Thus, she developed a new and better functioning ego-ideal as a result of the identifications that came in the wake of the *partial* separations—at least separations from more immature forms of object relationships. The new structure was manifested by a new sense of herself as a person with a future, with inner controls, with new and attainable goals, with a sense of pride, and with little need for self-punitive activities. In this latter respect, the prohibitive functions of superego-ego operations changed. The grief for Mrs. M. and the parents (and, unconsciously, a lost childhood) continued for some time, but Joan became less and less subject to the guilt and the defenses against guilt characterizing earlier behavior.

But these were not the only aspects of narcissism that became transformed. Clearly, Joan altered her narcissistic erotic investments so that they became compatible with a relatively non-incestuous erotic interest in a boy. Further, she altered the magical omnipotence—particularly expressed in involvement with the drug culture—and instead began to show her own burgeoning sense of competence as a woman.

In summarizing these changes, I do not mean to imply that they took place all at once. Joan continued to see me as regularly as she could until she left for college. Afterwards, her appointments were intermittent. Of course, the usual problems, confusions, and foolishness of late adolescence continued, but the trials could be dealt with on a later level rather than on the earlier one. Joan reached the beginnings of adult organization by achieving late adolescence. Going from the beginnings of adulthood to full adulthood took a long time. I believe that the therapeutic work was both psychoanalytic and psychotherapeutic in nature. Oedipal conflicts were analyzed to a considerable extent, but pre-oedipal conflicts were barely explored (see Adatto, 1958, 1966); the relationship with me (as a "new object") had a role in releasing growth process that could take place spontaneously thereafter.

ADOLESCENT ALTERATIONS OF THE EGO-IDEAL

I had originally thought that Joan was open in talking about her life—except about sex. Actually, she concealed a lot. Later, she told some of the things she had thought and done as a younger girl. But she told them as *memories*, in the context of concerns as an older person. They did not have the same immediacy or even the same meanings they had had before. The earlier contexts were lost forever. And this is the difficulty in reconstructing the life of the mind in early adolescence: Most young people in its midst—especially the girls—won't or can't tell us some important things and later they either can't remember at all or can't remember in the same ways. Concealment is an especially important trait in feminine development (Ritvo, 1976).

Concealment is a part of larger obstacle to understanding. Young adolescents are characteristically (and healthily) partly alienated from adults—including analysts, of course. Consequently, not much unmodified analysis of early adolescents is done. Perhaps not much should be done. These contraints limit analytic knowledge of mental events associated with the ego-ideal in early adolescence.

Complex conceptual realities limit discussions of the ego-ideal in adolescence. Every aspect of mind is related to every other aspect. The ego-ideal cannot be discussed sensibly aside from parallel discussions of the transformations of narcissism. And the ego-ideal is only a part of a larger system, the superego. The ego-ideal is like the carrot and the prohibitory functions of the superego (against destructiveness, incest, some forms of infantile sexuality) are like the stick. It is misleading just to talk about the carrot. Besides, the ego-ideal is a differentiated part of the ego—in fact distinguishable only when cleavage lines make boundaries discernible between the two (Spruiell, 1990). We can't talk about the carrot without the horse. And we can't talk about the carrot, stick, and horse without thinking of bodies and biology—and the world of which these bodies and organisms and motives and relationships and emotions are a part. We set up the concepts ego, id, and superego as useful abstractions (referring, we hope, to actually existing and coherent constellations of psychic functions). We must keep in mind that the ego-ideal is an abstraction, and we must also keep in mind that that abstraction refers to actual functions integrally related to the whole of the personality (Spruiell, 1990). Otherwise, we will lose Joan or any other real person in abstractions.

With these limitations in mind, some remarks need to be made about Joan's development *prior* to the alterations in adolescence, following what Joan and I learned reasonably reliably about her life from early childhood, what we could guess about it, and what, from analytic work with other adults and adolescents, we would consider to be very likely—although we were not able to analyze them in Joan's particular case. In what follows, I will combine these levels of empirical observations and reasonable inferences.

At the beginning, it is reasonable to assume that there are determinants of the ego-ideal from the genetic endowment and from prenatal events. Perhaps some day sociobiologists will help us understand the genetic elements; already psychoendocrinologists (e.g., Ehrhardt, 1973) have demonstrated that unusual prenatal hormonal environments, i.e., excesses or deficiencies of antigens, or proportions of estrogen to progesterone) seem to have surprising influences on the future development of certain interests thought in our culture to be feminine traits. More specifically, groups of women who had been exposed prenatally to actual or relative excesses of androgen (for example, in the case of the adrenogenital syndrome), tended to have little interest in bearing or caring for children. On the other hand, groups of women who had had a marked *deficiency* of androgens prenatally (because of a genetic defect preventing utilization of the hormones by individual cells) showed exactly the reverse—they were extremely "maternal" in nature. As for Joan, there were no signs of constitutional tendencies of an unusual nature. Nevertheless, it would be safe to assume that her ego-ideal, too, had its roots, its innate potentialities.

The specific flowering in childhood of Joan's ego-ideal, in terms of structure and function, and in terms of the mental contents of which it made use, had to do with the internalizations that followed specific but *tolerable* narcissistic frustrations, with resulting de-idealizations of others and de-idealizations of the self. These came about as a result of progressive reductions in the mother's part in regulating the stability of the mother-infant field. We assume there were strong motivations on both sides favoring separation and individuation—including, also, progressive limitations in infantile omnipotence and grandiose self-love.

Forced to recognize parental imperfections and her own, Joan, like most children, adapted by the useful building of internal structure. Inner structures replaced external interactions. The inner relations between ego and ego-ideal partially replaced the lost narcissistic relations between the child and parent. This is the reason Hartmann and Loewenstein (1962) described the superego as a "rescue operation for narcissism" (p. 61). On the other hand, in children less fortunate than Joan, overwhelming frustrations, or phase-*inappropriate* frustrations, can result in disorganization, collapse, retreat, or the internalization of poorly organized and integrated interactions.

As for the "content" of the ego-ideal, it is a mistake to think of it as a "container," filled with "contents." It is a reification of an abstraction to think of the ego-ideal as though it were a spatial and material entity. Contents—memories, feeling states, and values—are available to any psychic system, unless specific defensive compromises, such as repression, limit their access. Conversely, any psychic system, having access to the contents of the mind, will reflect the experiences of the individual.

In spite of the fact that her development was generally adequate, I would infer that the child, Joan, developed only a partially internalized ego-ideal. In many ways, she had *not* been particularly disappointed narcissistically as a little child. As a matter of fact, she had been excessively indulged and adored in sundry ways by both parents. But contrary to these indulgences, in a specific sense she had been disappointed harshly indeed. It has already been mentioned that analytic work during late adolescence revealed that she had been exposed more than ordinarily to primal scene experiences. She had been both overly stimulated and indulged—and yet neglected and given to understand too harshly that, however much she was loved in other ways, she was not loved by either parent as a whole female.

Joan's responses to what life had taught were in the form of characteristic compromise formations (like those of many more or less psychoneurotic individuals) that featured stern but brittle prohibitions, counterphobic responses, displacements (especially to horses), and selective repression of key fantasies—deriving from erotic pre-oedipal and oedipal (positive and negative) impulses, in order to bind inadequately resolved oedipal dilemmas. In terms of the superego and the ego-ideal, these compromise formations included either too much stick and too little carrot or else no stick temporarily and a carrot became grotesque. For the most part, she had to continue to rely on others for external regulation of her self-regard; she had not been able to develop reliable internal regulations that would be relatively autonomous from the sanctions, strictures, and values of others. It seems likely that unaltered aspects of infantile omnipotence helped preserve characterological counterphobic and optimistic trends.

I believe also that this caused Joan to have more than the usual difficulties developing an organization to deal with *inward* knowledge and feelings about sexuality. Instead, she developed in a way more characteristic of boys, with excessive externalization of sexuality, (e.g., the love of horses and horse shows so common in latency and early adolescence, but carried to an extreme). She tended to suppress awareness of sensations from inside—the sensations that amount to an inner core of feminine sexuality (Kestenberg, 1968).

Thus, Joan entered latency as a mercurial tomboy—oscillating widely between excesses and deficiencies of self-love, between omnipotent and impotent attitudes, and between manic-like excess of self-regard and bitter depression. Nevertheless, she was unconsciously able to find agreeable disguises for an intense penis envy and for a lack of stability and melding of narcissistic functions. And she was recognized by others for her loyalty and dependability. In short, she was a latency child who would be regarded as normal by most people and regarded by a professional as only mildly or moderately neurotic—a regular child of our times.

But pubescence, a growth spurt, budding breasts, pubic hair, finally menarche at 13—all signaled radical shifts in hormonal states. And, in turn, all sorts of behaviors paralleled these perceptions of an altered body image: the regressive reactivations of oedipal and pre-oedipal conflicts, the attempts at detachment from parental supplies and controls, the turn to the peer group, the development of outside heroes, the crushes—the whole panoply of early adolescent changes.

Joan reacted to all this in mostly ordinary ways, but she was handicapped by her psychoneurotic conflicts and untransformed aspects of narcissism. In other words, the combination of oedipal wishes that were stronger than usual for her age, childishly grandiose self-love, magical notions about the nature of her own power—either omnipotent or impotent—and that of others, and strong dependence on external standards for the regulation of self-esteem prevented her from coming to terms with a new body in a new world. These handicaps were augmented by the separation of her parents, with all the confusion and guilt and fear that brought to her.

Although she could turn to horses, be a pal to her father, compete with boys, and try to fight it out with her mother, she was not able to become a real part of the early adolescent social world of girls. She was not able to find very suitable figures or ideas to idealize in place of her parents (until she began to see me). She had to abandon pleasure in her own intelligence and destroy the excitement of learning. She maintained tenuous control not only over raw aggressive impulses (which I knew about early) but also over intense erotic impulses (as I learned later). She alternated between harsh self-recriminations, expiation, and religious resolution, and turning loose in screaming tantrums. I suspect that the tantrums both protected against and allowed for a disguised expression of erotic impulses. It is likely that the masturbatory fantasies at that time were cast in strongly sadomasochistic forms, with the expression of either the sadism or masochism consciously leaving the other hidden.

Comparing Joan's development with her peers, it was different only in degree. Most girls—like most boys—do not have to go through as much suffering in early adolescence, but many do and some endure much more. Most are able to manage with their girl friends; most can function as a part of a group; most have two parents more or less united and steady—a reliable-enough backstop on which to bounce their rebellious and compliant inclinations; most have parents who are not distraught, elated, disorganized, or whatever else separation and divorce might bring.

Compared to Joan, most girls have smoother, more gradual early adolescent changes. Menarche and other signs of puberty help as organizing events. Most girls are able to come to terms more easily with feminine rhythms and the steadily intensifying awareness of inner sexuality. A friendly environment provides them with heroes, peers, and settings to find out how to get to be grown-up women. Most have progressively more interesting contacts with boys, along with supplies of information, values, tactics, and support from groups of female peers (despite the internecine squabbles) about how to relate to boys—or, at least temporarily, do without them.

The growth spurt, taking place earlier in girls, seems to play a part in a resurrection of phallic inclinations, with an associated externalization of sexuality. It also seems likely that 12- and 13-year-old girls *need* a period of phallic consolidation. But the awareness of the growth of secondary sexual characteristics, particularly the breasts, along with the contrasts they see in the angular and muscular boys, combines with previous feminine experiences to urge a turning inward: a gradual renunciation of the use of gross muscular power in external conflicts, a turn to more subtle, verbal uses of influence, more of a tendency to nag and manipulate, more pouting, a turn toward receptiveness rather than intrusiveness, sometimes a turn away from group identifications in favor of shifting, intimate involvements with best friends, increased interest in those things dubbed feminine in our culture, and, compared to boys, less fear of homosexuality and more interests in romance.

Among the tendencies encouraged by these developments are two especially characteristic traits associated with femininity: concealment and tact. Ritvo (1976) has pointed out the adaptive nature of concealment for girls; it is powerfully reinforced at menarche, and the cultivation of "mystery" continues into adulthood, serving useful functions. Greenacre (1960) points out the growth of caution out of the little girl's ambivalence, a cautiousness that can eventually be transmuted into tactfulness.

These are only some of the obvious differences found normally between the sexes during development. These differences will lead to different qualities in ego/ego-ideal relationships. But there are no reasons to believe that there are important *structural* or *functional* differences in the ego-ideals of boys and girls.

As long as they can, most early adolescent girls and boys hold onto a marvelous notion that happens to be true but at the same time serves as a defense: "They're just kids." The defense is demolished ordinarily by the recognition of biological parity with adults: physical parity (and superiority), sexual parity (and superiority), and intellectual parity (and superiority).

The usually secret awareness—even kept by the young person from her own self—that one is adult, aggressively and sexually, can be accepted or defensively rejected. In either case, it acts as a psychological organizer, joining the other organizers, in forcing a kind of jelling of character at that time, however neurotic or normal that character might be. I believe that girls, for example, *know*, at least unconsciously, when they become able to have babies, when they become complete women in a biological, if not necessarily a psychological, sense. This knowledge may be, and often is, unwelcome. There may not be a readiness for the change. There may not be a readiness to know that the outside world also knows, and accordingly treats one differently as a late adolescent. The young person may find it astonishing, consciously at least, that different things are expected and demanded.

This coming together of inner and outer knowings—if the girl can bear it—disrupts whatever previous equilibrium there had been. A usually shorter, but sometimes longer, period of constructive turmoil ensues. Old icons and shibboleths come to be given up; new *partial* models (specific characteristics, not whole people) come to be found. The solutions that some are able to come to are as wondrous as those inwardly created as solutions by some five- or six-year-old children; these are solutions to oedipal dilemmas by way of further separation from parents and the acquisition by way of selective identifications of a new internal structure that replaces the old interaction. I believe that just as the prohibiting superego was born in the embers of the Oedipus complex, the basically adult ego-ideal is born in the embers of the fragmentations and impossible contradictions of early adolescence.

It is as if a 15-, 16-, or 17-year-old became capable of saying (we would be appropriately suspicious if any young woman really said such things), "I *shall* be a woman. I want to be a woman—with all the things that being a woman means to me. It's natural and good to be a woman in those terms. It's good, not bad, to be tender to a boy and to lust for him at the same time. It's good to put together my insides and my outsides. And it's good that, besides those private things, I can see a public place for me in the world. I have a future."

However, when the time came for Joan to meet these challenges and find these solutions, some time between 15 and 16, she could find only pseudo-solutions. Behind them she regressed and acted out her conflicts in disguised ways. Among the effects of the regression were reactivation of an unrealistic and phallic ego-ideal and the reactivation of cruelly harsh, but unreliable, superego strictures (Reich, 1953, 1954). She escaped from her own group into a "counter-culture." In drugs she found short-term answers and pseudo-answers to problems authentically answerable only through the inward reconstruction of an adult sort of ego-ideal. In the outlaw group she found support for the belief that there were *no* answers in the "straight" world of reality. Joan, like some other adolescents, was involved in the most dangerous aspect of the use of marijuana and certain other drugs: their capacities to dull the necessity for internal reorganization and to serve temporarily as chemical, ersatz ego-ideals.

Belatedly, after the confrontation with me about her use of drugs and after the "real-life" effects of acting out with Mrs. M., psychological growth resumed. She was then able to move from the childish world in which responsibility did not exist at all or was invested in parents or parent-like figures to the point that she took beginning responsibility for her own life. She was then able to move from a self-centered sort of love to a love in which she could give and receive pleasure without guilt. Then she was capable of seeing herself in a future world of adults.

In essence, Joan was able finally to become disillusioned about the magical expectations of childhood. Out of the morass of disillusionments, she was able to identify with qualities that could become useful later, and she was able to idealize these qualities, now her own, as she had previously idealized the persons who had seemed to have them. With these achievements, she became more independent, and more autonomous, in the regulations of her self-regard. She began to be an adult.

SUMMARY

Utilizing clinical experiences, I have attempted to demonstrate the reorganizations in the ego-ideal that take place as part of a larger set of reorganizations between early and late adolescence. The achievement of physical maturity acts as a sort of organizer of processes that, in normal and psychoneurotic individuals, occur in all parts of the psyche—particularly the ego-ideal. The reorganization and "melding" of the strands of narcissism take place and are accompanied by a shift in object love from one that is narcissistically based, or friendship that is aim-inhibited in nature to the capacity for a combination of feelings of lust and tenderness for a whole object of the opposite sex. The psychological indicator of the shift to late adolescence is the first "puppy love." Psychopathology can interfere with these changes, with serious results in later life.

The girl's ego-ideal is not different structurally or functionally from the boy's, but the contents utilized in ego/ego-ideal operations are obviously quite different and involve in the girl a more complex unification of inner and outer sexuality on an adult level.

REFERENCES

Adatto, C. 1958. Ego reintegration observations in late adolescence. *Int. J. Psycho-Anal.*, 39:172-177.

Adatto, C. 1966. On the metamorphosis from adolescence into adulthood. *J. Am. Psychoanal. Assn.*, 14:485-509.

Blos, P. 1962. *On Adolescence.* New York: International Universities Press.

Blos, P. 1974. The genealogy of the ego-ideal. *Psychoanal. Study Child.*, 29:43-88.

Brenner, C. 1982. *The Mind in Conflict.* New York: International Universities Press.

Ehrhardt, A. A. 1973. Maternalism in fetal hormones and related syndromes. In J. Zubin & J. Money, Eds., *Contemporary Sexual Behavior: Critical Issues in the 1970's.* Baltimore: Johns Hopkins University Press, pp. 99-115.

Greenacre, P. 1960. Woman as artist. *Psychoanal. Quart.*, 29:208-227.

Hartmann, H. & Loewenstein, R. M. 1962. Notes on the superego. *Psychoanal. Study Child.*, 17:42-81.

Kestenberg, J. 1968. Outside and inside: Male and female. *J. Amer. Psychoanal. Assn.*, 16:457-520.

Laufer, M. 1964. Ego ideal and pseudo ego ideal in adolescence. *Psychoanal. Study Child.*, 19:196-221.

Piaget, J. 1936. *The Origins of Intelligence in Children.* New York: International Universities Press, 1952.

Reich, A. 1953. *Narcissistic object choice in women. J. Am. Psychoanal Assn.*, 1:22-44.

Reich, A. 1954. Early identification as archaic elements in the superego. *J. Am. Psychoanal. Assn.*, 2:218-238.

Ritvo, S. 1976. Adolescent to woman. *J. Am. Psychoanal. Assn.*, 24:127-137.

Spruiell, V. 1972. The transition of the body image between early and late adolescence. In I. Marcus, Ed., *Currents in Psychoanalysis*. New York: International Universities Press, 1972.

Spruiell, V. 1975a. Three strands of narcissism. *Psychoanal. Quart.*, 44:577-595.

Spruiell, V. 1975b. Narcissistic transformations in adolescence. *Int. J. Psychoanal. Psychother.*, 4:518-536.

Spruiell, V. 1988. Indivisibility of Freudian object relations and drive theories. *Psychoanal. Q.*, 57:597-625.

Spruiell, V. 1990. The psychoanalytic situation: Sheltered freedom. Annual Freud Lecture, Psychoanalytic Association of New York, May 21, 1990.

Winnicott, D. 1969. The use of an object. *Int. J. Psycho-Anal.*, 50:711-716.

PART III

PSYCHOSOCIAL ISSUES

7 Female Adolescence and the Family: A Historical View

Lyman C. Wynne, M.D., Ph.D.
Laura Frader, Ph.D.

From a historical perspective, the changing position of the female adolescent within the family has followed closely the evolution of attitudes toward gender relations, and toward women and women's place in society in particular. These shifts mirrored the transition of families in Europe and America from the agricultural and protoindustrial societies of the period before the mid-18th century to the industrial and urban societies of the late 19th and 20th centuries. Changing views of female adolescence also have accompanied and simultaneously reinforced cultural stereotypes of women in the society at large.

In the period before industrialization (prior to the mid-18th century), limited educational and occupational choices and economic necessity often required both males and females to spend the period we now call adolescence within the confines of the family. Relatively little age-stage differentiation separated childhood from youth and youth from adulthood. In the 19th and early 20th centuries, in both Europe and America, the educational and psychological development of male adolescents became far less contained within the family. In contrast, by the latter 19th century, young girls were still socialized into domestic family roles that became increasingly discrepant with changing economic, demographic, and social factors in the extrafamilial culture, with important psychodynamic consequences for women.

Only in the second half of the 20th century have substantial alterations of stereotypes for female adolescents occurred. The growth of a larger and more affluent middle class, the influence of feminism and the women's movement, and the greater availability of education and experience for adolescent girls outside the family in school and peer groups have all radically altered the social world in which young women find themselves. These changes appear to have occurred at a faster pace than changes in the relationships of female adolescents with their families. Ambivalence about dependence and passivity versus autonomy and assertiveness on the part of female adolescents has thus become a psychological issue linked to an unequal pressure toward change and resistance to change, both within and outside the family.

FAMILY LIFE BEFORE INDUSTRIALIZATION

Generational Blurring and Generational Distinctions

Historians disagree about the extent to which 17th and 18th century observers viewed youth as a distinct life stage. Historical evidence suggests that one characteristic of the 17th and 18th century family was the so-called "continuum between generations," the blurring of distinctions between youth and adulthood. Indeed, according to some historians, "youth" was a relatively brief period barely worthy of recognition as a separate stage in the developmental life cycle (Demos, 1986; Demos & Demos, 1973; Kett, 1971). As John and Virginia Demos (1973) have said, in reference to the agrarian society of the Plymouth colony, "the child appears not so much as a child per se, but as himself a potential farmer; he is, then, a miniature model of his father" (p. 216). The same could be said of females; the adolescent girl often appeared as more of a copy of her mother than as an individual in the process of establishing a new identity. This did not mean, as John Demos says, that children had the same abilities as adults. Children were, for instance, given religious instruction and work appropriate to their age, and there was surely an understanding of age-related differences in experience and skill (Demos, 1986, p. 97). Still, in psychodynamic terms, the transition from youth to adulthood was marked not by a recasting of individual identity, but by the aging of an identity that already had been established.

On the other hand, other historical evidence suggests that adolescence or youth, especially in urban areas, was viewed as a distinct life stage with its own particular problems and characteristics. However, this was the case largely for males. Teenaged male apprentices in 18th-century London were recognized as a distinct age group notable for threatening the social peace by their boisterous activities (Gillis, 1974; Stone, 1977). Similarly, Barbara Hanawalt, writing about an earlier period, disputes Philippe Ariès' long-accepted, "dreary view of children passing into adulthood without experiencing adolescence or having their teenage years recognized as a separate phase of the life cycle" (Hanawalt, 1986, p. 188). She argues that adolescents' obligation to assume certain legal responsibilities shows that medieval English peasants did recognize a period between childhood and adulthood (Hanawalt, 1986).

Home-based Economy

Even if young people in the past experienced a period of transition in the passage from youth to adulthood and the law recognized this stage, age distinctions between youths and adults were often blurred in economic and family roles. The economic demands of protoindustrial rural life placed a considerable burden of responsibility on all family members, including male and female children between the ages of 10 and 18, to participate in the economic support of the family. This meant that among the great mass of middle- and lower-class families, the period we now know as adolescence was relatively brief; the assumption of adult functions could begin quite early. Although there are numerous variations in different countries and continents, some basic patterns may be discerned.

Especially in rural settings where workplace and dwelling were one and the same, participation in a system of family labor resulted in an interdependency of family members, particularly between young adolescents and adults. This interdependence developed around the performance of vital economic tasks as well as around the education of youths for the performance of adult roles and functions. The absence of significant choices for either employment or education outside of the family tended to make the family the center of both. With the exception of marriage (which usually meant leaving the home), no "graduation" or rite of passage within a family-based system of work and education marked the end of the training period and the beginning of adulthood. One stage blended quietly into the next. Parents and children of both sexes shared similar tasks and children often assumed the same economic roles as their parents.

Women's work was a vital and necessary part of the family economy in this period. For example, women whose husbands were cottage weavers in rural England usually carded wool and spun yarn or helped in the preparation of the cloth. Middle-class artisans often benefited from the partnership of their wives in a family enterprise. Children and youths of both sexes contributed to the "family producing economy" that characterized this period (Tilly & Scott, 1987).

Economic Roles of Youth

In the Plymouth Colony in colonial America, children began a process of technological training on the family farm that involved mastering the tools and trade of adults. This training, begun at age six or seven, normally lasted well into the teen years. For boys, this might consist of planting, plowing, or mending fences with the father; for girls, spinning or candlemaking was done under the direction of the mother (Demos, 1970).

In England, and on the continent as well, young adolescent girls performed a considerable amount of farm work under the direction of either parent—plowing, reaping, threshing, dairying, and caring for poultry (Anderson, 1974; Laslett, 1971; Tilly & Scott, 1987; Vann, 1977). They also assisted in protoindustrial household production in weaving, brewing, and garment-making (Grafteaux, 1975; Hellerstein, Hume, & Offen, 1981); and worked with their mothers, learning, by doing, the arts of soapmaking, preparation of medicines, brewing, and preserving. These tasks remained the special preserve of women in the home well into industrial revolution.

Indeed, from the standpoint of a successful family economy, the family itself was often dependent on the presence of youths of both sexes as laborers. Even after the development of capitalist agriculture and enclosures in England at the end of the 18th century had brought to an end many family farms and forced adults to turn to wage labor for survival, agricultural and industrial workers continued to rely on adolescent family labor when assistance was required (Pinchbeck, 1969; Smelser, 1968). Although work and training of youth in this period were sex-differentiated in content, both sexes carried out valued instrumental roles within a family setting.

Adult Availability at Home

The presence of both parents in the household meant that sex roles were not as sharply defined, in terms of their location inside or outside the home, as they became at a later stage in the development of the family under industrial capitalism. Fathers in the protoindustrial family-producing economy usually took a major part in the socialization of young children. Furthermore, during this period adolescents were likely to have contact with a wide variety of adults other than those in the nuclear family: the protoindustrial family often included boarders or relatives (Berkner, 1975; Laslett & Wall, 1972).

Thus, in addition to the parents, both non-kin and members of an extended kin group living in the household participated in the socialization of youths. In 18th-century Austrian stem families,* for example, aging parents lived with their married son and his family until death, and thus, by their active participation in the life of the household, were in a position to have considerable influence over the socialization of their grandchildren (Berkner, 1972).

Adolescent Socialization in a Family Setting

Although many individuals, both male and female, spent their adolescence in their families of origin, it is striking that considerable numbers of female and

---

*The term "stem family" was coined by the French sociologist Le Play (1871) to describe a specific type of extended family in which one child marries but remains at home to inherit the family property while the other children either leave to establish their own families elsewhere or stay in the household as celibates.

male adolescents in the past spent significant periods of time during their teens away from their biological families, working for other families as apprentices or as domestic servants. This practice was common to both continental Europe and Anglo-American cultures of the 17th and 18th centuries. In the absence of formal schooling in the Plymouth Colony, for example, even relatively well-to-do fathers sent their daughters and sons out to work in another household as servants. The employing family was expected not only to educate these youths in the basic work of domestic service, but also to teach at least two of the three R's (Demos, 1970).

In England and France, farmers sent their daughters to a neighboring farm family as domestic servants or rural cottagers sent their young girls to spin and weave in some neighboring household. In return, the youths of another family were taken in to work as domestic servants. In one carefully studied middle-class family, all five of the daughters had left home for either education or domestic service by age 14½, although they frequently returned home to visit their parents. Analysis of parish registers in England from the late 17th to the middle 18th century suggests that this pattern was quite common, not a rare exception. In one parish, the departure of teenaged youths from their families after the age of 13 was regarded as a definite drain on the resources of the parish (Macfarlane, 1970). Not all children who worked for another family during adolescence ceased to live at home. Both Hanawalt and Demos have called attention to the complex patterns of comings and goings that characterized the working lives of adolescent boys (Demos 1986; Hanawalt, 1986).

The system of "putting children out" did not necessarily indicate a weakening of family ties or a lack of concern for youths. In fact, the acceptability of domestic service, especially for female adolescents, lay partly in the fact that it offered the continued protection of a family and membership in a household (Laslett, 1971; Macfarlane, 1970; Shorter, 1975; Stone, 1977; Tilly & Scott, 1987). Furthermore, the establishment of ties to a new household did not mean that ties with one's own family of origin were broken or that these adolescent girls ceased to make a contribution to their biological families. Indeed, when domestic service was performed for a wage, girls regularly sent money home to their parents, a practice that is still common, even for young preadolescent girls, in nonindustrialized families of the Middle East, as in rural Lebanon.

Although this pattern was more widespread among the less prosperous families, it was not unusual among the families of the middle class who viewed household service as an opportunity for education combined with containment and income for their adolescent daughters (McBride, 1976). In addition, the system of "putting out" could involve the assumption of a protective parenting role on the part of the family in which the adolescent girl worked. As Bernard Bailyn (1972) pointed out:

> Apprenticeship was the contractual exchange of vocational training in an atmosphere of family nurture for absolute personal service over a stated period of years[,] . . . a condition . . . in which the master's roles and responsibilities were indistinguishable from the father's and where the servant's obligations were as . . . moral and as personal as [his own child's] . . . The master's parental concern for his servants and especially for his apprentices included care for their moral welfare as well as for their material condition (p. 17).

Still, the protective, parenting aspect of the master-servant relationship must not be exaggerated. Numerous young servant girls were subject to sexual harassment and sexual exploitation by their male employers. It is probably not entirely accidental that so many women who turned to prostitution in the 19th century were young women who had lost their virginity "in service" and were no longer considered marriageable (Sanger, [1858] 1939).

Apart from the economic and educational functions served by the system of "putting out" adolescents, the practice of giving over to another family the task of socialization may have served some important psychological functions. Since the gap between puberty (13-15 years of age for girls) and marriage (between 22 and 25 years of age) could be as much as 10 years, there often could be considerable tension within families during this period (Demos, 1970; Hajnal, 1965; Laslett, 1971; Macfarlane, 1970).* While youths experienced both physical maturation and early assumption of adult responsibilities, contributing to the family economy at home could delay adult independence and lead to obvious intragenerational conflicts. The comings and goings of adolescent boys and girls may have served to diminish the tensions inherent in changing patterns of authority as youths assumed adult roles in some areas and remained under the control of parents in other areas. "Children could be disciplined by strangers, outsiders, who found it easier to perform this task in the absence of intimate and already fixed emotional ties" (Macfarlane, 1970, p. 205). Finally, in an age when parents often died before children reached maturity, work outside their families of origin provided adolescents with a transition from the specific dependency on biological parents.

Even the rituals of courtship in the protoindustrial period (and in some areas into the 19th century) were regulated within the confines of family life (D'Emilio & Freedman, 1988, p. 73). The practice of "bundling," whereby a young couple was permitted to spend the night together in bed, fully clothed or with a "bundling board" between them, was practiced in rural England, France, and

---

*According to Demos (1970), the mean age at first marriage of females in the Plymouth Colony in the 17th and early 18th centuries was between 20 and 22 years of age; Laslett (1971) found the mean age at first marriage to be 24 in the 17th century in the English diocese of Canterbury.

Wales, as well as in 18th-century rural New England and Pennsylvania (D'Emilio & Freedman, 1988, pp. 22-23; Flandrin, 1975, pp. 172-181; Gillis, 1985, pp. 30-31). "Bundling served the needs of suitors who traveled long distances and called in small houses that offered neither privacy nor much heat" (D'Emilio & Freedman, 1988, p. 22). It also served as an introduction to sexual activity within the context of familial and community constraints that applied every bit as much to young men as to young women. Whereas bundling may have actually encouraged premarital sex (premarital pregnancy and illegitimacy both increased over the 18th and early 19th centuries [D'Emilio & Freedman, 1988, p. 73]), it was expected that if pregnancy did result the couple would marry.

Thus, adolescence for both males and females, even if spent in the household of a stranger, was still fixed within the psychological framework of family life. In the protoindustrial period, this life stage was not clearly marked off from either youth or adulthood; it involved the early assumption of adult roles, often with an early shift of direct dependence upon one's biological family to dependence upon alternative family settings.

CHANGES IN FAMILY LIFE WITH INDUSTRIALIZATION

The emergence of industrial capitalism brought fundamental changes to the nature of family life. The rise of the factory system in both Europe and America increasingly caused production to move outside the confines of the household and family. Although sectors of household production in some cases continued to survive until fairly late in the 19th century, overall, the separation of home from workplace resulted in a long-term sharpening of the gender division of labor and gender roles. Whereas men and women had earlier shared responsibilities for the economic and psychological support of the family, the separation of dwelling from place of work led to the view that men and women belonged in separate spheres: that men belonged in the public world of production and women belonged in the domestic arena, bearing and rearing children.

In the industrial period, these shifts in family functions also accentuated gender differences in adolescent socialization and brought female adolescence into sharper focus as a distinct life stage. These changes resulted in the formation of a body of thought that strongly influenced the socialization of female adolescents and resulted in greater dependence on, and confinement within, the biological family for females than for males.

Social Class Differences

Because the industrial revolution also sharpened class distinctions, the development of these sex differences affected working-class women differently than middle-class women. In the early 19th century, women of the working class and their adolescent daughters entered factories, particularly in textiles, or left home to work as agricultural wage laborers (Bouvier, [1936] 1983; Frader, 1987; Hellerstein, Hume & Offen, 1981; Pinchbeck, 1969; Tilly & Scott, 1987). In France, adolescent peasant girls migrated to large towns like Nîmes or Lyons to work (Heywood, 1988; Moch, 1983). Domestic service, as an alternative to factory work or agricultural work, came to be a regular, enduring occupation for many women rather than just a period of youthful acculturation and training (McBride, 1976). Working-class women and adolescents now spent the majority of their time outside the family.

The experience of middle-class young women, however, was different. As the standard of living for the middle class in general rose during the course of the century, middle-class families were liberated from dependence on the labor of their women and children. As the boundaries between the family and household, on the one hand, and the world of work and community, on the other hand, became more distinct, the 19th-century middle-class family became more reluctant to release its female youth into the harsh industrial world. Middle-class women and their adolescent daughters withdrew from the world of work to the privacy of the home (Smith, 1981). Even those middle-class women who chose to work outside their families often worked as governesses and thus remained within a family setting (Holcombe, 1973; Peterson, 1972).

Education

The separation of middle-class family life into masculine and feminine spheres coincided with increasing division between the sexes in the matter of education. Middle-class males in the 19th century left home at an early age for a classical liberal education or professional training. In fact, it was considered appropriate in this era for adolescent males to separate from their mothers in order to begin the serious task of adult socialization (Stone, 1977).* Thus, education became an area in which adolescence came to be recognized as a distinctive stage of development, especially for males.

For adolescent girls, however, education in the first half of the 19th century was still extremely limited. Marriage continued to be thought of as the only appropriate social role for women. Even with the appearance of boarding schools and finishing schools, most authors on the subject considered home education for adolescent girls as superior to schools. It was believed that girls could benefit only from prolonged contact with their mothers and that education within a

---

*The fact that young men left home for professional training and education should not be taken to mean that issues of dependency and family ties were nonexistent for males. Such middle-class youths often remained financially dependent upon their fathers until well into their twenties, a feature of their lives which could have important implications for father-son relations (Stone, 1977).

family setting was most appropriate to their future role as wife and mother (Dyhouse, 1981; Gorham, 1982; Hellerstein, Hume & Offen, 1981). Indeed, some writers saw education as one of the most important functions of the mother: "That the vocation of females is to teach has been laid down as a position which it is impossible to controvert. . . . It is in the domestick sphere that woman is inevitably a teacher. There she modifies . . . her dependents [and] every dweller under her own roof . . ." (Sigourney, 1838, p. 11). There she guided her daughter until she placed her daughter's hand in that of a husband.

Thus, the content of young girls' education was geared to their future role in the family and home. It reflected the underlying assumption that women's roles in the world were limited and that, aside from learning to read and write, only a scattered amount of knowledge in history, geography, literature, and the natural sciences was necessary. More useful were the "feminine accomplishments" of voice training, needlework, dancing, flower arranging, domestic economy, sewing, and knitting. Both in terms of formal education and in their psychological development, adolescent girls were educated not to become productive individuals but to be dependent and submissive ladies.

The reinforcement of a cultural stereotype was perpetuated by women themselves and figured prominently in the moral and practical education that girls received in the context of the family. A dramatic statement of this condition came from Frances Power Cobbe, who wrote in her memoirs in 1904: "Nobody believed that any of us could in later life, be more or less than an ornament to society. That a [girl] could become an artist or authoress would have been regarded as a deplorable dereliction" (Klein, 1971).

Women as Guardians of the Home

If home was separate from the workplace, in the literature of the 19th century it acquired the character of a haven, a refuge from the cruel outside world of work and industry. Perhaps no one expressed this idea more perfectly than the English writer John Ruskin (1865):

> . . . the man . . . must encounter all peril and trial; to him therefore must be the failure, the offence, the inevitable error; often he must be wounded or subdued; often misled and always hardened. But he guards the woman from all this; within his house, ruled by her, unless she herself has sought it, need not enter danger, nor temptation, nor cause of error or offence. This is the true nature of the home—it is the place of Peace; the shelter, not only from all injury, but from all terror, doubt and division (pp. 99-100).

Numerous social thinkers in Europe and America turned their attention to the importance of the home and the family as the center of social stability and moral order and made women their moral and domestic guardians (Hellerstein, Hume & Offen, 1981; Smith, 1989).

Domesticity

A direct outgrowth of the view of home as refuge from the outside world was the appearance of a discourse on domesticity in the early decades of the 19th century. This body of thought reinforced prevailing middle-class stereotypes of the feminine role, cemented the ties between women and the home, and indirectly established the specific goals of adolescent training. Increasing attention to adolescence as a significant developmental stage and period of training for the female coincided with the appearance of a literature devoted to the socialization of the female adolescent.

In England, the thinking about domesticity focused on the ideal of the Victorian lady; in America, upon the ideal of "true womanhood" (Welter, 1966). In her popular treatises on domesticity, *The Mothers of England, Their Influence and Their Responsibility* (1844) and *Women of England, Their Social Duties and Domestic Habits* (1839), Mrs. Sarah Stickney Ellis urged women, as the morally superior of the two sexes, to serve as the guardian of family affection and virtue within the Victorian home. Women had an important task: to provide a climate of warmth and emotional stability for their husbands and children. It was their duty to keep up an "appearance of outward order" and a "strong wall of confidence which no internal suspicion can undermine, no external enemy break through" (Ellis, 1844, p. 26). Devotion to her children as nurse, guardian, instructress, and domestic manager of all household affairs completed the tasks of the devoted wife and mother. Interestingly enough, at the same time that she was expected to serve as the pinnacle of virtue and home manager, her position with regard to her husband was a subordinate one; her thoughts must be forever focused on pleasing him. He, remembering "her character clothed in moral beauty," would be better able to pursue his role in the world of work (Ellis, 1839, p. 42).

The idea of "true womanhood" that appeared in America in the 1820s and 1830s also emphasized the domestic role for women, with additional stress placed on the attributes of piety, purity, and submissiveness. In an age during which the double standard of sexual behavior came sharply into focus, women became the repository of all innocence and virtue, the living expression of the victory of the spiritual over the sensual. All their work was to be morally uplifting. The one outside interest a woman could have that was not seen as a distraction from her family duties was religion. As one writer pointed out, "Religion is exactly what a woman needs, for it gives her that dignity which best suits her dependence" (Welter, 1966, p. 226).

The ideals of the Victorian woman and "true womanhood" reinforced and restated cultural presuppositions concerning the appropriate role for women. They are important in the present context because they also shaped attitudes toward the training of adolescent girls in the family. Conscientious parents were aided in the task of socialization by the increasing attention given to female adolescence as an important phase of development and by a growing body of literature written for young ladies, which attempted to impart the appropriate social rules.

Adolescence, Sexuality, and Threats to Feminine Virtue

Early in the 19th century, writers on child-rearing in Europe and America began to recognize the importance of puberty as a crucial time of life for "it is during this season more than any other that the character assumes its permanent shape and color" (Hawes, 1832, p. 35). Victorian physicians and social observers saw puberty as the critical period in the development of psychosocial gender differences. As one physician noted, "That which makes man more bold will generally awaken greater timidity in women. Puberty, which gives man the knowledge of greater power, gives to woman the conviction of her dependence" (Gorham, 1982, p. 86).

As the century progressed and as social conventions prohibiting the discussion of sexual maturation loosened, female adolescence was viewed in some of the literature on youth as a painful period of growth and adjustment (Clarke, 1873; Kett, 1971). Furthermore, physicians and observers were convinced that the sexual development of young women made them especially vunerable to disease and to negative influences on their character. Adolescent girls' sexuality also appeared as a sudden threat to the feminine virtue, which had been emphasized by the ideals of domesticity and "true womanhood."

The proliferation of books on manners and guidance for young ladies in the 19th century demonstrated an awareness of adolescence as a period of stress and as an important time in the development of identity years before G. Stanley Hall (1904) considered the specific attributes of adolescence in his pioneering work on this subject. Although many of these books were written in the first half of the century, they dealt with basic themes which emerged and reemerged throughout the end of the 1800s. Written specifically to complete the family-centered education given to middle-class adolescent girls by their mothers, these works showed that the maturation of the adolescent required the careful shaping of her personality to conform to the prevailing cultural stereotypes.

Among the many values common to the cultural definitions of womanhood—weakness, delicacy, piety, purity, selflessness and domesticity—two especially important themes emerged in the literature written for young ladies: the ideals of submission and self-control, on the one hand, and purity and virtue, on the other hand. Mrs. L. H. Sigourney (1838) spoke directly to the first of these themes in her *Letters to Young Ladies*:

> Submission to parents, teachers and superiors, harmony with brothers, sisters and friends, prepare the way for those more arduous relative duties which devolve upon our sex . . . It is still a higher attainment in the science of self-command to bear trials of temper with an unchanged cheerfulness of deportment (pp. 210-211).

"Equanimity" and "calmness" were important virtues to be cultivated by the fair sex; the female adolescent must learn to control strong feelings and maintain an appearance of utmost self-control.

If submission and control were important qualities, moral virtue and purity were equally so, especially given the physical changes of puberty that threatened to compromise them. Lydia Child, whose *Mother's Book* (1831) had wide circulation in 19th-century America, urged that mothers tell their daughters the facts of life before their teen years, for the lack of communication between mothers and adolescent daughters about "delicate subjects" could have undesirable consequences. Once the young girl had received this knowledge, however, her instinctive modesty must "prevent her from dwelling on the information until she was called upon to use it."

In a similar vein, other works warned young girls of the importance of preserving their virtue in the presence of men who, it was assumed, were more sensual and likely to despoil that virtue. One manual gave practical instructions: "Sit not with another in a place that is too narrow, read not out of the same book, let not your eagerness to see anything induce you to place your head too close to other person's" (Farrar, 1837, p. 293).

Not everyone followed these instructions, however. Courtship and sexuality for rural and working-class adolescent girls came more into the open in industrializing America and Europe. Although bundling persisted into the 19th century in rural and frontier areas in America and in some rural communities in Europe, in the period after about 1820, urban working-class courtship began to escape from the clutches of the family, mirroring the movement of urban working-class adolescent girls into factories and workshops. Courtship for these young women now took place in the dance hall, ice-cream parlor, or theater (D'Emilio & Freedman, 1988, p. 74; Peiss, 1990; Stansell, 1987, pp. 83-94). Freed somewhat from the constraints of family responsibilities and control, girls flirted and traded sexual favors for the promise of marriage (Stansell, 1987, pp. 86-87). In the same period, however, courtship for middle-class young women became more privatized and constrained. Polite visits in the parlor of the Victorian home characterized the courtship practices of the "proper" middle-class "young lady" (D'Emilio & Freedman, 1988, p. 75).

Thus, the socialization of the middle-class female adolescent in the 19th century, contained as it was within the family, encouraged submission and dependence as opposed to assertiveness, while at the same time giving attention to the adolescent girl's role as the more virtuous and moral of the two sexes. This combination of valued female stereotypes would seem to call for deliberate role-modeling by mothers in relation to their adolescent daughters, that is, through the powerful conscious and unconscious processes of identification. As we suggest below, these processes often had problematic psychodynamic consequences, particularly as developments in the society became increasingly discrepant with the discourse of "true womanhood." The requirement that morally virtuous, middle-class adolescent girls engage in charitable activities to assist poor women and that they regularly visit the aged and sick brought them into contact with the public world of benevolence and reform (Gorham, 1982; Perrot & Ribeill, 1985). Women's suffrage, the social reform movements in Europe and America, the increasing availability of public education for girls, and the visible evidence that not all girls obeyed the rules of polite conduct also created contradictions to the cultural construct of ideal womanhood toward the end of the 19th century. Yet, the persistent expression of these ideals in the literature for young ladies, as well as the persistent identifications within the family, continued to influence female adolescents well into the 20th century.

Even as social rules governing the passage from childhood to adulthood for young men in the 19th century facilitated independence from their families, the process of becoming an adult had a different meaning for young women. One task of the adolescent female was to learn to accept and cultivate passivity and dependence on the family and then to transfer that relationship from parents to husband (Cott, 1986). From one point of view, she was not to age at all, but to remain forever a child. In a period of expanding opportunities in education, employment, and individual development, the early training of adolescent girls for dependence and submission became increasingly dysfunctional.

DYSFUNCTIONAL CONSEQUENCES OF 19TH-CENTURY FEMALE SOCIALIZATION

Toward the end of the 19th century, the dysfunctional consequences of familial experiences in adolescence for later life of women became increasingly apparent. The discourse of "true womanhood" lasted well beyond the time when it was clearly adaptive. Especially in urban areas, modern industry took over the work formerly assumed by women and girls in the home (brewing, clothesmaking, baking, and soapmaking); women's domestic production (to the extent that it continued) became progressively devalued. The conscious practice of family limitation and a declining birthrate, together with the increased adult life expectancy began to leave a longer period of non-child-rearing (Banks, 1954). Although new labor-saving devices that emerged in the early 20th century eased the burden of housework, the requirement that women be domestic persisted. Thus, the socialization of adolescent girls no longer applied to the realities of their lives. The opening of service sector occupations to women in the late 19th and early 20th centuries made it possible for even middle-class women to work respectably outside the home for wages (Holcombe, 1973).

The inadequacy of familial preparation of female adolescents for later life was apparent not only in occupational and educational spheres but also in important aspects of emotional development. Most widely discussed, of course, was sexuality. The psychoanalytic formulation that conversion symptoms are related to sexual inhibitions was once regarded as based upon the interaction of female "castration anxiety" and the structure of family relationships, especially the Oedipal triangle. However, these family relationships were not viewed from a historical or social perspective. If the earlier formulation indeed involved a universal phenomenon, then major conversion phenomena presumably would not have sharply decreased in frequency during the 20th century in Europe and North America, as they in fact did.

Moreover, it is no accident that the late 19th century woman experienced the psychodynamic consequences of these discontinuities between early socialization and later emotional "reality" in the form of what 19th century clinicians described as "hysteria" and the so-called "female complaints" that fill the clinical histories of the period. As Smith-Rosenberg (1972) has pointed out, "It is quite possible that many women experienced a significant level of anxiety when forced to confront or adapt in one way or another to these changes. Thus, hysteria may have served as one option or tactic offering to particular women, otherwise unable to respond to these changes, a chance to redefine or restructure their place in the family" (p. 659).

To be sure, the tight corseting, poor diets, lack of fresh air and exercise, all part of genteel femininity in the 19th century, contributed to the neurological complaints, fainting, and gynecologic disorders that seem to have been common to Victorian women on both sides of the Atlantic. Yet, there is an undeniable psychodynamic component in these problems as well as in the depressions, "rheumatic attacks" and headaches described in the medical literature (Gilman, [1892] 1980; Showalter, 1985).

Joan Jacobs Brumberg (1982), in her study of chlorosis (a form of anemia), has called attention to the complex familial dynamics of girls' and women's "female complaints" in 19th- and early 20th-century America. As Brumberg points out, "chlorosis represented an entire conception of the female adolescent, rather than a simple anemia" (p. 1468). The diagnosis was often made solely on the basis of age and appearance, without any blood test, and chlorosis was frequently viewed as a "nervous disorder" rather than as a nutritional or blood disorder. As one observer pointed out, "It occurs most frequently at the time of puberty, because the system is then in such a transition. . . ." (Brumberg, 1982, p. 1471).

In addition, the significance for adolescent girls of invalidism, neurasthenia, and chlorosis was that these pathologies were common "among mothers, aunts, teachers, and family friends, who conditioned the psychological orientation and experience of younger women" (Brumberg, 1982, p. 1472). Thus, adult women, by unconscious or conscious role-modeling, perpetuated the stereotype of the sickly, delicate Victorian woman for their adolescent daughters, nieces, and students.

The psychodynamic discontinuities had many other consequences that still are very much a matter of public concern and debate. The 19th-century ideal of tacit compliance and dependency, stemming from childhood and adolescent socialization, has been dysfunctional for adult women needing and seeking autonomy and the minimal assertiveness important for self-esteem. The life of Florence Nightingale provides an interesting example of one reaction against the rigid sex-role socialization of female adolescents in the 19th century (see Allen, 1975), but there are many others (Gorham, 1982). Ticho (1976), for example, discussed this issue from a psychoanalytic viewpoint. She believes that the issue of female autonomy gradually became significant after World War I when young women first began to leave the parental home in order to live alone, rather than to marry. From the psychodynamic standpoint, dependency on the family of origin was replaced without interruption by dependency upon husband or employer, so that needs for autonomy did not become an explicit and widespread issue until the early 20th century.

At an accelerating pace, particularly since World War II, the restructuring of Western society has made the 19th-century ideal for female adolescence and subsequent womanhood increasingly anachronistic. The relevant changes on many levels have been widely discussed. These changes include the rapid increase in numbers of women entering the job market, particularly from the middle class. Previously, working women often were regarded as unfortunate victims of deprived economic circumstances, with consequences that were widely assumed to lead to delinquency or other misfortunes in their offspring. Only very recently has a new ideal begun to emerge, partly as a result of the continued economic necessity of wage-earning for women, regardless of whether they are married or single.

This changing occupational situation for women has been interwoven with greatly expanded educational opportunities for adolescent girls and young women. It is often forgotten that in rural America, prior to World War II, an eighth-grade education for girls was regarded as entirely appropriate for life's later needs. In urban America during those years, the educational expectation was more commonly high school; only since World War II has a college education for girls been regarded as valid and necessary in the middle class. Entering the job market, going away to school, greater ease of travel, and affluence for a higher proportion of the population in the Western world—have all been associated with bringing adolescent and young adult women out of the home setting. Earlier educational differences, accentuated by military service during the two World Wars, had enabled male adolescents and young adults to achieve this extrafamilial life far more fully.

The problem of the lingering ideals of domesticity goes beyond both occupational skills and educational competence. Psychodynamically, the internalization of outmoded gender stereotypes continues to create intrapsychic barriers for women's success outside of the home. An example is women's tendency to take low-level jobs inappropriate for their education and intelligence, as well as inadequate for their personal satisfaction. In our view, such sabotaging of one's own potentialities has at least part of its source in adolescent internalization of values, often related to role models from an earlier generation. Here we are, of course, referring to the consequences of historical, dysfunctional residues within individuals, a point that in no way discounts the realistic, political, economic, and logistical problems of changing roles throughout both adolescence and adulthood in times of rapid social transformation (Bardwick, 1971).

Looking back over the past two centuries, one is struck by the fact that current changes in family life and socialization involve a return to some of the features of the protoindustrial families discussed earlier in this chapter. Once again, occupational activities of both men and women are positively valued for their wage contribution to the family. To be sure, legislation is still needed to prevent discrimination against women, to mandate equal pay for work of comparable worth, and to provide women with freedom from sexual harassment in the workplace. The important point is that equivalency is now perceived by much of the dominant middle class as a rightful goal, while until quite recently lower pay for women could be justified on the grounds that the woman's primary role should be in the home and not as a wage earner. However, changes in family values and the family role of female adolescents lag behind role changes in the broader economic structure.

With both parents often working at the same time when there are young children and adolescents in the home, a revised view about sharing the responsibilities of child rearing also harks back to the protoindustrial era. On the other hand, such sharing in home activities is sometimes criticized as unisexual, especially when a redefinition of gender roles is still transitional. Female adolescence is now far less often perceived as a time for building skills in domesticity and certainly there is less preoccupation about maintaining feminine adolescent virtue and purity.

Another feature of protoindustrial family life that may be reappearing is the continuum of generations, particularly in the intimate working together of parents and adolescents within a family setting. In the past this involved a blurring of generational boundaries, although there was little confusion about age-related differences in experience and skill. In recent years, there also appears to be a blurring of generational boundaries in family life, affecting both male and female adolescents, just as in the protoindustrial era, but now on a rather different basis. Clinically, one has the impression that there has been a steady increase in the extent to which parents abdicate their parental roles and "parentify" the children of both sexes, giving them age-inappropriate responsibilities. Many family thera-pists have noted that adolescents and even children often set the rules for house-hold life; a common goal in family therapy is to help the family establish or reinforce functional boundaries between the generations. Current blurring of generational roles includes a diffusion of authority, with ambiguity about who sets the rules and who instructs whom.

In 19th-century industrial society, the sexual division of labor between parents inside the home versus outside the home meant that authority in day-to-day family life was often exerted by the mother, with the father in the role of "enforcer." In those contemporary families where shorter working hours mean increased participation of the father in child-rearing and discipline, the issue of how authority is exerted is often unclear and disputed between the sexes, thus affecting the role-modeling for adolescent offspring of both sexes.

Margaret Mead (1970) once observed that while in historical periods of slow cultural change learning of the culture is passed on from the older generation to the younger, in periods of very rapid change the younger generation may in certain respects become better informed about current realities and in a sense educate and transmit the new culture to their elders. Some observers have sug-gested that this has taken place with respect to changing attitudes toward racism, sexuality, the use of drugs, and popular music and art. This kind of generational reversal tends to confuse and blur the uniform and consistent transition from older to younger generations that presumably still must take place in less visible aspects of psychological development. Even in the educational world, many a college-educated parent has been chagrined at having to learn "new math" from a grade-school offspring.

Still another aspect of generational changes in educational processes has been described as a "graying of the schools," in which parents, particularly house-wives with grown or partly grown children, return for further education in increasingly large numbers, often sharing in classroom activities with students one or two generations their junior. What is notably different about such activi-ties, compared to the continuum of the generations of the distant past, is that they take place predominantly outside the home. (Curiously, one might speculate that television is turning out to counteract this trend. Despite the seeming aridity and passivity of the countless hours spent in front of the television set, the impact on family life of television, compared to extrafamilial peer activities of both adolescents and parents, is a factor whose consequences are not yet clear.)

On the other hand, the development of the contemporary female adolescent does differ markedly from both the 19th-century industrial period and the preceding era in a crucial feature, namely, her life is no longer primarily contained within a family setting, either that of the biological family or of another household. School and peer group activities obviously have a much greater role in socialization, but, as we have seen, they historically took on this importance for females later than for males.

The extent to which these changes are taking place varies along ethnic, racial, religious, and social class lines, so that one should be careful not to overlook exceptions to these generalizations. For example, the tendency to retain earlier feminine ideals for teenage girls in standards of conduct, dress, and education appears to be more characteristic of certain cities of the southeast United States than for other parts of the country. The relative lack of economic and educational opportunities for Black and Hispanic adolescent girls, especially in times of economic recession, has made working out a balance of independence and dependence and its psychodynamic consequences very different than for White middle-class adolescent girls. Finally, the changing shape of the modern family—the increasing numbers of single-parent families, lesbian and gay households, and female-headed households across class, racial, and ethnic lines—has begun to alter our definitions of the contemporary family itself and to change the context in which adolescent girls of all backgrounds mature socially and psychologically.

SUMMARY

The education and psychological development of all adolescents, male and female, was primarily contained within a family setting in protoindustrial Europe and America. Associated with economic and occupational changes that occurred as a result of industrialization, a sharp increase in sex-role differences led to a 19th-century emphasis upon domesticity, morality, and the guardianship of the home to be inculcated during girls' adolescence. However, the narrowness of these ideals left adult women ill-prepared for subsequent economic and social changes and prone to a variety of symptomatic difficulties ranging from somatic complaints to phobias and depressions.

The changes in the 20th century, most notably since World War II, have included a renewed blurring of sex-role differences in adolescents, with a new balance needed between autonomy and assertiveness, on the one hand, and dependency and passivity, on the other. A view of current ethnic, religious, regional, and class differences in family life and in adolescent socialization suggests that 19th-century social constructions of womanhood are clearly anachronistic. Homophobia, hostility to an Equal Rights Amendment, claims about the alleged death of the family, and politically conservative efforts to reassert the primacy of the family often appear to be expressions of a wish to return to a 19th-century definition of gender roles. These changes are taking place at a historical moment when family boundaries have become blurred. Adolescents now leave their families of origin for peer group and other extrafamilial activities, not to live and work in service and education with another family. In this context, adolescent female psychological development seems destined to take new paths beyond the confines of the family, and certainly beyond the family as it was known in the past.

REFERENCES

Allen, D. R. 1975. Florence Nightingale, towards a psychohistorical interpretation. *J. Interdiscipl. Hist.*, 6:23-45.

Anderson, M. 1974. *Family Structure in 19th Century Lancashire*. Cambridge, England: Cambridge University Press.

Bailyn, B. 1972. *Education in the Forming of American Society*. New York: Norton.

Banks, J. A. 1954. *Prosperity and Parenthood, A Study of Family Planning Among the Victorian Middle Classes*. London: Routledge and Kegan Paul.

Bardwick, J. 1971. *Psychology of Women: A Study of Bio-Cultural Conflicts*. New York: Harper & Row.

Berkner, L. 1972. The stem family and the developmental cycle of the peasant household: A 19th century Austrian example. *Amer. Hist. Rev.*, 77:389-418.

Berkner, L. 1975. The use and misuse of census data for a historical analysis of family structure. *J. Interdiscipl. Hist.*, 5:721-738.

Bouvier, J. 1936. *Mes Mémoires*. Paris: Maspero, 1983.

Brumberg, J. J. 1982. Chlorotic Girls, 1870-1920: A Historical Perspective on Female Adolescence. *Child Development* 53:1468-1477.

Child, L. 1831. *The Mother's Book*. New York: Arno Press Reprints, 1971.

Clarke, E. H. 1873. *Sex in Education, or A Fair Chance for Girls*. Boston: J. R. Osgood.

Cott, N., Ed., 1986. *Root of Bitterness: Documents in the Social History of American Women*. Boston: Northeastern University Press.

D'Emilio, J. & Freedman, E. 1988. *Intimate Matters: A History of Sexuality in America*. New York: Harper & Row.

Demos, J. 1970. *A Little Commonwealth: Family Life in Plymouth Colony*. New York: Oxford.

Demos, J. 1986. *Past, Present and Personal*. New York: Oxford.

Demos, J. & Demos, V. 1973. Adolescence in historical perspective. In M. Gordon, Ed., *The American Family in Social-Historical Perspective*. New York: St. Martin's Press.

Dyhouse, C. 1981. *Girls Growing Up in Late Victorian and Edwardian England*. London: Routledge.

Ellis, Mrs. S. S. 1839. *The Women of England, Their Social Duties and Domestic Habits*. London: Fisher, Son and Co.

Ellis, Mrs. S. S. 1844. *The Mothers of England, Their Influence and Their Responsibility*. London: Fisher, Son and Co.

Farrar, Mrs. E. 1837. *The Young Lady's Friend*. Boston: American Stationers' Co.

Flandrin, J-L. 1975. *Les Amours paysannes*. Paris: Juillard.

Frader, L. L. 1987. Women in the industrial capitalist economy. In R. Bridenthal, C. Koonz, & S. Stuard, Eds., *Becoming Visible: Women in European History*. 2nd ed. Boston: Houghton Mifflin.

Gillis, J. 1974. *Youth and History*. New York and London: Academic Press.

Gillis, J. 1985. *For Better, For Worse: British Marriages, 1600 to the Present*. New York and Oxford: Oxford University Press.

Gilman, C. P. 1892. "The Yellow Wallpaper." In Ann J. Lane, Ed., (1980) *The Charlotte Perkins Gilman Reader*. New York: Pantheon.

Gorham, D. 1982. *The Victorian Girl and the Feminine Ideal*. Bloomington: Indiana.

Grafteaux, S. 1975. *Mémé Santerre*. Verviers: Marabout.

Hajnal, J. 1965. Europen marriage patterns in perspective. In D. V. Glass & D. E. C. Eversley, Eds., *Population in History*. Chicago: Aldine.

Hall, G. S. 1904. *Adolescence: Its Psychology and Its Relations to Physiology, Anthropology, Sociology, Sex, Crime, Religion and Education*. New York: D. Appleton.

Hanawalt, B. 1986. *The Ties that Bound. Peasant Families in Medieval England*. Oxford and New York: Oxford University Press.

Hawes, J. 1832. *Letters to Young Men*. Hartford, CT: Cooke and Co.

Hellerstein, E., Hume, L. P. & Offen, K., Eds. 1981. *Victorian Women: A Documentary History*. Palo Alto: Stanford.

Heywood, C. 1988. *Childhood in Nineteenth Century France*. Cambridge and New York: Cambridge University Press.

Holcombe, L. 1973. *Victorian Ladies at Work*. Hamden: Archon.

Kett, J. 1971. Adolescence and youth in nineteenth century America. In T. Rabb & R. I. Rotberg, Eds., *The Family in History: Interdisciplinary Essays*. New York: Harper & Row, pp. 95-110.

Klein, V. 1971. *The Feminine Character: The History of an Ideology*. Urbana, IL: University of Illinois.

Laslett, P. 1971. *The Worlds We Have Lost*. New York: Scribners.

Laslett, P. & Wall, R., Eds. 1972. *Household and Family in Past Time*. Cambridge, England: Cambridge University Press.

Le Play, P. F. G. 1871. *L'Organisation de la Famille selon le vrai modele signale par l'histoire de toutes les races et de tous les temps*. Paris: A. Mame et Fils.

Macfarlane, A. 1970. *The Family Life of Ralph Josselin*. New York: Norton.

McBride, T. 1976. *The Domestic Revolution: The Modernization of Household Service in England and France, 1820-1920*. New York: St. Martins.

Mead, M. 1970. *Culture and Commitment: A Study of the Generation Cap*. Garden City, N.Y.: Natural History Press/Doubleday & Co. Inc.

Moch, L. P. 1983. *Paths to the City*. Beverley Hills: Sage.

Peiss, K. 1990. 'Charity girls' and city pleasures: Historical notes on working-class sexuality, 1880-1920. In E. C. Dubois & V. Ruiz, Eds., *Unequal Sisters: A Multicultural Reader in U.U. Women's History*. New York: Routledge.

Perrot, M. & Ribeill, G., Eds., 1985. *Le Journal Intime de Caroline B*. Paris: Arthaud, Montalba.

Peterson, M. J. 1972. The Victorian governess. In M. Vicinus, Ed., *Suffer and Be Still: Women in the Victorian Age*. Bloomington, IN: Indiana University Press.

Pinchbeck, I. 1969. *Women Workers in the Industrial Revolution*. New York: Kelly.

Ruskin, J. 1865. *Sesame and Lilies*. New York: Homewood Press, 1902.

Sanger, W. 1858. *A History of Prostitution*. New York: Eugenics Publishing Company, 1939.

Shorter, E. 1975. *The Making of the Modern Family*. New York: Basic Books.

Showalter, E. 1985. *The Female Malady*. New York: Pantheon.

Sigourney, Mrs. L. H. 1838. *Letters to Young Ladies*. New York: Harper.

Smelser, N. 1968. *Social Change in the Industrial Revolution*. Glencoe, IL: Free Press.

Smith, B. 1981. *Ladies of the Leisure Class*. New Brunswick: Princeton University Press.

Smith, B. 1989. *Changing Lives*. Lexington, MA: Dorsey.

Smith-Rosenberg, C. 1972. The hysterical woman: Sex roles and role conflict in 19th-century America. *Soc. Res.*, 39:652-678.

Stansell, C. 1987. *City of Women: Sex and Class in New York 1789-1860*. Urbana: University of Illinois Press.

Stone, L. 1977. *Family, Sex and Marriage in England, 1500-1800*. New York: Harper & Row.

Ticho, G. R. 1976. Female autonomy and young adult women. *J. Amer. Psychoanal. Assoc.*, 24:139-155.

Tilly, L. A. T. & Scott, J. 1987. *Women, Work and Family*. New York: Methuen.

Vann, R. T. 1977. Towards a new life style: Women in preindustrial capitalism. In R. Bridenthal & C. Koontz, Eds., *Becoming Visible, Women in European History*. 1st ed. Boston: Houghton Mifflin.

Welter, B. 1966. The cult of true womanhood. *Amer. Quart.*, 18:151-174.

8 Cultural Factors in Adolescent Girls' Development: The Role of Ethnic Minority Group Status

Pamela A. Sarigiani, Ph.D.
Phame M. Camarena, Ph.D.
Anne C. Petersen, Ph.D.

In contrast to early models of adolescent development (e.g., Freud, 1953; Hall, 1904), recent work in adolescence has been characterized by an increasing interest in the gender-specific developmental issues of girls (this volume; Gilligan, Lyons & Hanmer, 1990) and an increased awareness of the importance of context for shaping the developmental experience of all adolescents (Bronfenbrenner, 1977; Garbarino, 1986). Two major themes of this recent work have been: (1) the special psychological adjustment challenges faced by girls making the transition to womanhood and (2) the ways in which features of the context interact with these normative developmental transitions to shape individual adjustment.

Although there is not complete agreement on the causes or significance of the sex differences, the majority of recent studies confirm that, relative to boys, the period of adolescence represents an especially significant challenge for the psychological adjustment of girls (McGrath, Keita, Strickland & Russo, 1990). At the global level, this challenge is manifested in girls' higher incidence of depressive mood across the adolescent years (Kandel & Davies, 1982; Petersen, Sarigiani & Kennedy, 1991).

These sex differences in global indicators of mental health are not generally presumed to arise directly as a function of one's sex category. Rather, most current developmental models highlight the ways in which features of the social context interact with normative transitions to shape individuals' adjustment to

Acknowledgments: We gratefully acknowledge the assistance of Maria Eugenia Fonseca; Phame Camarena's work on this paper was supported by NIMH Grant MH 38142-08S1.

138

developmental challenge. For example, in Petersen and Taylor's (1980) model, psychological adjustment to pubertal change is dependent on the ways in which the social world attaches meaning and significance to particular physical changes. In that light, it is not surprising that the timing of puberty relative to peers has emerged as an important predictor of psychological adjustment or that the opposite nature of these effects for girls and boys (late girls and early boys related to positive adjustment) reflects cultural standards of desirability (Brooks-Gunn & Petersen, 1983; Simmons & Blyth, 1987). In like manner, the norms and expectations of the social world are implicated in girls' adjustment to other normative transitions of adolescence such as changing social roles and sexual status (Katz, 1986).

ADOLESCENT GIRLS' ADJUSTMENT IN CULTURAL CONTEXT

Although the importance of the social world as a significant developmental factor is now widely accepted, there is still a dearth of published data that systematically consider the role of different cultural contexts in shaping girls' adjustment to the developmental challenges of adolescence. By far, the majority of research on adolescent adjustment has been focused on "normal" samples drawn from white, middle-class, suburban contexts (Feldman & Elliott, 1990; Powers, Hauser & Kilner, 1989). Similar focus on white, middle-class girls and women has characterized the research on female development (Reid & Comas-Diaz, 1990). Although critical for advancing our understanding of female development and adjustment, these studies have provided a rather narrow perspective on the wide range of experiences of adolescent boys and girls in America.

As the proportion of American youth becomes increasingly represented by youth who are *not* white, middle class, and suburban, it is becoming even more important to consider the adjustment experiences of girls located within other subcultural contexts of the larger American society (Elliott & Feldman, 1990). This point is reflected in contemporary society's struggle to generally accommodate issues of cultural "diversity" (Fineman, McCormick, Carroll & Smith, 1991).

Because psychologists and psychiatrists traditionally have not been concerned with or trained to consider the influence of culture, there is a real danger of ethnocentrism—that some of the new work with diverse groups may misrepresent the meaning of adolescent girls' experience (Spencer & Dornbusch, 1990). Drawing from the ideas of sociology and cultural anthropology, we can find it possible, however, to analyze and interpret data on girls' adjustment to adolescent transitions in different cultural contexts in ways that are both culturally sensitive and developmentally sound (Gibbs & Huang, 1989a).

Cultural to Immediate Context

First, it is important to recognize that culture does not have its primary influence on female development in direct ways. That is, being an African-American or Native American does not directly "cause" any particular developmental outcome. Rather, societal constraints and cultural values and norms are reflected in, and transmitted through, the more immediate contexts (family, peers, schools, neighborhoods) that adolescent girls inhabit (Bronfenbrenner, 1977).

Diversity Within Cultural Context

Second, there is a tendency in empirical research to categorize and summarize findings related to a particular group as if they represent some reality of experience for all members of that group. In actuality, members of minority groups within American society represent a tremendous diversity, not only between, but within, groups as well. This point is especially important because of the potential to misattribute causality to cultural values that may more reasonably represent issues of economics or social class across different ethnic or racial groups (e.g., Spencer & Dornbusch, 1990).

The Nature of Outcomes

Finally, the larger American culture, as well as the scholarly and clinical subcultures, has well-established norms about what healthy adjustment is and is not. The danger is that if these same norms of good and bad are applied to minority groups that represent different social realities and/or cultural values, the experience of the adolescent and the interpretation of the observer may be at odds. For the researcher or practitioner, this issue of culturally relevant standards is manifested in a need to examine girls' adjustment in terms of a "fit" within a context and a willingness to consider the potentially positive influence of cultural contexts that are typically associated with negative images (Gibbs & Huang, 1989b; Lerner, 1984).

REVIEW OF RESEARCH

With these cultural propositions in mind, it is now possible to turn to the body of research that explicitly acknowledges issues of adolescent female development within various American cultural groups. The goal here is not to exhaustively review all available literature on all possible minority groups. Rather, the goal is to sample from groups that represent differences in cultural traditions and heritage to illustrate the ways in which cultural context can shape the adjustment challenges faced by adolescent girls. These challenges include: (1) adjusting to transformations of the physical body, (2) adapting to changing expectations for self and social roles, and (3) negotiating new standards and consequences of sexuality.

Adjusting to the Changing Body

As the most universal feature of adolescent development, pubertal change represents a developmental challenge that adolescent girls in all cultural contexts must confront. Culture is, however, critical as it "may facilitate or hinder the young person's adjustment to the biological changes of puberty and may influence whether these changes become a source of pride or of anxiety and confusion" (Conger & Petersen, 1984, p. 92). In other words, whether viewed from larger cultural standards or from social comparisons with friends, the social world is a pervasive influence that shapes the significance of actual pubertal changes as well as reactions to a new physical appearance. Furthermore, although previous research has generally demonstrated the importance of immediate social contexts (e.g., school systems, ballet dancing) as influences on girls' adjustment to pubertal changes (Brooks-Gunn & Warren, 1985; Simmons & Blyth, 1987), scant research has focused on how these immediate contexts might be shaped in different cultural or ethnic groups (Brooks-Gunn & Reiter, 1990).

That the significance of actual pubertal events can be profoundly shaped by culture is clearly indicated in anthropological studies of pubertal rites and transitions (Brooks-Gunn & Reiter, 1990). Although not traditional in American culture, puberty can be a formal time of celebration, and a social marker which facilitates role transitions into womanhood (Richards & Petersen, 1987). For example, at the time of their first and second menstruation, Navaho girls traditionally participated in a four-day religious ceremony that marked their attainment of womanhood status for family and tribe (Driver, 1970).

It is important to note that the traditions of the Navaho represent only one of hundreds found within Native American tribes and that the degree to which these traditional rites and customs are still followed by individual families and communities varies considerably (Reeves, 1989). For instance, with an increased movement of youth toward urban areas and away from tribal lands, the potential for modified traditions is great. In general, this movement may be leading to a loss of "the ritual power" associated with past puberty rites (LaFromboise, Heyle & Ozer, 1990). Although the degree to which these kinds of rites and traditions are still manifested may vary widely, the Native American families and communities that have cultural traditions of puberty as a socially celebrated marker of womanhood are still likely to frame the experience of pubertal change quite differently than most contemporary American families where menarche and associated physical changes are likely to be approached with privacy, anxiety, and awkwardness (Brooks-Gunn & Reiter, 1990).

In addition to the way in which the cultural context frames the pubertal experience, there is some evidence that actual pubertal development may show variation across racial groups. Although not incontrovertible, there are a number of large-scale studies which suggest that black girls are more likely to develop secondary sex characteristics at a younger age than white girls (Foster, Voors, Webber, Frerichs & Berenson, 1977; Harlan, Harlan & Grillo, 1980).

In the most recent studies, Udry, Halpern and Campbell (1991) reported that although black and white adolescent girls had the same hormonal levels, black girls were more physically developed at the same age. Although these results could be a function of ethnocentrically biased ratings, the consistency of these more recent reports is suggestive of a real but small difference. Such a difference would be important to consider because the development of secondary sex characteristics provides cues to family and friends, and influences the timing of reactions to the developing adolescent girl (Brooks-Gunn & Reiter, 1990). The relative timing of these physical changes may be linked to earlier (as compared to the larger culture) expectations for adult behaviors and roles with consequences for psychological adjustment. Note, however, that these issues are related to racial characteristics directly and are not necessarily linked to cultural factors per se.

In addition to adjusting to actual physical change, the adolescent girl must also adjust to a changing physical appearance. This new physical appearance is evaluated on standards created within cultural contexts and supported by family, friends, and other social contacts. Importantly, almost all cultures have different standards for what is attractive or desirable (Fallon, 1990). Adolescent girls within different ethnic and racial groups are, therefore, presumably evaluating themselves on the standards of their own groups. There is some evidence to suggest that, to a large degree, a culturally specific reference group is used by American girls in ethnically and racially distinct groups.

The problem is, however, that many of these girls also may begin to compare themselves to the broader American standards of beauty that may be both unrealistic and physically unattainable (Root, 1990). For example, the lean, long-legged standard prevalent for girls in the United States (Faust, 1983) has been linked to results showing more body image problems for early developing girls, the group least likely to attain the standard (e.g., Petersen, Kennedy & Sullivan, 1991). In contrast, early developing girls in Germany do not suffer from such a negative body image (Silbereisen, Petersen, Albrecht & Kracke, 1989), presumably because of a different, more curvaceous, and attainable standard of beauty.

American standards of physical beauty still are primarily a standard of white features and body types (Nielsen, 1991). At a time when fitting in and feeling accepted are particularly important, deviating from the cultural standard may be difficult for adolescent girls. Indeed, Phinney (1989) reported that for the African-American adolescent girls in her study, realizing that white standards of beauty (particularly hair and skin color) did not apply to them was an important part of ethnic identity resolution. Similarly, Japanese-American girls may feel self-conscious about their racial characteristics and may, in extreme cases, resort to artificial means of creating a Western-looking double eyelid (Nagata, 1989).

At the far end of body-image concern, Attie, Brooks-Gunn and Petersen (1990) propose that eating problems are most likely to occur in adolescence due to the convergence of physical changes and psychosocial challenges confronting the adolescent. This is an area where the role of the cultural context has been reported to play a significant and opposite role. Consider in this connection that while non-majority girls may be forced to confront a culturally conflicting set of standards for appearance, the incidence of anorexia nervosa has rarely been reported in minority populations (Silber, 1986). As Silber explains, anorexia and bulimia are generally presumed to be disorders of the white, middle-to-upper-middle class.

It is important to consider the potential variability within cultural context in adjustment to one's changing body. For instance, whether ''white'' or other cultural standards of comparison are used may be dependent on the degree to which girls' immediate social references and judges (i.e., family and friends) are located within culturally segregated or integrated communities (Silber, 1986).

This same issue is manifested in the incidence of adolescent girls' eating disorders. Although the overall incidence of eating disorders found in African-American populations has been very low, recent studies show evidence of an increasing trend (Hsu, 1987; Pumariega, Edwards & Mitchell, 1984). As Root (1990) asserts, ''whereas the cultural context may afford 'protection' to the group, it does not necessarily protect specific individuals'' (p. 527). Factors which may contribute to the increasing vulnerability for eating disorders among racial or ethnic groups include: seeking acceptance from the larger mainstream culture, particularly for the upwardly socially mobile; isolation and loss of culture in immigrant families; and the impact of the mass media in perpetuating negative stereotypes about women of color. This results in women reacting against these stereotypes and adopting the white standard (Root, 1990).

In his analysis of seven black and Hispanic adolescent females with anorexia nervosa, Silber (1986) pointed out that the family histories of all cases belonged to the upper middle class or were upwardly mobile. The black patients were the only black adolescents in their peer groups. The Hispanic adolescent girls with eating disorders all were recent immigrants to the United States. These findings reinforce the idea that it is not membership in an ethnic or racial group which causes outcomes; rather, one's particular social location and socialization are more proximal influences.

Ethnocentrism also can influence the perceived nature of outcomes. As pointed out by Silber (1986), the diagnosis of eating disorders may be delayed in ethnic groups because of cultural stereotypes that these problems only exist in the white, upper middle class populations. Similarly, cultural stereotypes may result in a thin Asian-American woman being overlooked in assessment of an eating disorder (Root, 1990).

In a related vein, the way in which the majority culture views the ethnic group also has implications for girls' adjustment. For example, negative stereotypes about the natural features of women of color may result in extreme efforts to sever connection to one's ethnic culture, resulting in distorted body image and eating issues (Root, 1990).

Adjusting to Changing Social Roles

The physical changes of puberty act as a social cue for the maturational attainment of womanhood and help set the stage for a changing definition of self. Although the nature and meaning of "womanhood" varies considerably across cultures, all adolescent girls must negotiate and adjust to new sets of expectations and norms for the performance of social roles (Katz, 1986). Within contemporary American culture, this adjustment challenge largely consists of balancing expectations for work and family roles.

The emphasis on family ties and family roles is a particularly strong theme in the social roles of many ethnic groups. In Hispanic families, there is an emphasis on "familism," the cultural value that deems the family as the primary social unit and a critical source of personal support (Busch-Rossnagel & Zayas, 1991). The important role of the extended family in the lives of African-American families has long-term historical roots (Smith, 1989). Similarly, in Native American families, strong family ties exist along both vertical and horizontal dimensions—extended family members such as grandparents, uncles, and cousins may play important roles in everyday life (Katz, Carruthers & Forrest, 1979; Red Horse, 1983).

In considering these issues with specific reference to adolescent girls, it is important to remember that family as well as other social relationship connections have been described as being particularly central to the development of girls and women (e.g., Belle, 1982). This relational emphasis is consistent with the cultural expectations of most ethnic groups within the United States where the transition to womanhood traditionally focuses on preparation for roles of mother, wife, and kin-keeper. Mirande and Enriquez (1979) noted that throughout her life the Mexican-American female is prepared for marriage and motherhood. Differences in sex-role socialization for Mexican-Americans become particularly pronounced at adolescence, when adolescent girls are likely to remain close to home and to be protected in their extrafamilial contacts (Ramirez, 1989).

In addition to differences in socialization for family roles, ethnic groups may differ in their socialization for work roles. In the United States, a strong emphasis on middle-class values of achievement and competition may strongly contrast with the traditional value systems of minority groups. As LaFromboise, Heyle & Ozer (1990) point out, the work ethic of the majority culture, which is focused on individual achievement and competition, perhaps at the expense of family ties, conflicts with Native American values which emphasize "observance of tradition, responsibility for extended family and friends, cooperation, and group identification" (p. 464). For the Asian-American, an emphasis on educational success as preparation for later work is more highly valued. It is interesting to note, however, that this work success is not seen as "personal gain"; rather, individual achievement is valued for the honor it brings one's family (Liu, Yu, Chang & Fernandez, 1990).

It is also important to consider issues of variability in examination of adolescent girls' adjustment to changing social roles. Generalizations about expectations for work and family obviously are not true for every member of various cultural groups. For example, when one considers Hispanic youth, the heterogeneity of this group in terms of cultural backgrounds and nationalities must be recognized (Busch-Rossnagel & Zayas, 1991). Suarez-Orozco (1987) pointed out the importance of recognizing variability when considering school performance among Hispanic youth. In his study of Central American immigrants, he found that they did not face the same school problems as many of their counterparts born in the U.S. He suggests that these adolescents feel a sense of responsibility to parents and family members. This sense of responsibility, along with the personal experience of overcoming the hardships of war, helped promote these students' motivation to do well in school.

This cultural heterogeneity is also illustrated within the Asian-American groups. Although Asian-Americans have been labeled as the "model minority" for their educational and work achievements, not all Asian cultural groups within America or all Asian-Americans within any group aspire or live up to popular images of success. Although Japanese and Chinese youth have long traditions of success in American educational systems, recent Cambodian or Laotian immigrants may not have the family backgrounds or social supports that make this same kind of achievement possible (Liu et al., 1990; Phinney, 1989).

The importance of socioeconomic status as an influence on cultural expectations and values for adult social roles is also critical to consider. Almost all authors who consider issues of ethnic and racial groups are careful to point out the confounding overlap between poverty and cultural group (e.g., Spencer & Dornbusch, 1990; Gibbs & Huang, 1989a). Specifically, approximately one-third of Native American, African-American, and Hispanic-American individuals live below the poverty level, in contrast to approximately 10 percent of white Americans (U.S. Department of Health, 1990; Wetzel, 1987).

Again, although these statistics paint a general picture of economic distress, there is considerable within-group variability. Although Asian-Americans as a group have only 10 percent of families below the poverty level, over 35 percent of Vietnamese families were found to be under the poverty level in the 1980 census (U.S. Department of Commerce, 1990). In a similar vein, Bell-Scott and Taylor (1989) point to the fact that although a great deal of existing research has focused on low-income black adolescents, new research is just now beginning to recognize the variety of environments from, and in which, African-Americans may come live (e.g., rural, urban, suburban).

The contribution of socioeconomic status is crucial for understanding the nature of outcomes for adolescent girls. Although black and Hispanic youth are more likely to drop out of school than white youth and are less likely to graduate from high school, this is largely linked to socioeconomic factors. For example, nonpoor black youth drop out of school at only a marginally higher rate than do white youth, and among all poor youth, dropout among blacks is lower than for whites (Wetzel, 1987). Similarly, Gibbs (1985) found that a greater proportion of both black and white girls from higher socioeconomic backgrounds expected to complete junior college or to obtain a college degree than did girls from lower socioeconomic backgrounds.

The salience of close family ties in influencing the nature of outcomes in adjustment to changing social roles for girls also should be considered. Although lack of emphasis on individual achievement may conflict with the majority culture, this emphasis on family ties likely plays a protective role. The low suicide rate among Hispanics has been attributed to both a concern for family honor and to the protectiveness of close family ties (Smith, Mercy & Warren, 1985). Schumm, McCollum, & Bugaighis (1988) found that the Mexican-American adolescents in their sample reported more satisfaction with family life than did the Anglo adolescents. Given the importance of family relations and relationship issues in general in the lives of girls, and considering the links of relationships to mental health (e.g., McGrath et al., 1990) Mexican-American girls may be provided with an important protective factor which may reduce their risk for depression.

Smith (1989) suggests that the extended family role in black families has diminished, isolating many black women from important sources of support. This has implications for adolescent girls as they take on adult roles. Similarly, LaFromboise, Heyle, & Ozer (1990) pointed out that despite the difficulties in reservation life, the American Indian woman in her own cultural context may benefit from having social support from extended family and from living in an environment where people share similar values and practices. For those who live away from the reservation or from tribal community supports, geographic and cultural isolation may lead to adjustment problems. Furthermore, the pursuit of higher education by women may result in another loss of connection with the culture, for American Indian men without a college degree are unlikely to marry college graduates; given the very low college completion rates for Native Americans, the significance of this becomes clear (LaFromboise et al., 1990).

In this vein, it is important to recognize the importance of acculturation as a critical issue for adolescent girls negotiating role transitions. In other words, while increased integration with the larger American culture provides new opportunities for gain (primarily economic), these can be offset by losses resulting from the positive freatures of traditional cultural values.

At the opposite end, acculturation issues are reflected in the special needs of minority adolescent girls who have recently immigrated to the United States. Here the concern is for problems of alienation and adjustment to a new environment far removed from some traditional sources of support. Zambrana and Silva-Palacious (1989) reported significant gender differences in the stress reactions of recent Mexican-American adolescent immigrants. Specifically, they found that adolescent girls were more likely than boys to frame their experience in terms of family loss and change. Given the salience of extended family and social networks described above and the importance of peer relationships for girls, the particular challenges facing immigrant adolescent girls are important to consider.

Adjusting to the Sexual Self

Intricately linked to both the changing body and new expectations for social roles, adolescent girls of all cultural groups must adjust to new definitions of self as a sexual being with reproductive capabilities. Cultural attitudes toward sexuality in general, expectations concerning the sexual behavior of adolescent girls in particular, and norms for adolescent childbearing all are transmitted to adolescent girls through interactions with, and observations of, models within the family, peer, school, and community contexts (Chilman, 1983).

One important dimension in which cultures vary regarding attitudes toward sexuality is in their relative degree of permissiveness versus restrictiveness. The traditional cultures represented by ethnic minority groups residing within the United States generally can be characterized as sexually restrictive in comparison to sexuality attitudes of the majority culture (Katchadourian & Lunde, 1980). Huang and Ying (1989) reported that in many Chinese-American families, sexuality remains a taboo subject. Most children in traditional Filipino-American families receive little direct sex education from parents and other elders. Furthermore, a considerable concern of Filipino-American parents is that their daughters maintain a good reputation and that their chastity not come into question (Santos, 1983).

Similarly, in traditional Mexican-American families, discussions between parents and children about sexuality and reproduction rarely occur; overt evidence of sexual behavior is considered to be a form of disrespect for the household (Vega, Hough & Romero, (1983). Premarital virginity is deemed an important feminine virtue and knowledge about sexuality may be viewed as inappropriate for girls from traditional Mexican-American families and communities (Mirande & Enriquez, 1979; Scott, Shifman, Orr, Owen & Fawcett, 1988).

With regard to norms and expectations of the African-American community, it has been suggested that in comparison to whites, blacks hold more permissive attitudes toward sexuality (Ladner, 1972). In contrast, Harrison (1990) asserts that although there has been a prevailing norm within the black community to not reject a person on the basis of the marital status of his or her parents, the attitude that parenthood is best reserved for marriage has also existed simultaneously. Harrison described this norm as dating back to the 1940s and as being derived from the values and attitudes of the rural South. However, the impact of increased urbanization, economic stress, and the decline in the influence of the black church has contributed to the increased vulnerability for high-risk sexual behavior and adolescent parenthood among blacks.

The influence of socioeconomic status is relevant to consider when examining cultural context variability in adjustment to the sexual self of the adolescent girl. For example, Scott-Jones, Roland & White (1989) pointed out that differences reported between blacks and whites in sexual activity and pregnancy are likely due to socioeconomic differences. Similarly, Leigh, Weddle & Loewen (1988) reported that most of the literature about the sexual activity of blacks has focused on lower socioeconomic samples. In their investigation of black adolescent girls, they found that higher level of mother's education, higher family income, and living with both parents at age 14 were variables related to a later timing of transition to sexual intercourse. The absence of middle-class families in the teen's neighborhood has been found to be a correlate of adolescent parenthood among blacks (Duncan & Laren, 1991).

In addition to the influence of socioeconomic factors, the role of acculturation also is important to consider in understanding cultural context variability in sexual attitudes and behavior. Amaro (1988) found that SES, degree of religiosity, and degree of acculturation were linked with reproductive attitudes in the Mexican-American women in her sample. This was illustrated by the finding that in comparison to women with more traditional attitudes towards sex, women with more liberal attitudes had more education, higher status jobs, lower levels of religious affiliation, and a greater bicultural affiliation.

Independent of etiology, the fact remains that minority adolescents as a group are more likely than their majority counterparts to begin sexual activity earlier and to become mothers during the teenage years (Katchadourian, 1990; Malone, 1986). Importantly, however, even though cultural values and expectations may not have caused these outcomes, the reactions of immediate contextual agents, including family and friends, may be framed in part by culture-related issues.

Mexican-American adolescent mothers were found to have more daily contact with extended family, less likely to be living alone, and more likely to be living with a spouse or a boyfriend than were non-Hispanic white mothers (Becerra & de Anda, 1984). Furthermore, de Anda, Becerra & Fielder (1988) found that Mexican-American adolescent mothers shared close emotional bonds with the baby's father, who often responded positively to the pregnancy; in contrast, non-Hispanic white adolescents' boyfriends tended to have negative reactions towards the pregnancy. These authors suggested that cultural differences regarding family bonds and responsibility for children resulted in more stable and supportive partners for the Mexican-American adolescents.

Becerra and de Anda (1984) also point to the role of acculturation in influencing sexuality. They found that the Mexican-American adolescents in their study who were in the process of acculturation were more likely to state that their pregnancy was unplanned, the least likely to use contraception, but the most likely to know when pregnancy was likely to occur. Becerra and de Anda suggested that these adolescent girls were caught between the world view of their ethnic heritage and that of the majority culture.

The negative outcomes that may be experienced by the ethnic minority girl as she adjusts to her changing sexual self are real and cannot be ignored. For example, a substantial percentage of Native American women seeking mental health services have been the victims of incest, rape, and sexual assault (U.S. Department of Health and Human Services, 1988). The high incidence of drug and alcohol use among Native American adolescents (Edwards & Egbert-Edwards, 1990; Katz et al., 1979) coupled with the tendency of Native American women to self-medicate with alcohol and drugs underlines the importance of including issues such as the experience of sexual violence in the assessment and treatment of depression in these women (McGrath et al., 1990).

Furthermore, the negative outcomes associated with teen pregnancy cannot be ignored. Adolescent mothers are particularly unlikely to be adequately prepared for the responsibilities of childrearing and are likely to experience disruptions in their development and educational attainment (Furstenberg, 1991). Nevertheless, although much research on adolescent pregnancy and parenthood has focused on negative outcomes, it is important to remember that many of the differences between adolescent mothers and later childbearers existed prior to pregnancy. As Furstenberg (1991) pointed out, "teenage mothers are more likely than later childbearers to have grown up in extreme poverty, to have a background of family instability, and to have encountered academic and social problems in school" (p. 132). Furstenberg suggested that the incentives for postponing parenthood are substantial only if young women really believe that they have a strong prospect of making it into the middle class. Additionally, the meaning of teen pregnancy is quite different when the anticipated age of adult roles is quite young. For some young adolescent mothers, motherhood may be seen as the ticket to adulthood (Ladner, 1972).

CONCLUSIONS: PRACTICAL APPLICATIONS FOR RESEARCH AND INTERVENTION

This chapter began with a stated concern about the need to examine the role of cultural context as an influence on the adjustment challenges of adolescent girls. What emerges in this brief review is a recognition of the complexity of cultural contexts as developmental influences. Given this complexity, the review was not intended as an analysis of all issues related to all cultural groups; rather, the literature reviewed was used to illustrate important ideas that have practical applications for the future study of, and intervention in, the lives of adolescent girls.

Research Applications

The present emphasis on adjustment to the normal developmental challenges of adolescence is intentional and important. Most of the research on ethnic groups has tended to focus on the problems of minority youth (Spencer & Dornbusch, 1990). The simple fact is, however, that most adolescent girls from culturally different backgrounds are *not* pregnant, abusing drugs, or attempting suicide. That is not to say, however, that minority girls are not confronted with special challenges. Certainly there is some evidence to suggest that women from racial and ethnic minority groups are somewhat more likely to experience depression or other negative mental health outcomes; however, given the multiple oppressions of sexism, racism, and economic disadvantage that these women are likely to experience (McGrath et al., 1990), the degree to which they do not manifest greater problems is a tribute to their strength and resilience.

The emphasis on normative developmental challenges is also important because it allows for a specific focus on the issues facing girls. Problem-centered research (with the exception of sexuality/pregnancy) has tended to focus on issues more salient and common for boys, such as delinquency and drugs. Furthermore, because boys are typically the most visible members of youth culture groups, girls often have been overlooked in previous work on youth (Brake, 1985). Because past research on ethnic groups has been characterized by a marked absence of any gender-specific focus, it is important for future work to consider gender and ethnicity simultaneously (Reid & Comas-Diaz, 1990).

The review of this past work also highlighted the fact that, even in the face of incredible cultural variability across and within cultural groups, there is a common set of issues important for framing the experience of girls. Although the particular norms and expectations may vary from group to group, all of these girls face a potential conflict between cultures that can influence their ability to adjust to their adolescent transitions (Phinney, Lochner & Murphy, 1990). Additionally, for all of these girls, although cultural heritage may provide an initial foundation, the power of forces such as parents' educational backgrounds or financial resources can overwhelm the influence of traditional cultural values (e.g., Harrison, 1990).

It is clear that additional work is needed on all groups that represent cultural difference from the white, suburban, middle-class reference that has recently provided the norms of development. This includes groups which may not be ethnically or racially different, but who may still represent cultures in stark contrast. For example, the plight of rural America's girls is not well documented or understood; however, the little research that does exist suggests that these girls also may be facing challenges similar to those of ethnic minorities (e.g., Petersen, Offer & Kaplan, 1979; Sarigiani, Wilson, Petersen & Vicary, 1990). Similarly, the work on all of these groups must not be seen in terms of static models. The face of minority life is changing across America and research needs to stay abreast of the significance of these changes.

Intervention Applications

As the proportion of minority youth continues to grow, helping professionals need to increase their awareness of the incredible variety of cultural backgrounds represented in today's youth. They need to learn about the ways in which family, friends, schools, and communities transmit the norms, values, and expectations which give different meanings to girls' developmental experiences. Helping professionals also need to be able to see beyond skin color or ethnic label to appreciate the diversity within groups and the economic and social forces that shape individual experience. Finally, the culturally sensitive helping professional must understand the adjustment of minority girls in terms of the fit within their own contexts and not in terms of some artificial standard from within one's own world.

Drawing from these lessons of culture, it is possible to develop intervention strategies that match rather than clash with the culture of origin. If a culture emphasizes extended familial connections, then utilize family members beyond the traditional nuclear family. If a culture stresses involvement in the community, then draw from resources within the community. In either case, recognizing additional sources of support will not only help in the remediation of distress, it also will lead to a reaffirmation of the importance of one's background and heritage (e.g., Gibbs & Huang, 1989b; Red Horse, 1983). Finally, the effective helper needs to be an active student who continues to learn from adolescents and their families about the potential goals and strategies that will best maximize the adjustment of girls in ways that are both developmentally and culturally sound.

REFERENCES

Amaro, H. 1988. Women in the Mexican-American community: Religion, culture, and reproductive attitudes and experiences. *J. Community Psychology*, 16:6-20.

Attie, I., Brooks-Gunn, J. & Petersen, A. C. 1990. A developmental perspective on eating disorders and eating problems. In M. Lewis & S. M. Miller, Eds., *Handbook of Developmental Psychopathology*. New York: Plenum.

Becerra, R. & de Anda, D. 1984. Pregnancy and motherhood among Mexican-American adolescents. *Health and Social Work*, 9:106-123.

Belle, D. 1982. The stress of caring: Women as providers of social support. In L. Goldberg and S. Breznitz, Eds., *Handbook of Stress*. New York: Free Press.

Bell-Scott, D. & Taylor, R. L. 1989. Introduction: The multiple ecologies of black adolescent development. *J. Adol. Research*, 4:119-124.

Brake, M., 1985. *Comparative Youth Culture*. London: Routledge & Kegan Paul.

Bronfenbrenner, U. 1977. Toward an experimental ecology of human development. *Amer. Psychol.*, 32:513-531.

Brooks-Gunn, J. & Petersen, A. C., Eds. 1983. *Girls at Puberty: Biological and Psychosocial Perspectives*. New York: Plenum.

Brooks-Gunn, J. & Reiter, E. O. 1990. The role of pubertal processes. In S. S. Feldman & G. R. Elliott, Eds., *At the Threshold: The Developing Adolescent*. Cambridge, MA: Harvard University.

Brooks-Gunn, J. & Warren, M. P. 1985. Effects of delayed menarche in different contexts: Dance and nondance students. *J. Youth Adol.*, 14:285-300.

Busch-Rossnagel, N. A. and Zayas, L. H. 1991. Hispanic adolescents. In R. M. Lerner, A. C. Petersen & J. Brooks-Gunn, Eds., *Encyclopedia of Adolescence*. Vol. 1. New York: Garland.

Chilman, C. 1983. *Adolescent Sexuality in a Changing American Society*. New York: Wiley.

Conger, J. J. & Petersen, A. C. 1984. *Adolescence and Youth: Psychological Development in a Changing World*. New York: Harper & Row.

de Anda, D., Becerra, R. M. & Fielder, E. P. 1988. Sexuality, pregnancy, and motherhood among Mexican-American adolescents. *J. Adol. Research*, 3:403-411.

Driver, H. E. 1970. *Indians of North America*. 2nd ed. Chicago: University of Chicago.

Duncan, G. J. & Laren, D. 1991. Neighborhood and family influences on teen births and dropping out. *Effects of neighborhood poverty on the development of children and adolescents*. Presented at the biennial meeting of the Society for Research in Child Development, Seattle, WA.

Edwards, E. D. & Egbert-Edwards, M. 1990. American Indian adolescents: Combating problems of substance use and abuse through a community model. In A. R. Stiffman & L. E. Davis, Eds., *Ethnic Issues in Adolescent Mental Health*. Newbury Park, CA: Sage.

Elliott, G. R. & Feldman, S. S. 1990. Capturing the adolescent experience. In S. S. Feldman & G. R. Elliott, Eds., *At the Threshold: The Developing Adolescent*. Cambridge, MA: Harvard University.

Fallon, A. 1990. Culture in the mirror: Sociocultural determinants of body image. In T. F. Cash & T. Pruzinsky, Eds., *Body Image: Development, Deviance, and Change*. New York: Guilford.

Faust, M. S. 1983. Alternative constructions of adolescent growth. In J. Brooks-Gunn & A. C. Petersen, Eds., *Girls at Puberty: Biological and Psychosocial Perspectives*. New York: Plenum.

Feldman, S. S. & Elliott, G. R. 1990. Progress and promise. In S. S. Feldman & G. R. Elliott, Eds., *At the Threshold: The Developing Adolescent*. Cambridge, MA: Harvard University Press.

Fineman, H., McCormick, J., Carroll, G., & Smith, V. E. 1991. The new politics of race. *Newsweek*, pp. 22-26, May 6.

Foster, T. A., Voors, A. W., Webber, L. S., Frerichs, R. R., & Berenson, G. S. 1977. Anthropometric and maturational measurement of children, ages 5-14 years in a biracial bommunity—the Bogalusa Heart Study. *American J. Clinical Nutrition*, 30:582-591.

Freud, S. 1953. *A General Introduction to Psychoanalysis*. New York: Permabooks.

Furstenberg, F. F. 1991. As the pendulum swings: Teenage childbearing and social concerns. *Family Relations*, 40:127-138.

Garbarino, J. 1986. *Adolescent Development: An Ecological Perspective*. Columbus, OH: Charles Merrill.

Gibbs, J. T. 1985. City girls: Psychosocial adjustment of urban black adolescent females. *SAGE: A Scholarly Journal on Black Women*, 2:28-36.

Gibbs, J. T. and Huang, L. N. 1989a. A conceptual framework for assessing and treating minority youth. In J. T. Gibbs & L. N. Huang, Eds., *Children of Color: Psychological Interventions with Minority Youth*. San Francisco: Jossey-Bass.

Gibbs, J. T. & Huang, L. N., Eds., 1989b. *Children of Color: Psychological Interventions with Minority Youth*. San Francisco: Jossey-Bass.

Gilligan, C., Lyons, N. P., & Hanmer, T. J., Eds. 1990. *Making Connections*. Cambridge, MA: Harvard University.

Hall, G. S. 1904. *Adolescence*. New York: Appleton-Century-Crofts.

Harlan, W. R., Harlan, E. A., and Grillo, P. 1980. Secondary sex characteristics of girls 12 to 17 years of age: The U.S. Health Examination Survey. *J. Pediatrics*. 96:1074-1078.

Harrison, A. 1990. High risk sexual behavior among black adolescents. In A. R. Stiffman & L. E. Davis, Eds., *Ethnic Issues in Adolescent Mental Health*. Newbury Park, CA: Sage.

Hsu, L. K. G. 1987. Are the eating disorders becoming more common among blacks. *Internat. J. Eating Disorders*, 6:113-124.

Huang, L. N. & Ying, Y. W. 1989. Chinese American children and adolescents. In J. T. Gibbs L. N. Huang, Eds., *Children of Color: Psychological Interventions with Minority Youth*. San Francisco: Jossey-Bass.

Kandel, D. B. & Davies, M. 1982. Epidemiology of depressive mood in adolescence. *Arch. Gen. Psychiatry*, 39:1205-1212.

Katchadourian, H. A. 1990. Sexuality. In S. S. Feldman & G. R. Elliott, Eds., *At the Threshold: The Developing Adolescent*. Cambridge, MA: Harvard University Press.

Katchadourian, H. A. & Lunde, D. T. 1980. *Fundamentals of Human Sexuality*. New York: Holt, Rinehart & Winston.

Katz, P. A. 1986. Gender identity: Development and consequences. In R. D. Ashmore & F. K. Del Boca, Eds., *The Social Psychology of Female-Male Relationships*. New York: Academic Press.

Katz, P., Carruthers, H., & Forrest, T. 1979. Adolescent Saulteaux-Objibway girls: The adolescent process amidst a clash of cultures. In M. Sugar, Ed., *Female Adolescent Development*. New York: Brunner/Mazel.

Ladner, J. 1972. *Tomorrow's Tomorrow: The Black Woman*. Garden City: Doubleday.

LaFromboise, T. D., Heyle, A. M., & Ozer, E. J. 1990. Changing and diverse roles of women in American Indian cultures. *Sex Roles*, 22:455-475.

Leigh, G. K., Weddle, K. D., & Loewen, I. R. 1988. Analysis of the timing of transition to sexual intercourse for black adolescent females. *J. Adol. Research*, 3:333-344.

Lerner, R. M. 1984. *On the Nature of Human Plasticity*. New York: Cambridge University Press.

Liu, W. T., Yu, E. S. H., Chang, C. F., & Fernandez, M. 1990. The mental health of Asian American teenagers: A research challenge. In A. R. Stiffman and L. E. Davis, Eds., *Ethnic Issues in Adolescent Mental Health*. Newbury Park, CA: Sage.

Malone, T. E. 1986. *Report of the Secretary's Task Force on Black and Minority Health: Volume VI: Infant Mortality and Low Birthweight* (GPO No. 491-313/44711). Washington, D.C.: U.S. Government Printing Office.

McDermott, J. F., Robillard, A. B., Char, W. F., Hsu, J., Tseng, W. S., & Ashton, G. C. 1983. Reexamining the concept of adolescence: Differences between adolescent boys and girls in the context of their families. *Amer. J. Psychiatry*, 140:1318-1322.

McGrath, E., Keita, G. P., Strickland, B. R., & Russo, N. F., Eds. 1990. *Women and Depression: Risk Factors and Treatment Issues*. Final report of the American Psychological Association's National Task Force on Women and Depression. Washington, D.C.: American Psychological Association.

Mirande, A. & Enriquez, E. 1979. *La Chicana*. Chicago: University of Chicago Press.

Nagata, D. K. 1989. Japanese American children and adolescents. In J. T. Gibbs & L. N. Huang, Eds., *Children of Color: Psychological Interventions with Minority Youth*. San Francisco: Jossey-Bass.

Nielsen, L. 1991. *Adolescence: A Contemporary View*. 2nd ed. Fort Worth, TX: Holt, Rinehart and Winston.

Petersen, A. C., Kennedy, R. E., & Sullivan, P. 1991. In M. E. Colten and S. Gore, Eds., *Adolescent Stress: Causes and Consequences*. Hawthorne, NH: Aldine de Gruyter.

Petersen, A. C., Offer, D., & Kaplan, E. 1979. The self-image of rural adolescent girls. In M. Sugar, Ed., *Female Adolescent Development*. New York: Brunner/Mazel.

Petersen, A. C., Sarigiani, P. A., & Kennedy, R. E. 1991. Adolescent depression: Why more girls? *J. Youth Adol.*, 20:247-271.

Petersen, A. C. & Taylor, B. 1980. The biological approach to adolescence: Biological change and psychosocial adaptation. In J. Adelson, Ed., *Handbook of the Psychology of Adolescence*. New York: Wiley.

Phinney, J. S. 1989. Stages of ethnic identity development in minority group adolescents. *J. Early Adol.*, 9:34-49.

Phinney, J. S., Lochner, B. T., & Murphy, R. 1990. Ethnic identity development and psychological adjustment in adolescence. In A. R. Stiffman & L. E. Davis, Eds., *Ethnic Issues in Adolescent Mental Health*. Newbury Park, CA: Sage.

Powers, S. I., Hauser, S. T., & Kilner, L. A. 1989. Adolescent mental health. *Amer. Psychol.*, 44:200-208.

Pumariega, A. J., Edwards, P., & Mitchell, C. B. 1984. Anorexia nervosa in black adolescents. *J. Amer. Acad. Child Psychiat.*, 23:111-114.

Ramirez, O. 1989. Mexican American children and adolescents. In J. T. Gibbs & L. N. Huang, Eds., *Children of Color: Psychological Interventions with Minority Youth*. San Francisco: Jossey-Bass.

Red Horse, J. 1983. Indian family values and experiences. In G. J. Powell, J. Yamamoto, A. Romero, & A. Morales, Eds., *The Psychosocial Development of Minority Group Children*. New York: Brunner/Mazel.

Reeves, M. S. 1989. The high cost of endurance. *Education Week*, 8:2-4.

Reid, P. T. & Comas-Diaz, L. 1990. Gender and ethnicity: Perspectives on dual status. *Sex Roles*, 22:397-408.

Richards, M. & Petersen, A. C. 1987. Biological theoretical models of adolescent development. In V. B. Van Hasselt & M. Hersen, Eds., *The Handbook of Adolescent Psychology*. Elmsford, NY: Pergamon.

Root, M. P. P. 1990. Disordered eating in women of color. *Sex Roles*, 22:525-536.

Santos, R. A. 1983. The social and emotional development of Filipino-American children. In G. J. Powell, J. Yamamoto, A. Romero, & A. Morales, Eds., *The Psychosocial Development of Minority Group Children*. New York: Brunner/Mazel.

Sarigiani, P. A., Wilson, J. L., Petersen, A. C., & Vicary, J. R. 1990. Self-image and educational plans of adolescents from two contrasting communities. *J. Early Adol.*, 10:37-55.

Schumm, W. R., McCollum, E. E., Bugaighis, M. A., Jurich, A. P., Bollman, F. R., & Reitz, J. 1988. Differences between Anglos and Mexican American family members on satisfaction with family life. *Hispanic J. Behav. Sciences*, 10:39-53.

Scott, C. S., Shifman, L., Orr, L., Owen, R. G., & Fawcett, N. 1988. Hispanic and Black American adolescents' beliefs relating to sexuality and contraception. *Adolescence*, 23:667-688.

Scott-Jones, D., Roland, E. J., & White, A. B. 1989. Antecedents and outcomes of pregnancy in black adolescents. In R. L. Jones, Ed., *Black Adolescents*. Berkeley, CA: Cobb & Henry.

Silber, T. J. 1986. Anorexia nervosa in Blacks and Hispanics. *Internat. J. Eating Disorders*, 5:121-128.

Silbereisen, R. K., Petersen, A. C., Albrecht, H. T., & Kracke, B. 1989. Maturational timing and the development of problem behavior: Longitudinal studies in adolescence. *J. Early Adol.*, 9:247-268.

Simmons, R. G. & Blyth, D. A. 1987. *Moving into Adolescence: The Impact of Pubertal Change and School Context.* New York: Aldine-De Gruyter.

Smith, E. S. 1989. African American women and the extended family: A sociohistorical review. *Western J. Black Studies,* 13:179-183.

Smith, J. C., Mercy, J. A., & Warren, C. W. 1985. Comparison of suicides among Anglos and Hispanics in five Southwestern states. *Suicide and Life-Threatening Behavior,* 15:14-26.

Spencer, M. B. & Dornbusch, S. M. 1990. Challenges in studying minority youth. In S. S. Feldman & G. R. Elliot, Eds., *At the Threshold: The Developing Adolescent.* Cambridge, MA: Harvard University Press.

Suarez-Orozco, M. M. 1987. "Becoming somebody": Central American immigrants in U. S. inner-city schools. *Anthropol. and Education Quart.,* 18:287-299.

Udry, J. R., Halpern, C., & Campbell, B. 1991. Hormones, pubertal development, and sexual behavior in adolescent females. Reproduction as social development in adolescent females. Symposium presented at the biennial meeting of the Society for Research in Child Development. Seattle, WA.

U.S. Department of Commerce. 1990. *Statistical Abstract of the United States: 1990.* (110th ed.). Washington, D.C.: U.S. Government, p. 39.

U.S. Department of Health and Human Services. 1988. *Indian Health Service: Chart Series Book.* Washington, D.C.: U.S. Government.

U.S. Department of Health and Human Services. 1990. *Indian Health Service: Regional Differences in Indian Health 1990.* Washington, D.C.: U.S. Government, p. 19.

Vega, W. A., Hough, R. L., & Romero, A. 1983. Family life patterns of Mexican-Americans. In G. J. Powell, J. Yamamoto, A. Romero, & A. Morales, Eds., *The Psychosocial Development of Minority Group Children.* New York: Brunner/Mazel.

Wetzel, J. R. 1987. *American Youth: A Statistical Snapshot.* W. T. Grant Foundation Commission on Youth and America's Future. Washington, D.C.

Zambrana, R. E. & Silva-Palacious, V. 1989. Gender differences in stress among Mexican immigrant adolescents in Los Angeles, CA. *J. Adol. Research,* 4:426-442.

9 Issues of Autonomy in Adolescence: The "Superwoman"

Alayne Yates, M.D.

During the past three decades, we have witnessed a significant shift in the position of women within the culture. Women serve on executive boards, cabinets, ministries, on medical school faculties, and as officers in the Armed Forces. Although women remain greatly outnumbered in top faculty and managerial positions (Blum & Smith, 1988), the overall change is dramatic. The improvement is largely due to the women's movement. This shift has brought women a new presence, a new power, but also some very high expectations for self development.

With their rise in status, women have come to demand a great deal of themselves. In the upper socioeconomic bracket, many women want to achieve professionally, gain a place of respect in the community, marry and raise a child or two, and handle any problems that arise, competently and efficiently, by themselves. When these self-reliant women become depressed or dissatisfied with themselves and enter therapy, they appear distinctly different from the women patients of years past. Their discomfort is with disconnection and lack of fulfillment from their many responsibilities, rather than problems within relationships.

Women's proven ability to succeed, shoulder to shoulder with men, has certainly affected the adolescent girl's perception of herself and her anticipation of what she should be able to accomplish in adult life. If she is to live up to her self-expectations, she will need to be independent, assertive, persistent, and perfectionistic. Perhaps she has already acquired persistence and perfectionism as women have cultivated these qualities from time immemorial, in the context of gathering food, cooking, and caring for a family. She is not as likely to have acquired independence and assertiveness, which are traditionally male values. Yet, if she is to succeed in the male arena, she must be able to speak out in groups, attend college away from home, and compete openly with men. These demands can occasion considerable anxiety. However, many young women have

157

learned to master their anxiety and move toward greater autonomy and self-reliance (Rothchild, 1979).

Establishing independence is a particular problem for women. The problem is made even more acute by the value placed on independence in the culture at large. People in the United States score higher than people in any of a number of other nations in the value they place on independence and personal freedom (National Opinion Research Poll, 1989). We reward individuals who are autonomous and mobile, who can move away from their family of origin and establish themselves on the basis of their independent achievements. In fact, the term "achievement" tends to be synonymous with "independent achievement."

In the past, psychoanalysts have underlined the importance of independence by associating it with maturity, health, and the successful resolution of developmental conflicts (Deutsch, 1944; Freud, 1931). Until recently, they have tended not to recognize conflicts associated with extreme independence: that it can be an emotional liability as well as an advantage. This chapter will address this issue by examining the dilemma of two young, high-achieving women who are struggling to maintain a very separate state.

BETSY*

Betsy, the youngest of three children, was born to a mother who taught history part time at a prestigious college and a father who was a busy physician. Betsy's mother enjoyed having children and especially liked "fussing over" little girls. In contrast to her older brother, Brad, Betsy was never a behavior problem. When Brad hit Betsy, she ran to her mother, protesting vigorously. The mother always found some activity to distract and quiet her. Betsy had many interests that her mother fostered, including art, crafts, cooking, swimming, taking care of animals, and reading. When Betsy's mother would depart for her teaching job, she left Betsy with plenty of activities so that she wouldn't be lonely. Betsy performed well in school, in spite of the fact that she often forgot her pencils and papers. She seemed like a happy child who continued to need her mother to structure her day and keep her organized.

When Betsy was 12 years of age, her mother began an extramarital affair with an English professor in the college where she taught. Betsy's parents separated and reconciled. When her mother was away, Betsy seemed lost, ate a lot and gained considerable weight. Her father encouraged her to take on some household responsibilities and during the next several years she seemed able to adapt. When she was 14, her parents divorced, her mother moved to Great Britain, and Betsy was placed in a boarding school. She did not see her mother, although

---

* From Yates, 1991, pp. 44–47.

they corresponded. On school holidays she stayed with her father. With academic progress she was accepted at a university, moved there, made a few friends, and began to date another student.

When Betsy was a college junior, her father suggested that she think seriously about her future and a career. Betsy visited her mother for the first time since the divorce. She had hoped that an interesting job might be available in Great Britain, but she was disappointed and her mother offered her little support. When she returned to school, she was worried about her future and how she would be able to make it on her own. She took a part-time job in merchandising and began to jog every morning, rain or shine. She studied even more diligently and earned straight A grades for the first time. In the six months prior to her graduation, she embarked on a diet, along with several of her friends. She considered herself fat and was delighted to finally be able to lose weight. She began to weigh herself daily and to carefully monitor calories.

Shortly after graduation, Betsy took a job as an apprentice buyer in a large department store. She followed a demanding schedule, worked diligently, and soon was promoted to assistant buyer. She took on extra duties and often worked during the weekend to the exclusion of social events. She continued to diet and ran 15 miles a week regardless of weather conditions. Through persistence and perseverance, she became the youngest buyer ever in her department store (Yates, 1991).

Betsy was well cared for in her early life and was closely identified with, and dependent on, her mother. The precipitous separation from her mother in early adolescence made her more independent, whether she liked it or not. However, her greatest surge in autonomy occurred as she anticipated leaving college and establishing herself on her own.

PATRICE

Patrice, the youngest and only girl among three children had a father who was a financial consultant and a homemaker mother who did considerable volunteer and civic work. The family engaged in many activities together, often attending the gymnastic meets in which the two boys were involved. Patrice thought that her father, who had been a gymnast in his youth, preferred her brothers. She, in turn, felt closer to, and favored by, her mother. Her brothers thought that she was favored by both parents.

Although Patrice had problems in spelling and penmanship, she managed to do well in her other subjects. By the time she reached sixth grade she had two best friends who shared many common interests such as boys, cooking, bicycle riding, drama, and writing poems for the school newspaper. At high school graduation, she was on the honor roll and was the only senior chosen as a junior counselor at camp. She entered a large state university some distance from home.

Patrice's mother began to sew a college wardrobe for Patrice six months before she left for the university. The two women often talked together about what college would be like. Patrice thought she was fat and wanted to be as slim as she imagined college girls were, so she began to diet. During this period, Patrice felt closer to her mother than she had for many years, but she continued to be very active socially with peers.

Patrice greatly missed her parents and friends when she first arrived on campus. She felt better once classes began and she could bury herself in homework. She joined several clubs and engaged in extracurricular activities. Even though she did not need the money and was already feeling somewhat overloaded, she took a part-time job as a waitress. As a result of snacking on leftovers that she brought from work, she gained back all the weight she had lost. Eventually, she stopped waitressing, studied more in the library (away from the refrigerator), and overscheduled herself even further. She stopped "messing around" with her friends and dropped out of all extracurricular activities because it was time to "get serious" about life. She considered joining the Peace Corps because it would be a challenge, and she always worked her best under those conditions.

Betsy and Patrice were raised in affluent, high-achieving families. They appeared to have been well cared for as children and their lives were reasonably stable. They were close to, and relied upon, mothers who encouraged them toward greater independence. They did well in school and developed close ties with peers. As they addressed the issue of "Who am I," they began to strive to live up to "superwoman" self-expectations by developing "masculine" attributes of competitiveness, assertion, independence, and vocational challenge.

The high self-expectations of Betsy and Patrice seemed to fuel their chronic dissatisfaction with body and self. As they surrounded themselves with projects to prove their worth, they dropped out of relationships and became progressively more alone. They operated essentially on their own and rarely asked for help. It was as if they could not achieve up to their high self-expectations and also preserve a network of close, caring relationships.

The price Betsy and Patrice paid for success was the loss of connectedness. In the past, they had found gratification in caring relationships, but now they had little time or energy left to pursue them. This arrangement seemed to work for them up to a point. Their high achievement earned them plaudits at home and ever escalating tokens of success at school. Eventually, however, they found themselves in a uniquely modern straightjacket. They felt alienated and alone, and they questioned their goals. Betsy felt "caught in a box"; she began to entertain thoughts of suicide. Patrice worried about her inability to sustain pleasure through relationships with men. When these young women sought help, they presented conflicts about independence and identity.

AUTONOMY AND AFFILIATION

The analytic community has become more aware of conflicts in women between independence, defined as a capacity for autonomous functioning, and attachments to others (Notman, Zilbach, Miller & Nadelson, 1986). Recently, authors such as Gilligan (1982) have begun to question the emphasis on independence for women when it is accompanied, as it usually is, by a deemphasis on close relationships and interpersonal care. Gilligan suggests that in our society maintaining a state of self-sufficiency has become a moral ideal. This sets adults at odds with the human condition and fosters what is called the culture of narcissism. This is similar to Macoby's (1977) description of contemporary individuals driven by success, who want to be known as winners but who have developed scant capacity for personal intimacy and social commitment. However, overly self-reliant persons do not necessarily present the psychodynamic features of the narcissistic character (Yates, 1991).

Gilligan bases her concern on studies of different groups of men and women. Men and women medical students (Gilligan & Pollak, 1988) seem to view life differently from one another. Men tend to associate intimacy with danger while women view relationships as safe, but are threatened by thoughts of losing or being without a relationship. In the legal profession, women's concern for caring can be a distinct liability. When attorneys advance an effective argument they should not question whether and how much it will hurt the other person's feelings, but many women attorneys do. Eventually, they find that they need to suppress empathy and concern for others in order to compete successfully (Jack & Jack, 1988). Instead, they need to emphasize mastery, a characteristically masculine basis for self-esteem (Zilbach, Notman, Nadelson, et al., 1979). This is not an easy task, since women have been raised to expect and enjoy connectedness.

Women often pay a price when they operate within a framework of masculine values. They may begin to feel detached and isolated (Gilligan & Pollak, 1988), conflicted over issues of loyalty and care (Gilligan, Johnson & Miller, 1987), or experience depression and a sense of worthlessness. They pay a price because, in order to be successful in a man's world, they must negate their primary femininity (Kleeman, 1976; Roiphe & Galenson, 1981), the early, unconflicted, preoedipal sense of being female (Notman et al., 1986). Gilligan (1987) states that an orientation toward achievement can effectively preempt an orientation toward relationships and care.

A woman's concept of herself begins with her early identification with her mother as a nurturant figure. Unlike her brother, she does not need to relinquish her preoedipal ties to mother in order to establish a gender identity. Her development within this relationship allows her to develop a rich network of interconnectedness, identification, and empathy (Blos, 1980). If her transitions are smooth, she should, in adolescence and adult life, continue to derive a positive sense of self by being close to, and by caring for, others. However, if she is to compete in the business or professional arena, she must operate in a manner that contradicts her early experience in interconnectedness.

Male and female development can be seen as proceeding along two differing developmental lines (Notman et al., 1986). Although both boys and girls form an initial, close relationship with the mother, boys must disidentify with the mother (Stoller, 1976) if they are to achieve a masculine identity. This means that boys must relinquish the pleasure and protection they derive through the relationship with the mother. In order to do this, they may need to distance themselves from her. They may renounce closeness and begin to distrust intimate relationships. This limits the range of empathy and identification boys are able to develop (Blos, 1969). When boys mature, they may be limited in their ability to give and receive within caring relationships. On the other hand, they may be better suited than girls for the business and professional world, at least as it is currently constituted.

Although girls remain identified with the mother, they are able to differentiate from her by acquiring a different set of internal representations through their experience with others (Notman et al., 1986). This means that girls continue to grow within, and through, close relationships. Because their early emotional development is different from boys, they should not necessarily be expected to adapt in the same manner or to take on the same moral perspective as boys. Johnston (1985) demonstrates that this is indeed the case. In solving problems presented in two of Aesop's fables, boys prefer justice strategies such as focusing on identifying conflicting rights, while girls prefer care strategies such as responding to the needs of the individuals involved.

ADOLESCENCE

Adolescence has been called the second separation-individuation process (Beattie, 1988; Blos, 1967) in which adolescents must learn, once again, to manage the tension between ego growth and the desire to regress. Adolescence also provides a second chance to rework unfinished oedipal and preoedipal conflicts (Eissler, 1958). Whether youths address oedipal or preoedipal issues depends upon the gender-specific developmental format. Boys have established a greater separation early on; in adolescence they tend to retest oedipal issues as they find a sphere of power and freedom that is separate and distinct from that of the parents. Girls have never become as separate; in adolescence they remain more concerned with preoedipal, often romanticized, issues of inter-relatedness.

Gilligan, Lyons & Hanmer (1990) describe the erratic development of autonomy in the adolescent girl. At age 11, she is "bossy," outspoken, and sure of herself. She knows who she is and what she thinks. By age 16, she no longer "knows" what she thinks. This represents a certain disconnection from her own thoughts and feelings, a by-product of becoming a logical thinker and excluding intuitive concepts. This disconnection often is accompanied by distancing and greater conflict within the relationship to mother. Some young women continue to vacillate between these two perceptual modes. Some choose separation and the values related to independent achievement; others choose connection and the values related to caring.

In the best solution, women are able to bridge the gap between value systems, incorporating the modes of separation and connection as compatible aspects of the self. In this case, they enjoy the emotional benefits of close relationships and use the energy and optimism this affords to develop themselves as leaders and independent achievers within the educational or vocational world.

ROLE STRAIN AND INCREASED ACTIVITY

"Superwomen" tend to forfeit gratification from close relationships as they strive toward excellence in male-invested educational and vocational arenas. If we assume that in women this degree of independence necessarily entails conflict over issues of dependency, then we would need to address how this conflict is translated in everyday life. As Betsy and Patrice began to consolidate their character (Blos, 1969) and life goals, both girls presented an increase in activity, asceticism, and the need to control the body. As they became more involved in independent endeavors, they became progressively more alone in spite of the fact that they remained sensitive to, and concerned about, the feelings of others. They acted as if their self-control would be threatened if they took the time to invest in relationships.

The issues that these young women face are contained in a series of events that occurred when Patrice was a freshman in college. Her mother, to whom she had been extremely close, was to have a hysterectomy right before Patrice's final exams. Without hesitation, Patrice left school and returned home. She remained at home for the following week, in spite of the fact that she would have to take make-up exams. She did poorly (by her standards) on two exams and, therefore, decided to attend summer school instead of returning home for summer vacation. She made this choice even though she continued to dearly miss her friends and family. During the summer she studied hard, avoided many social events, dieted, and worked part time as a waitress. She was uncomfortable when she had nothing to do. When she had time to herself she would snack, more or less continuously. Later, Patrice consciously took on more responsibility to enhance her resolve to lose weight.

Patrice needed to maintain herself as a self-reliant, achieving young woman in spite of her need for caring relationships. Engaging in various activities helped her to maintain a separate state. It provided an immediate, fairly effective defense against dependent longings, often expressed as hunger. Being independently active removed Patrice from the condition of dependency and it directly reinforced her separateness. She felt soothed by certain simple, repetitive activities such as running. She enjoyed a sense of efficacy and felt better about herself when her work was recognized and rewarded. Engaging in activity brought a sense of purpose and organization. Activity, then, became a major source of gratification and protection in the absence of caring relationships.

The psychological literature lends support to the association between independence and multiple activities. Timko, Streigel-Moore, Silberstein, et al. (1987) described a group of "superwomen," university students who list a number of roles that they see as central to their self-concept. The number of roles selected was correlated with the value that these "superwomen" placed on certain masculine attributes (strength, leanness, competitiveness, dominance, etc.), values that are prized by the culture and are associated with upward mobility and success.

OVERUSE OF ACTIVITY

Engaging in activity is a means by which young "superwomen" maintain homeostasis in the face of emotional deprivation. However, when the need for care is acute, these women can overuse activity to the point of physical and emotional exhaustion. Dieting and exercise are two of the many activities that young "superwomen" tend to undertake. When they overinvest in diet or exercise, their endeavors can take on a distinctly ascetic cast. A high school junior, an "A" student, studied until midnight and awoke at 4:30 AM to run five miles, rain or shine, before breakfast. Breakfast consisted of an apple or half a grapefruit. She ate a salad for lunch. She worked out on weights after school, and then consumed a piece of chicken and vegetables for dinner. Her diet and exercise schedule never varied.

The goal of diet and exercise activity is to control the body. Early in development it is the body that needs to eat, rest, and be cared for. It would seem that the real issue for "superwomen" is to control the dependent longings that reside in the body so that they can be as independent as possible. They try not to eat, rest as little as possible, and avoid social relationships, a construct that easily translates into asceticism. Building on Anna Freud's (1946) concept of asceticism as a valuable defense of adolescence, Mogul (1980) describes how adolescents employ asceticism to establish a sense of strength and freedom from dependence on the parents. He suggests that asceticism becomes pathological only when it is an end in itself.

If this theory is correct, then our "superwomen" would be more likely than other women to present as compulsive exercisers or eating disordered. In fact, the "superwomen" university students described by Timko et al. (1987) were more likely than other students to present disturbed eating attitudes and behaviors. A separate study by Steiner-Adair (1986) showed that high school girls who embrace the image of "superwoman" are those who report disordered eating attitudes and behaviors on the Eating Attitudes Test (EAT). Conversely, those students who are oriented toward relationships and care, rather than independence or success, do not demonstrate disordered eating attitudes or behaviors. Gilligan (1987) uses this study to suggest that vulnerability to the eating disorders occurs when young women focus on issues of perfection and control and are unable to recognize the importance of interpersonal connection.

These several studies suggest that there is a cadre of bright, high-achieving young women who strive for greater independence in part by renouncing the importance of close interpersonal relationships. In order to achieve an extremely independent state, they may tightly control the body and renounce the need for food and rest. They can express this in various forms of asceticism, including disturbed eating and exercise behaviors (Yates, 1991).

ROLE STRAIN AS A FUNCTION OF CULTURAL PRESSURE

Adolescent males, as well as females, may experience role strain when they attempt high levels of independent achievement. In our study of compulsive athletes, we found that men employed activity to maintain a separate state in a fashion similar to women (Yates, 1991). Men who demanded a great deal of independent achievement of themselves were more apt to overuse exercise to the point of self-harm, a condition that we thought was analogous to the eating disorders. This suggests that women are not the only ones adversely affected by the expectation of extreme independence. Men have dependency needs and they do assign value to connectedness (Gilligan & Pollak, 1988). In a technological culture that overvalues independence and independent achievement, men, as well as women, may be susceptible to the overuse of diet, exercise, and other activity.

This chapter has addressed upper socioeconomic adolescent women. However, the same forces probably apply to all women who are sensitive to cultural values, who are upwardly mobile and who strive toward greater independence. Although we do not have the necessary studies to support this contention, we do know that the incidence of eating disorders is greater among high-achieving university women and that it increases sharply in immigrant women who are attempting to achieve in an industrialized nation without the family and community supports of their homeland (Yates, 1989).

THERAPY

In individual therapy, adolescent "superwomen" display many strengths, but they also present many problems. They try to be as independent of the therapist as possible. They work diligently at solving their problems as if therapy were another responsibility, another challenge, another item on their interminable list. This effectively prevents them from receiving the compassion and concern of the therapist and it protects them from being gratified through the relationship. They value the therapist but they seem emotionally disconnected and they expect very little. It is the completion of the task that is "supposed" to be fulfilling.

The therapist may view "superwomen" as narcissistic because of their style of distant relatedness and the aura of self-sufficiency. The therapist may feel ineffectual, removed from the therapy, bored and frustrated. However, the transference that these young women develop tends to differ from the mirroring or idealizing transferences that Kohut (1977) describes in narcissistic patients. "Superwomen" avoid basking in the therapist's approval as narcissistic patients often do (suggesting a mirror transference). Instead, they deflect or diminish the therapist's positive comments as if they were undeserving of the recognition. They do not find power in the relationship with the therapist and they certainly do not deny that the therapist is a separate person, as in the idealizing transference.

In therapy, "superwomen" use their self-sufficiency as a defense against the powerful draw of the relationship. They are afraid that they might need the therapist. They defend by assuming that the therapist wishes them to manage their own problems, i.e., they try to be "on top of the therapy" by figuring things out before the therapist can. This is their method of maintaining control and a position of autonomy. They do not necessarily mean to devalue the therapist and they do not dislike it when the therapist interrupts. They may even be relieved when this occurs. They hear the therapist's comments and may integrate them into their understanding of themselves. Although these young women tend to be emotionally disconnected, they do not present the non-relatedness, the internal deadness, or the disdainful aloofness of the narcissistic patient.

SUMMARY

The women's movement has borne fruit in the past 30 years. As a group, women have become more effective and more powerful than ever before. With this, some adolescents have begun to adopt extraordinarily high self-expectations for independence and achievement. As these young "superwomen" strive to meet these goals, they may deinvest in relationships and become overly involved in many activities. If this process continues, they may question their identity and suffer from alienation or depression.

REFERENCES

Beattie, H.J. 1988. Eating disorders and the mother-daughter relationship. *International J. Eating Disorders*, 7:453-460.

Bernstein, D. 1983. The female superego: A different perspective. *International J. Psychoanalysis*, 64:187-201.

Blos, P. 1967. The second individuation process of adolescence. *Psychoanal. Study Child*, 22:162-186.

Blos, P. 1969. Character formation in adolescence. *Psychoanal. Study Child*, 23:245-263.

Blos, P. 1980. Modifications in the traditional psychoanalytic theory of female adolescent development. *Adolescent Psychiatry*, 8:8-24.

Blum, L. & Smith, V. 1988. Women's mobility in the corporation: A critique of the politics of optimism. *Signs*, 13:3-5.

Deutsch, H. 1944. *The Psychology of Women*, Vol. 1. New York: Grune and Stratton.

Eissler, K.R. 1958. Notes on problems of technique in the psychoanalytic psychotherapy of adolescents. *Psychoanal. Study Child*, 13:223-234.

Freud, A. 1946. *The Ego and the Mechanisms of Defense*. New York: International Universities Press.

Freud, S. 1931. Female Sexuality, *Standard Edition*, 21. London Press and the Institute for Psychoanalysis: London, 1961, pp. 225-246.

Gilligan, C. 1982. New maps of development: New visions of maturity. *Amer. J. Orthopsychiat.*, 52:199-212.

Gilligan, C. 1987. Adolescent development reconsidered. In C.E. Irwin, Ed., *New Directions for Child Development*, no. 37. San Francisco: Jossey-Bass.

Gilligan, C., Johnson, D.K., & Miller, B. 1987. Moral voice, adolescent development, and secondary education: A study at the Green River School. *GEHD Center Monograph #3*.

Gilligan, C., Lyons, N.P., & Hanmer, T.J. 1990. *Making Connections: The Relational Worlds of Adolescent Girls at Emma Willard School*. Cambridge, MA: Harvard University Press.

Gilligan, C. & Pollak, S. 1988. The vulnerable and invulnerable physician. In C. Gilligan, J.V. Ward, & J.M. Taylor, Eds., *Mapping the Moral Domain*. Cambridge, MA: Harvard University Press.

Jack, D. & Jack, R. 1988. Women lawyers: Archetype and alternatives. In C. Gilligan, J.V. Ward, & J.M. Taylor, Eds., *Mapping the Moral Domain*. Cambridge, MA: Harvard University Press.

Johnston, D.K. 1985. Two moral orientations: Two problem-solving strategies: *Adolescent's solutions to dilemmas in fables*. Unpublished Ph.D. dissertation, Harvard Graduate School of Education.

Kleeman, J. 1976. Freud's views on early female sexuality in the light of direct child observation. *J. Am. Psychoanal. Assoc.*, 24:3-27.

Kohut, H. 1977. *The Restoration of the Self*. New York: International Universities Press.

Macoby, M. 1977. *The Gamesman: The New Corporate Leaders*. New York: Simon and Schuster.

Mogul, S.L. 1980. Asceticism in adolescence and anorexia nervosa. *Psychoanalytic Study Child*, 35:155-175.

National Opinion Research Poll, 1989. National Opinion Research Center. Chicago: University of Chicago.

Notman, M.T., Zilbach, J.J., Miller, J., & Nadelson, C.C. 1986. Themes in psychoanalytic understanding of women: Some reconsiderations of autonomy and affiliation. *J. Am. Acad. of Psychoanal.*, 14:241-253.

Roiphe, H. & Galenson, E. 1981. *Infantile Origins of Sexual Identity*. New York: International Universities Press.

Rothchild, E. 1979. Female power: Lines to development of autonomy in adolescent girls. In M. Sugar, Ed., *Female Adolescent Development*. New York: Brunner/Mazel.

Steiner-Adair, C. 1986. The body politic: Normal female adolescent development and the development of eating disorders. *J. Am. Acad. Psychoanal.*, 14:95-114.

Stoller, R. 1976. Primary femininity. *J. Am. Psychoanal. Assoc.*, 24:59-77.

Timko, C., Streigel-Moore, R.H., Silberstein, L.R., & Rodin, J. 1987. Femininity/Masculinity and disordered eating in women: How are they related? *International J. Eating Disorders*, 6:701-712.

Yates A. 1989. Current perspectives on the eating disorders: History, psychological and biological aspects. *J. Am. Acad. Child & Adol. Psychiatry*, 28:813-828.

Yates, A. 1991. *Compulsive Exercise and the Eating Disorders: Toward an Integrated Theory of Activity*. New York: Brunner/Mazel.

Yates, A. 1992. Comparing obligatory to nonobligatory runners. *Psychosomatics*, 33(2):180-189.

Zilbach, J. J., Notman, M., Nadelson, C., & Miller, J.B. 1979. *Reconsiderations of Aggression and Self-Esteem in Women*. Paper presented at International Psychoanalytic Assoc., New York.

10 Female Delinquency

Graciela Viale-Val, Psy.D.
Carrie Sylvester, M.D., M.P.H.

In this chapter we will review the literature on female delinquency and examine factors which contribute to gender differences in the commission of serious offenses. We will find that studies of the characteristics of female offenders have been scarce and have produced apparently contradictory findings.

Lack of reliable statistics, inadequate theoretical models to guide the study of disordered adolescent behavior, and variability in data collection methods have contributed to controversy which permeates most discussions of gender differences in criminal activity. Given the number of social and cultural factors interacting with individual differences, it is not surprising to find a lack of consensus about the relative importance of different risk factors and their cumulative contribution to adolescent maladjustment. The literature on female delinquency published in the last three decades also tends to reflect the feminist perspective, particularly in the writings of "pro-feminist criminologists."

We will address current controversies and examine the differential treatment of female delinquency by researchers, the courts, and the penal system, as well as the possible impact of the "women's movement" on the prevalence of female delinquency. The focus of our discussion will be on delinquent behaviors defined as "illegal activities that are committed by a child or adolescent" (Henggeler, 1989), but relevant information from studies of disruptive behavior disorders and antisocial personality disorder is included.

EPIDEMIOLOGY OF DELINQUENT BEHAVIOR AND GENDER DIFFERENCES

Official statistics of arrests and incarceration, victimization data, and self-report measures of delinquency show that girls are much less prone to delinquent behavior than boys (Henggeler, 1989; Nagel & Hagan, 1983; Rutter & Giller,

1984; West, 1967) and are less likely to participate in violent crimes (Hamparian, Schyster, Dinitz & Conraad, 1978). Some reports have suggested, nevertheless, that women tend to have a higher *rate* of arrests for violent crimes than men (Herjanic, Henn & Vanderpearl, 1977; Rappenport & Lassen, 1966) and that the *pattern* of delinquency is identical for both groups (Cernkovich & Giordano, 1979). Recent statistics have been used to demonstrate that female delinquency is on the rise and that women and girls are more frequently involved in violent crimes than in the past (Adler, 1975; Fagan, Jones, Hartstone, Rudman & Emerson, 1981; McClelland, 1982).

Excellent reviews of the controversy on the relative usefulness of statistics based on official arrests data, victimization data, and self-reports completed by "normal adolescents" or by incarcerated offenders have been done by Nagel and Hagan (1983) and by O'Brien (1985). Briefly stated, the reviewers stress that these sources of information on the prevalence of criminal activities have been found to be deficient in important areas. For example, statistics based on crime reports may reflect the influence of sex and race biases on the rate of arrests or regional factors such as the professionalism of the police force. Surveys of victims of crime are likely to be affected by the severity and nature of the crime and the relationship of the victim to the offender. Self-reports of delinquency, which can add to the understanding of unreported offenses, are not based on standard methodology and may be weighted toward the reporting of less serious or quite trivial offenses. Thus, even the most reliable statistics about female crime are flawed, and studies based on self-reports, incarceration, arrest data, and court data are not comparable (Benedek, 1979).

According to statistics of arrests for the five years from 1986 to 1990, there was an eight percent increase in the total number of arrests of juveniles for all offenses, while adult arrests increased by 19 percent (Federal Bureau of Investigation, 1990). Adult men accounted for 78 percent of all arrests, and for 89 percent of violent crimes during 1990. During that same period, male arrests went up by 18 percent while female arrests increased by 24 percent. Seventy-eight percent of women's arrests for index offenses (serious criminal activity) and 19 percent of all women's arrests in 1990 were for larceny-theft.

The number of adult men and women in jails has also continued to increase in the past decade. On June 30, 1989, an estimated one of every 249 men and one of every 2,578 women residing in the United States of America were in local jails. Women constituted approximately nine percent of the jail inmates, 5.4 percent of federal and state prison inmates, and 13 percent of persons under correctional supervision (Bureau of Justice Statistics, 1990a).

Regarding juvenile arrests, statistics for 1986 to 1990 show an 8.1 percent increase in the number of male arrests for all crimes and a 7.4 percent increase for female arrests (Federal Bureau of Investigation, 1990). Boys outnumbered girls in arrests for all types of offenses except for runaway and prostitution. The ratio of boy to girl arrests for violent crime was 8.1:1 during 1986 and 7.5:1 in 1990, while the ratio of 3.3:1 for all offenses was unchanged. Currently available juvenile court statistics indicate a three percent increase in girls' property crimes and an eight percent decline in girls' drug cases between 1986 and 1987 (Office of Juvenile Justice and Delinquency Prevention, 1990).

In 1987, boys were involved in four of five delinquency cases processed, but the offense profiles of male and female delinquency cases were very similar. Both male and female delinquency case rates increased with age through 16 years. Although the boys' rate continued to climb with age, case rates for girls peaked at age 16 years and then, except for drug offenses, declined. There was a two percent decrease in the number of youth formally processed for status offenses between 1986 and 1987. Boys accounted for the majority of liquor law violations (78 percent) whereas girls had a higher rate of runaway (63 percent). Because referred youth were more likely to be adjudicated and placed in detention for runaway than for other status offenses, girls were detained and placed out of their homes more often than boys.

It is notable that only about one-third of the petitioned status offense cases are adjudicated and that a minority of cases result in placement or probation. Only a small portion of court-referred adolescents are formally processed by the courts. Girls referred for delinquency are more likely to be processed informally than are boys (whose cases are more likely to be waived to criminal court where there is formal legal representation and, thus, more protection from arbitrary detention.) Girls are also more likely to be placed in private custody.

In 1987, the ratio of boys to girls held in public custody was 6.4:1 whereas the ratio for youth held in private custody was 2.2:1 (Office of Juvenile Justice and Delinquency Prevention, 1987). Approximately 39 percent of the juveniles held in long-term state youth correctional institutions during 1987 had been incarcerated for violent crimes. Another 24 percent were incarcerated for burglary. Almost 60 percent of these adolescent boys and girls reported that they used drugs regularly and an estimated 48 percent said they were under the influence of drugs and alcohol at the time of the offense that led to their incarceration (Bureau of Justice Statistics, 1990b).

Narrowing of the differences in the ratio of male to female delinquency and, recently, the relative increases in the participation of girls and young women in a broader range of crimes have been found to be based primarily on self-report data. As noted, these tend to encompass less severe delinquent behaviors and status offenses such as running away, truancy, parental defiance, shoplifting, and drug-related offenses. Even though relative increases in female delinquency have been used to support conclusions that female delinquency is becoming more serious and widespread, there are pitfalls in relying on percentage or relative increases when the starting point is very low, i.e., relative increases in women's crime rates may be more apparent than real because the base rates for female crime are much lower (Steffensmeier, 1978).

Another perspective on the assumption that female delinquency is becoming more similar to that of males was provided by Cernkovich, Giordano, and Pugh (1985). They found that more boys than girls self-reported engaging in delinquent behaviors other than disobeying or defying parents, running away from home, and using "hard" drugs. Nevertheless, what seemed to differentiate boys and girls was not the type of antisocial act, but the frequency of involvement in those acts. Similarities were due mostly to the high percentage of both sexes admitting to involvement in minor offenses, whereas the ratios of male to female involvement were considerable higher for more serious offenses. They also found racial differences in the pattern and frequency of involvement in antisocial activities. White girls reported higher rates of involvement in antisocial activities, but less participation in more serious offenses against person than non-white girls.

Curran (1984) has argued that changes in statistics used to support the notion of an increase in female criminality and delinquency as a result of the influence of the "women's movement" can be explained instead by the changes in the status of juveniles in the criminal system. He attributes the percentage increase in the commission of violent crimes to the removal of status offenses from the Juvenile Act in 1976. The reduction in total offenses results in the relative inflation in violent crimes committed by girls. Adjusted statistics show that the rise for girls has been less than the rise in boys' violent criminal activity. He also points to the effect of recent changes in how the juvenile system views "traditional female offenses" and in a "law-and-order" approach which has resulted in a higher rate of arrests and convictions, particularly for girls.

Nagel and Hagan (1983), in their review, found evidence indicating that adolescent girls are participating in a broader variety of delinquent activities. They concluded that "in a relative sense, there is evidence that women are becoming more like men in their levels of involvement in crime, particularly younger women and in the area of property crime, especially petty theft and fraud." They noted, however, that these changes were from very small absolute frequencies to slightly higher frequencies and that as seriousness of crime increases, so does the difference between the levels of male and female participation among adolescents and adults.

These conclusions are not intended to minimize the significance of changes in the past two decades in female involvement in a wider range of delinquent activities, nor of the significant increase in arrests for drug abuse offenses. Traditionally, it had been thought that women's involvement in drug dealing was rare, but FBI investigations (Federal Bureau of Investigation, 1987) and interviews with drug-using women found that approximately 72 percent had been dealing drugs and that a large percentage had initiated the dealing prior to their drug use (Hunt, 1990). Observers have noted that as many as 85 percent of incarcerated women have a drug problem and attribute crowding in women's prisons to an increase in drug abuse among women (Bureau of Justice Statistics, 1990b; Church, 1990).

In summary, although there has been considerable disagreement concerning the question of whether the assumed increase in the participation of women and girls in criminal behavior is a fact or a "social invention" (James & Thornton, 1980), women and adolescent girls have consistently been shown to be less likely to commit crimes in general, and less likely to commit serious or violent criminal acts.

THEORETICAL BASES FOR GENDER DIFFERENCES IN DELINQUENCY

According to a popular theory, girls and women have traditionally been more likely to have been confined to their homes and kept under more strict supervision and, thus, have had less opportunity to become involved in illegal activities. In the second half of this century, increased emancipation and participation in the workforce have provided women more opportunity to commit "white collar," or property, crimes (Henggeler, 1989; Price, 1977; West, 1967; Zedner, 1991). In reviewing convictions for girls in 18th and 19th century England, Zedner (1991) concluded that female crime, like male crime, was primarily determined by socioeconomic situation, habitat (rural or urban), and opportunity. Noting that women have traditionally outnumbered men in arrests for sexual or "moral" crimes such as prostitution and drunkenness, Zedner comments that as long as women have been judged by a standard of "ideal femininity," society has demonstrated lower tolerance for female "moral" deviance.

Another popular theory, discussed in more detail later in this chapter, proposes that gender differences in the frequency of arrests and incarceration can be explained by differential treatment by the judicial system. This is based on a paternalistic societal stance toward women, under which they are treated with more leniency by the police and the courts.

Several studies have been conducted to explore the hypothesis that disparity in character traits such as passivity and compliance, as well as role socialization, accounts for gender differences in the frequency and types of offense. Horwitz and White (1987) postulated that differences in gender identity are related to the expression of psychopathology. Identification with a traditional feminine role characterized by helplessness, submissiveness and dependence would make girls more vulnerable to depression, anxiety, and psychophysiological symptoms; identification with the male role characterized by dominance, assertiveness, and independence would result in aggressive, antisocial behavior.

Interestingly, Horwitz and White (1987) found that identification with traits traditionally associated with the opposite sex did not produce pathology associated with that sex, nor did girls with masculine identities demonstrate higher rates of delinquent behavior. In other words, the least amount of psychopathology is found among boys and girls who have both feminine and masculine traits and gender identifications. Further, careful study of relevant clinical syndromes casts doubt on the utility of gender-bound trait definitions in deviant populations. Cloninger and Guze (1970) reported early and promiscuous sexual behavior in adult sociopaths, with increased prostitution in *both* sexes. Conversion disorder, or so-called "hysteria," has also been reported to be prominent in men with antisocial personality disorder (Guze, Woodruff & Clayton, 1971a).

Thornton (1982) noted that criminology literature reflects a pervasive view of masculine and feminine traits as polar opposites rather than human traits with a complex, overlapping relationship. In his study, he found no relationship between gender traits and frequency of delinquency. He also found that gender traits did not explain why boys or girls commit status offenses. There was a slight and interesting difference in property offenses in that less masculine boys and more masculine girls were slightly more likely to commit property offenses. When sex was considered, there was only a very weak association between masculine gender traits and aggressive offenses. Gender traits and opportunity, or decreased parental social control, were not related to the rate or type of offenses for girls, so that increasing masculine traits in girls did not seem to lead to increased opportunity to commit crimes.

Others such as West (1967) have emphasized the relationship between female delinquency and the psychological maladjustment resulting from adverse family environments. He noted that gender differences in crime involvement have always existed. He observed that the small minority of girls who do become actively delinquent and whom he characterized as "unhappy misfits" generally present more difficult problems than delinquent boys and they more often come from "very disordered or conflicted homes."

Simons, Miller, and Aigner (1980) hypothesized that the same psychosocial theories of criminal deviance that might explain male delinquency would serve to explain female delinquency. Thus, the same variables would account for delinquency in both groups, except that girls, in accord with their lower rate of criminality, would exhibit fewer of those variables or characteristics. They conducted a self-report survey of delinquent behavior and indices for the following four theories of crime and delinquency.

Anomie is a term for a hypothesis that simply states that a person's perception that legitimate means of success are inaccessible is related to criminal behavior. Differential association theory hypothesizes a relationship between one's associates and one's values and behavior. Control theory postulates that the degree of alienation from societal values and rejection by parents is somehow related to increased criminality. Labeling theory suggests that delinquent acts are an adaptation to negative labels imposed by significant persons in the social environment. Female respondents were much lower in self-reported delinquency.

Results of this study indicated that, except for increased female anomie, differences in the incidence of self-reported delinquent behavior were due to girls being less exposed to factors such as parental rejection and teacher labeling that were associated with deviance in boys. Values of friends and teacher labeling were especially strongly associated with male delinquency. They pointed out that these results do not address why girls are differentially exposed to these adverse circumstances.

Findings by Simons and colleagues (1980) are particularly interesting with respect to anomie, or expected achievement, and teacher labeling in the light of the above discussion of Horwitz and White's (1987) review and Thornton's (1982) results regarding gender traits. It has been reported that poor academic performance is almost uniformly associated with antisocial personality disorder regardless of sex (Guze, Woodruff & Clayton, 1971b). "Feminine" compliance and attention to teachers is especially associated with academic achievement in the earlier grades when teacher labeling is developing, whereas "masculine" traits such as assertiveness become important in feminine academic achievement, especially in adolescence. It might be hypothesized that, in the case of academic achievement that is associated with low predilection for delinquent activity in both sexes, a healthy mixture of so-called masculine and feminine traits would be associated with greater success and less adolescent deviance.

While this is not intended to be a comprehensive review of the theories that have attempted to explain gender differences in criminal behavior, it suggests the complexities facing future researchers given the lack of agreement concerning the true magnitude and nature of those differences and the multiplicity of cultural, socioeconomic, interpersonal, and individual factors that affect adolescents.

GENDER BIAS IN THE JUVENILE COURT SYSTEM

Most investigators seem to agree with the observation that adult and adolescent females are likely to be treated in a different manner than males by the police, the courts, and the correctional system. Moreover, it is commonly assumed that differences in arrest rates reflect, at least partially, the reluctance of police and courts to treat female offenders punitively (Benedek, 1979; Lewis, Shanok, and Pincus, 1982).

Research, however, seems to contradict these assumptions. Kashani, Daniel, Reid, et al. (1984) found that, whereas boys were admitted to group homes for offenses against property and persons, girls were more likely to be admitted for status offenses and promiscuity. Numerous studies have documented that women are treated more punitively by the courts, and that female delinquents are more often punished for their sexual behavior and for status offenses than their male counterparts (Rutter & Giller, 1984). Girls are disproportionately incarcerated and are more likely to be placed for less serious offenses than boys; as a result, Rutter and Giller concluded ''that it is unlikely that the male preponderance in delinquency is an artifact of police or court leniency towards females'' (p. 121).

In a comprehensive review of the impact of gender on courts' decisions at different stages in the criminal process of adults, Nagel and Hagan (1983) noted that no studies addressed these issues prior to 1970. Additionally, even though most of the recent studies are based on theories characterized as ''chivalry/ paternalism'' or ''evil woman,'' there has been lack of agreement about definitions and measurement of these concepts. Also, many studies have failed to take into consideration severity of offense, prior criminal record, occupation, employment, and age of the offender.

Sex differences in the pretrial stage seem to favor women only in the handling of misdemeanors and victimless crimes. Once the decision to proceed to trial is made, being male is correlated with being convicted for less serious crimes. During the sentencing stage, women are more likely to receive suspended sentences or probation in misdemeanor court, but few sex differences are found in length of incarceration. Nagel and Hagan (1983) conclude that the aggregate of findings showing less severe outcomes for women in the case of less severe offenses is consistent with the ''chivalry/paternalism'' theories; whereas, in the case of serious offenses, deviation from ''traditional female patterns of behavior'' results in placement in the ''evil woman'' category so that favorable court treatment is no longer offered. They further note that no research has addressed whether or not changing patterns in female involvement in crime and sex role attitudes have had an impact on the differential treatment of the sexes by the courts.

With regard to the juvenile system, McClelland (1982) has also called attention to the complex interaction of gender differences with other factors such as age, ethnicity, and social class that appear to influence the handling of adolescents by the police and courts. Chesney-Lind (1977) goes even further in pointing to ways in which ''extralegal paternalism'' places greater expectations for ''obedience and chastity'' on girls than on boys. Using official statistics and results from previous surveys and studies, she concludes that gender bias reflected in judicial paternalistic interest in girls' sexuality results in harsher and ''degrading'' treatment of girls in the juvenile system and the violation of the ''civil rights of most of the girls who have come into its jurisdiction.'' Chesney-Lind (1977) asserts that status offenders should be removed from court jurisdiction and referred to community agencies.

Alder (1984), however, cautions that referral of adolescents to ''diversion agencies'' would result in an increase in the proportion of female involvement with youth services for less severe misconduct or no offense behavior. In Alder's (1984) opinion, greater diversion of girls for status offenses reflects a differential treatment based on gender differences and another means of societal control of "inappropriate sex role behaviors" in girls. Rather than providing protection and opportunities for troubled adolescents, diversion programs are likely to place these adolescents at risk of stigmatization and contribute to their greater recidivism. Thus, Alder believes that protective interventions mask harsher treatment of girls than boys.

For the most part, arguments pointing to the "sexualization" of female criminality (Alder, 1984; Armstrong, 1977; Miller, 1979; Price, 1977; Zedner, 1991) have lacked empirical support. Teilmann and Landry (1981) reviewed the arrest histories of a random sample of juveniles arrested by police departments in California, Arizona, Illinois, Delaware, and Washington in a study conducted to examine the nature and extent of gender bias, taking into account the type of offense committed and the juvenile's prior record. Results of this study revealed no consistent sex bias and wide variations across the different sites. Since status offenders, regardless of sex, were more likely to receive "harsher treatment" than delinquent offenders, there was no evidence of gender bias. In partial support of the "sexualization" theory, the authors noted that there was a consistently high rate of referral for runaway and "incorrigibility" across sites and sexes.

In addition, data collected in one site as part of a study of a diversion program showed that girls were more likely to be arrested for runaway than boys. Self-reports from girls compared with boys also indicated that girls were "over-arrested" for runaway and incorrigibility. The authors attributed these findings to parental bias in the referral process.

An alternative explanation based on impressions from data collected about adolescent girls incarcerated in Illinois is that courts are more prone to place girls under protective custody whenever their behavior continues to place them at risk of sexual exploitation or physical danger (Viale-Val, Rosenthal, Lynch, et al. 1991). Girls were repeatedly incarcerated for the same minor offenses whenever they persisted in running away from their homes or from less restrictive placements. These girls reported being repeatedly raped and victimized while on the run. For some of these girls, the high frequency of past runaway behavior and promiscuity that was often associated with a history of sexual abuse and substance abuse represented a chronic pattern of self-destructive behavior rather than an exercise of the right to sexual freedom as some feminist criminologists suggest.

From a legal perspective the lengths of incarceration for these girls may appear punitive, but court decisions could clinically be viewed as protective. Chronic runaway behavior, as the primary coping strategy for most of these girls, rather than the nature of the offense appears to be the primary factor affecting decisions to incarcerate delinquent girls except, perhaps, for more serious or violent crimes.

In summary, despite commonly accepted notions about the influence of gender biases in the juvenile system, few empirical studies have been found to support this. Studies on differences in the attitudes of police, courts, and other juvenile authorities toward girls across different geographical areas, length of incarceration, outcomes of incarceration, and differential treatment of girls in the correctional system are needed.

RISK FACTORS: FAMILY AND EPIDEMIOLOGICAL

Numerous studies have highlighted the role of family variables as "causes" or correlates of delinquent behavior. Additionally, individual characteristics and variables such as early school failure, age of first arrest, and seriousness of the first offense have been identified as predictors of more serious and frequent criminal activity (Farrington, 1987; Ganzer & Saranson, 1973; Hanson, Henggeler, Haefele et al. 1984). Methodological deficiencies in sampling procedures, questionable reliability and validity of self-report instruments, use of one or few sources of information about delinquent behavior and family variables, inconsistent definition of delinquency, and poor definition of a host of family factors have resulted in contradictory findings. These inconsistencies have perpetuated controversy surrounding the nature and magnitude of the relationship between child-rearing practices and juvenile delinquency (McCord, 1982).

Whether conduct disorder or oppositional defiant disorder clearly predict later antisocial behavior or criminality has been controversial (Loeber, 1991), but antisocial personality disorder does have its onset in childhood or early adolescence (Behar & Stewart, 1982; Mitchell & Rosa, 1981). Therefore, studies of childhood disorders using DSM-III or III-R criteria and well standardized diagnostic and/or screening instruments are reviewed.

Costello (1989) noted that the rate of conduct disorder varied according to the method used to make the diagnosis. She presented aggregate data demonstrating that *relative* risk factors may be discerned from checklist studies, but *absolute* rates of disorder may be inflated using that methodology.

Offord, Boyle, and Racine (1989) used multiple checklists to examine correlates of psychiatric disorders, including sex, in 3,294 children ages four to 16 years. Family dysfunction had a strong independent relationship to conduct disorder. Other major factors included parent arrested and age 12 to 16. Other less important factors were low income and failed a grade.

Further information about risk factors for conduct disorder was developed in an eight-year longitudinal parent and child interview study of 776 children by Velez, Johnson, and Cohen (1989). As in the Offord study (1989), the effect of sex was considered as a factor by them, but it was overshadowed by other factors. Thus, differences between girls and boys, although examined, were not found to be important in this study which did not take adjudication specifically into account. In addition to low socioeconomic status, mother's, but not father's, low education predicted conduct disorder. Parental sociopathy was another important factor. *Mother never having been married was twice as important as divorce in predicting conduct disorder.* In addition, seven or more (of 23) life events (a measure of general chaos in a child's life) in the preceding two years increased by a factor of three the risk for developing conduct disorder.

A recent provocative study of conduct disorder or oppositional defiant disorder looked for male and female differences in reported parenting style. Rey and Plapp (1990) used the Parental Bonding Instrument, which assesses dimensions of parental care and "overprotection," defined as the degree of unwarranted control. They studied 62 normal controls (37 percent female), 49 oppositional disordered (46 percent female), and 62 conduct disordered (46 percent female). The conduct-disordered adolescents assigned their parents to affectionless control (low care/high overprotection) twice as often as controls. No difference was found between disordered boys and girls. This was interpreted to reflect the view that coercive family processes have an important role in the development and/ or maintenance of conduct problems.

They also noted Patterson's (1982) observation that parents of children with conduct disorders are more punitive than parents of normal children, and that coercive interchanges are more prolonged, more likely to involve other family members, and less likely to lead to resolution. Similar to the study of Simons and associates (1980), this one looked at these issues in samples of already affected individuals selected to be balanced for sex as a variable, rather than examining at-risk individuals to clarify which factors cause differential rates of these problems in boys and girls. Therefore, although differences in a variety of family and epidemiological variables are not especially pronounced between boys and girls with disruptive disorders, these findings cannot be generalized to other at-risk children.

Family variables most frequently linked to delinquency are similar to those noted above. They are "broken homes" (Farrington, 1987; Offord, Abrams, Allen & Poushinsky, 1979; Offord, 1982; Weeks, 1940; West, 1967); "family or parental discord" (McCord, 1979, 1982); parental criminal history (McCord, 1979; Offord, Allen & Abrams, 1978; Offord et al., 1979); parental psychopathology (Offord et al., 1978; Offord, 1982); parental rejection (McCord, 1979, 1982; Simons, et al. 1989); substance abuse in the family (Pollock et al., 1990); and "systemic" variables such as family cohesion and personal growth dimensions (LeFlore, 1988; Tolan, 1988). The link between these variables and delinquent behavior has been attributed to the lack of parental supervision resulting from parental psychopathology or "insufficient parenting" (Offord et al., 1979).

McCord (1982) has pointed out the many deficiencies in studies on the broken homes hypothesis, primarily the failure to control for other variables that may account for the relationship between broken homes and criminality, such as exposure to family conflict, maternal rejection, and paternal deviance. Indeed, Mednick, Baker and Carothers (1990), in an 18-year follow-up study of 410 Danish males, found that stability of the family constellation following divorce, not divorce *per se*, was a significant predictor of later criminal behavior, even after controlling for the effects of paternal crime and socioeconomic status. Downward drift in socioeconomic status following divorce and paternal criminal record were independently associated with adolescent criminality.

Although most studies of family and epidemiological risk factors have been only of boys, or have failed to consider gender in the analysis, several authors have noted that families of delinquent girls appear to be more dysfunctional, and that the impact of disrupted or dysfunctional families seems to be of greater significance for girls (Henggeler, Edwards & Borduin, 1987; Offord et al., 1979; Wallerstein, 1991). Offord and associates (1979) studied a sample of girls placed on probation and matched controls from the same schools. The most striking difference between the families of delinquents and of controls was the frequency of broken homes (66.1 percent *vs.* 22 percent) that were mostly caused by separation, divorce, or parental desertion. Parental handicaps such as mental illness, criminality, and welfare history seemed to have their major effect in delinquency production in girls through contributing to a broken home.

In a more recent study of adolescents on probation, Offord (1982) attempted to determine the contribution of family factors in the production of delinquent behavior. Interview data were collected from parents or guardians of delinquent and control subjects who were matched for school performance. He found no support for the theory that the emotional consequences of poor school performance, such as low self-esteem, play a part in the genesis of delinquency in either sex. Instead, the deprived family environment appeared to produce both delinquency and academic difficulties.

Another possibility, or course, is that academic limitations are related to other etiological factors found in low-income families. One of these is compromised perinatal circumstances, which are well known to differentially impact boys (who have more disruptive disorders and delinquency) far more than girls. Families of delinquents were significantly more likely than those of controls to be broken and/or have parental mental illness, to have fathers involved with the law, and to contain parents with a welfare history. For girls, the families of delinquents were characterized by multiple parental disabilities when compared with families of controls. Offord (1982) concluded, again, that ''the most powerful distinguishing characteristic between delinquent families and controls was the frequency of broken homes.''

Noting that greater frequency of broken homes and family disruption has been reported in female delinquents compared with male delinquents in several studies, Offord (1982) hypothesized that the disruption of the home may be more devastating for girls because of their identification with the traditional feminine roles of wife and mother, and because of their greater difficulty becoming economically and emotionally independent of the family. He reasoned that since the frequency of delinquency is higher in boys, fewer disruptions such as those due to parental mental illness or welfare history may play a role in their delinquency. Major disruptions, as measured by broken homes, are needed instead, to promote delinquency in girls.

This is consonant with the findings of Ganzer and Saranson (1973) that delinquent girls came from more disorganized and socially less adequate families than delinquent boys. Moreover, Kalter, Riemer, Brickman, et al. (1985) found that adolescent girls who experienced divorce in their families reported engaging in more rebellious, delinquent-like behaviors than girls whose parents stayed married. Kalter and associates (1985) suggested "that parental divorce may interfere with a girl's accepting and valuing her femininity, which in turn may result in sexually precocious/promiscuous behavior as a restitutive attempt, or may lead to a denial of one's sexuality." They hypothesized that conflicts related to separation may be expressed in "rebellious and antisocial actions, or conversely, in a regressive retreat from adolescent striving" (p. 543).

The impact of family disruption on children is complex as reviewed by Wallerstein (1991). The results of recent studies suggest that many girls who experience family disruption early have more satisfying relationships with their mothers than do boys. This reverses, nevertheless, when mothers remarry, although many mother-daughter relationships tend to reconstitute two years after the mother's remarriage. However, she summarized other results which indicate that in later adolescence girls and boys from divorced families experience similar unhappiness and low achievement.

Despite the many studies that have highlighted the role of family factors in the background of juvenile delinquents, it is important, in the light of the above described reports, to consider the work of Farnworth (1984) who concluded on the basis of a self-report study of black adolescents that there was little evidence to support the broken-homes thesis of delinquency among *nonmainstream* groups. According to her, one of the major limitations in empirical studies that support the broken-home thesis (in studies employing records of official contact with the law as a measure of delinquency) is that stability of the home is routinely included as a criterion for legal intervention. Farnworth did, however, show that both parents being employed and father present reduced risk for both sexes. She also found that family size and mobility adversely affected boys, but not girls, and suggested that family structure was not as important as personal relationships resulting from family disorganization.

Studies on the relationship between delinquent girls and their parents have shown that, though delinquent youths in general tend to view their parents more negatively than controls, the relationships of delinquent girls with their mothers are characterized by higher rates of conflict, hostility, and ambivalence than those of boys with their mothers (Henggeler et al., 1987; Kroupa, 1988). Henggeler and associates (1987) also found that the fathers of female delinquents were rated as more "neurotic" and dominant than the parents of the controls, and their families were more dysfunctional that those of male delinquents. These findings mirror some of those described for children with disruptive disorder, and lend support to the concept that multiple, continuous family difficulties may be more salient than whether a family is broken.

Only recently has the literature on female delinquency examined the impact of physical and sexual abuse in the development of these adolescents (Lewis, Yeager et al., 1991; McManus, Alessi, Grapentine, et al., 1984; Myers, Burket, Lyles, et al., 1990). Two consecutive studies on the mental health needs of incarcerated adolescents (Viale-Val, Rosenthal & Clay, 1986; Viale-Val et al., 1991) showed that incarcerated adolescent girls were more likely to have a history of sexual abuse (50.1 percent *vs.* 1.8 percent) and physical abuse (41.7 percent *vs.* 22.5 percent) than were incarcerated boys. Moreover, only a small minority of the girls came from homes where parents were still married (8 percent) and one-third of the parents had never married. The family history of these girls reflected instability and a high prevalence of parental psychiatric disorders, substance abuse, and criminality. Girls tended to be older at the time of their first arrest and had fewer arrests than boys prior to their index incarceration.

In summary, despite their methodological deficiencies, studies on the relationship between family disruption and discord and disruptive behavior in girls has been amply documented. Nevertheless, as Glasser (1979) points out, theories postulating that one or multiple factors account for most criminal offenses fail to provide useful explanations. He addresses the need for an integrated theory that would explain a large and diverse range of offenses, which "would be preferable to a multicausal theory which merely lists broad factors without suggesting the manner in which they are interrelated" (p. 218). Along the same lines, Offord (1982) emphasizes the need to study mechanisms by which family variables contribute to the risk for antisocial behavior. These concerns parallel Wallerstein's (1991) description of the complex methodological and conceptual issues pertaining to research on divorce and its impact on children.

RISK FACTORS: PSYCHOPATHOLOGY

Much of the recent literature on criminality in women has focused on the possible relationship between their antisocial behavior and psychopatholgy

(Zedner, 1991). Stephenson, Blakely, and Nichol (1973) assessed psychiatric status and treatment needs of a random sample of 50 children "charged with delinquency." Thirty-two percent of those assessed were found to be "emotionally disturbed" and 36 percent to have had "some previous emotional disturbance." The implications of this study are limited because demographic characteristics were omitted and gender differences were not examined.

McManus and colleagues (1984) investigated the prevalence of psychiatric disturbance in a sample of 40 male and 31 female "seriously delinquent" adolescents from the Michigan training school system with a history of violence or recidivism. Using age at first offense and the total number of adjudicated offenses as criteria to determine the severity of delinquency, they found that their sample of female adolescents was as seriously delinquent as the boys, but the girls had fewer adjudicated violent offenses. Twenty boys and 21 girls reported that they had made suicide attempts within the past year. Neither the severity of the suicidal tendencies, the number, or seriousness of the attempts was related to sex of the subjects (Alessi, McManus, Grapentine, 1984a, 1984b).

In this study, girls were more likely to receive diagnoses of polysubstance abuse and major depression or dysthymia, although most were considered to be secondary depressions. Male subjects were more likely to be diagnosed as exhibiting aggressive conduct disorder, schizophrenia or schizotypal personality disorder, or residual attention deficit disorder. Both received similar rates of diagnoses of substance abuse and/or alcohol abuse/dependence (63 percent) and of borderline personality disorder (15 male and 11 female), although borderline personality disorder was in the context of other major disorders.

Lewis and colleagues (1982) compared the "neuropsychiatric status" of incarcerated white girls (19) and boys (35), many of whom had been psychiatrically hospitalized previously. Boys were more likely to have used lethal weapons and inflicted permanent injury on their victims than girls. They found no differences in the psychiatric, neurological, or educational status of boys and girls. It should be noted that subjects in this study had either been referred for psychiatric evaluation or placed on a secure unit because of the severity of their aggressive behaviors. Thus, as in the previous study, these findings may not be applicable to the majority of adolescent boys or girls in correctional facilities.

When 120 incarcerated adolescents were systematically examined for depression (Chiles, Miller & Cox, 1980; Miller, Chiles & Barnes, 1982), more girls were found to be depressed than boys (29 percent and 20 percent). Girls reported suicide attempts two and a half times more often than boys. When depressed, girls were more likely to attempt suicide than were depressed boys. Girls who did not "act out" were more likely to attempt suicide than boys who did not "act out" even though high levels of disruptive behavior were equally related to suicide attempts in both sexes. Thus, the lack of disruptive behavior was viewed as being more related to severity of depression in the adolescent female subjects than in boys.

Others have also focused on the prevalence of depressive disorders and suicidal behavior among juvenile delinquents. Kashani, Manning, McKnew (1980) studied 71 boys and 29 girls admitted to a juvenile center for evaluation and detention. They found that 56 percent of the 18 subjects who met DSM-III (American Psychiatric Association, 1980) criteria for major depressive episode were girls. The prevalence of depressive symptoms such as appetite disturbances, fatigue, and suicidal ideation among delinquent girls was found to be three times that in boys.

Two recent studies of female delinquents have provided additional evidence of the frequency and severity of psychiatric disturbances in this population. Fifteen adolescent girls committed to a nonsecure residential program were interviewed by Myers and his collaborators (1990) using a child structured interview to obtain DSM-III diagnoses. In addition to conduct disorder, 87 percent of the subjects met substance abuse criteria and two-thirds met criteria for major depressive episode. Other frequent diagnoses included any anxiety disorder (47 percent), adjustment disorder with depressed mood (13 percent), and, specifically, separation anxiety disorder in seven percent.

In the first study dedicated to a representative sample of incarcerated female adolescents who had not been referred for clinical evaluation, Viale-Val and associates (1991) obtained similar results. Structured interviews and a battery of well-standardized self-report instruments were administered to 43 girls admitted to the only Illinois state correctional facility for adolescent girls. Additional demographic information, family history, and offense records were obtained by review of their correctional records. In addition to conduct disorder, a large percentage of the subjects met criteria for substance abuse/dependence disorder (76 percent), affective disorders (60 percent), and a history of assaultive and/or suicidal behavior (93 percent). Seventy-eight percent of the subjects admitted to previous suicide attempts, and 33.3 percent had a history of psychiatric hospitalization.

In tragic concordance with recent studies of family discord focusing on the prevalence of sexual and physical abuse in the disrupted families of delinquent girls, results from studies focusing on individual psychopathology are sobering. Lewis and colleagues (1982) noted differences in the history of placements of her subjects. *All* of the girls had been placed outside the home prior to their incarceration versus 71.9 percent of the boys. Incarcerated girls were also more likely to have been abused than boys. Similarly, McManus and colleagues (1984) observed that girls in their study were more likely to have experienced physical abuse or neglect than the boys, and to have been permanently removed from the home by the age of 10. Girls also tended to have experienced a significantly higher number of stressful events. This recalls the previously described results of Velez and associates (1989) that demonstrated an association between increased life stress and conduct disorder in both sexes.

Viale-Val and colleagues (1991) also reported that other highly prevalent problems in incarcerated adolescent girls included sexual abuse (50.1 percent), promiscuity (46 percent), unplanned pregnancy (45.8 percent), runaway (91 percent), and rape (42 percent). Ninety-two percent of the girls came from broken homes, demonstrating a high prevalence of severe psychiatric disturbance in the context of chaotic families.

These findings raise great concern about this population that is at high risk for medical problems often related to the sexual behavior (Council on Scientific Affairs, 1990). These victimized girls are likely to remain at risk for premature death, including morbidity and mortality from suicidality and substance abuse (Marohn, Locke, Rosenthal, et al. 1982; Yeager & Lewis, 1990). Moreover, Lewis and associates (1991) found that most continued to be involved in unstable and violent relationships. As mothers, these girls were neglectful or abusive and, thus, unable to care for their children.

These findings suggest that institutionalized delinquent girls constitute an "atypical" subgroup of externalizing troubled girls. A considerable amount of severe psychiatric disturbance and potentially self-destructive behavior apparently goes undetected in female adolescents admitted to correctional settings. Despite methodological limitations, the implications of accumulated evidence suggest that incarcerated adolescent girls are more prone to substance abuse, affective disturbances, and suicidal behavior than boys. Therefore, even though relatively few girls are incarcerated, they constitute a highly dysfunctional group with a very poor prognosis.

COMMENT

Despite a great deal of research, the prevailing controversy on gender differences in delinquency and its correlates is far from resolved. Further, the mechanisms by which environmental factors interface with individual congenital and developmental differences remain poorly understood. Attempts to bridge the conceptual gap have been made by several researchers and theorists.

In noting the stability of multiple problem behaviors and the progression into more serious difficulties from childhood through adolescence, Allen, Aber and Leadbeter (1990) point to the need to focus on developmental correlates of risk status. Failure to achieve central developmental tasks are said to lead to an enduring risk for problem behaviors. According to attachment theory and psychodynamic formulations based on infant research, children construe internal representations of themselves in relationship to others. When those "internal working models" are based on relationships with unpredictable, unavailable, or abusive parents, the child learns a model of relationships in which "anger and insecurity are the central features."

Bowlby (1973) postulates that the stages of protest and anger due to separation or insecure attachment are followed by emotional detachment, or apathy. Hypothetically, such detachment might be related to a lack of empathy for victims and/or disregard for self, which seem to be present in many delinquent acts. Faced with the developmental task of achieving further separation and greater autonomy, adolescents who are impaired due to earlier insecure attachment might be unable to maintain a sense of relatedness and face additional strains in the relationship with parents. Allen and collaborators (1990) invoke research findings in support of the opinion that adolescent delinquency reflects an inability to achieve autonomy without the context of positive relationships with parents or, subsequently, with other adults in the community.

Recent formulations in self-psychology, in addition, have shifted the emphasis from the centrality of developmental separation-individuation tasks toward an emphasis on the need for sustaining relationships throughout the life span (Socarides & Stolorow, 1984/85). Failures in the availability of these sustaining relationships early in life would place individuals at higher risk at future major developmental turning points such as adolescence. Families of delinquent children, in particular of delinquent girls, have been described as neglectful, abusive, and exposing the child to the modeling influence of emotionally disturbed, alcoholic, and antisocial parents. Disrupted marriages further expose girls to the presence of unrelated men, with the potential for further victimization that is probably etiologically related to adolescent runaway and prostitution.

Clinical data show that the impact of inadequate or abusive parenting and childhood trauma translates into severe psychological deficits and concomitant emotional difficulties that, in turn, contribute to perpetuation of psychopathology and social maladjustment across generations. Hyperarousal, difficulty modulating and tolerating painful affects, identification with the aggressor and/or the victim, and inability to maintain a sense of worth are the common aftermaths of child abuse (Krystal, 1988; Shengold, 1989). Whereas boys may attempt to fill deficits resulting from their frustrated developmental needs by reorganizing themselves around driven activity, girls are more prone to seek the restoration of their damaged self-image through sexual contacts. Adolescent girls also tend to seek restoration of the disrupted ties with the maternal self-object by having babies who inevitably are doomed to fail to fulfill their mother's fantasies.

CONCLUSION

We conclude that adolescent girls remain much less likely to be involved in delinquent behavior than boys despite many significant changes in societal standards and family constellations. For the most part, the literature shows that similar family and social risk factors are present in the backgrounds of male and female delinquents. Yet, it seems to be generally believed that the family backgrounds of delinquent girls are even more chaotic, abusive, and rejecting than those of boys. Running away from abusive homes, truancy, and substance abuse not only appear to precipitate entry of these girls into the juvenile justice system, but also continue to place them at risk for further victimization. Likewise, delinquent girls have been found to remain at high risk for premature death, severe psychopathology, and chaotic life styles. *Indeed, lack of an appropriately nurturing, protective, mentally stable and economically successful parent seems to be a major risk factor for both sexes in the face of family disruption*, whereas no compelling evidence was found for the argument that the feminist movement has somehow contributed to an increase in adolescent female crime.

Research, treatment, and preventive measures need to address the impact on female development of the increase in family violence, the rising divorce rate, and economic factors which force more mothers into the workplace without adequate social supports. Girls remain a minority among delinquent youths. Accumulated knowledge, nevertheless, highlights the severity of family and individual psychopathology in this group, as well as the lasting repercussions on future generations of the deviant adjustment and emotional impairment of these girls.

REFERENCES

Adler, F. 1975. *Sisters in Crime: The Rise of the New Female Criminal.* New York: McGraw-Hill.

Alder, C. 1984. Gender bias in juvenile diversion. *Crime and Delinquency*, 30:400-414.

Alessi, N. E., McManus, M., Brickman, A. & Grapentine, W. L. 1984a. Suicidal behavior among serious juvenile offenders. *American J. Psychiatry*, 141:286-287.

Alessi, N. E., McManus, M., Grapentine, W. L. & Brickman, A. 1984b. The characterization of depressive disorders in juvenile offenders. *J. Affective Disorders*, 6:9-17.

Allen, J. P., Aber, J. L., & Leadbeater, B. J. 1990. Adolescent problem behaviors: The influence of attachment and autonomy. *Psychiatric Clinics of North America*, 13:455-467.

American Psychiatric Association. 1980. *Diagnostic and Statistical Manual of Mental Disorders (Third Edition).* Washington, D.C.: American Psychiatric Association.

Armstrong, G. 1977. Females under the law—"Protected" but unequal. *Crime and Delinquency*, 4:109-120.

Behar, D. & Stewart, M. A. 1982. Aggressive conduct disorder: The influence of social class, sex, and age on the clinical picture. *Acta Psychiatrica Scandinavica*, 65:210-220.

Benedek, E. 1979. Female delinquency: Fantasies, facts, and future. *Adolescent Psychiatry*, 7:524-539.

Bowlby, J. 1973. *Attachment and Loss. Vol. 2: Separation, Anxiety, and Anger.* New York: Basic Books.

Bureau of Justice Statistics. 1990a. *Jail Inmates: 1989.* Washington, D.C.: U.S. Government Printing Office.

Bureau of Justice Statistics. 1990b. *BJS Data Report: 1989.* Washington, D.C.: U.S. Government Printing Office.

Cernkovich, S. A. & Giordano, P. C. 1979. A comparative analysis of male and female delinquency. *The Sociological Quarterly,* 20:131-145.

Cernkovich, S. A., Giordano, P. C. & Pugh, M. D. 1985. Chronic offenders: The missing cases in self-report delinquency research. *Journal of Criminal Law and Criminology,* 76:705-732.

Chesney-Lind, M. 1977. Judicial paternalism and the female status offender. *Crime and Delinquency,* 4:121-130.

Chiles, J., Miller, M., & Cox, G. 1980. Depression in an adolescent delinquent population. *Archives of General Psychiatry,* 37:1179-1184.

Church, G. J. 1990. The view from behind bars. *Time. Fall Special Issue:* 19-22.

Cloninger, C. R. & Guze, S. B. 1970. Psychiatric illness and female criminality: The role of sociopathy and hysteria in the antisocial woman. *American J. Psychiatry,* 127:303-311.

Costello, E. J. 1989. Developments in child psychiatry epidemiology: Introduction. *J. Amer. Acad. Child Adol. Psychiatry,* 28:836-841.

Council on Scientific Affairs 1990. Health status of detained and incarcerated youths. *J. Amer. Med. Assoc.,* 263:987-991.

Curran, D. J. 1984. The myth of the ''new'' female delinquent. *Crime and Delinquency,* 30:387-399.

Fagan, J., Jones, S. J., Hartstone, E., Rudman, C., & Emerson, R. 1981. *Background Paper for the Violent Juvenile Offender Research and Development Program.* Washington, D.C.: U.S. Department of Justice.

Farnworth, M. 1984. Family structure, family attributes, and delinquency in a sample of low income, minority males and females. *J. Youth Adol.,* 13:349-364.

Farrington, D. P. 1987. Predicting individual crime rates. *Crime and Justice: An Annual Review of Research,* 9:53-102.

Federal Bureau of Investigation, U.S. Department of Justice. 1987. *Uniform Crime Reports.* Washington, DC: Government Printing Office.

Federal Bureau of Investigation, U.S. Department of Justice. 1990. *Uniform Crime Reports.* Washington, DC: Government Printing Office.

Ganzer, V. J. & Saranson, I. G. 1973. Variables associated with recidivism among juvenile delinquents. *J. Consult. Clin. Psychol.,* 40:1-5.

Glasser, D. 1979. A review of crime-causation theory and its application. *Crime and Justice: An Annual Review of Research,* 1:203-237.

Guze, S. B., Woodruff, R. A., Jr., & Clayton, P. J. 1971a. A study of conversion symptoms in psychiatric outpatients. *Amer. J. Psychiatry,* 127:643-646.

Guze, S. B., Woodruff, R. A., Jr., & Clayton, P. J. 1971b. Hysteria and antisocial behavior: Further evidence of an association. *Amer. J. Psychiatry,* 127:957-960.

Hamparian, D. M., Schyster, R., Dinitz, S., & Conraad, J. P. 1978. *The Violent Few: A Study of Dangerous Juvenile Offenders.* Lexington: Lexington Books.

Hanson, C. L., Henggeler, S. W., Haefele, W. F., & Rodick, J. D. 1984. Demographic, individual, and family relationship correlates of serious and repeated crime among adolescents and their siblings. *J. Consult. Clin. Psychol.*, 52:528-538.

Henggeler, S. W. 1989. *Delinquency in Adolescence*. Newbury Park: Sage.

Henggeler, S. W., Edwards, J., & Borduin, C. 1987. The family relations of female juvenile delinquents. *J. Abnorm. Child Psychol.*, 15:199-209.

Herjanic, M., Henn, F. A., & Vanderpearl, R. H. 1977. Forensic psychiatry: Female offenders. *Amer. J. Psychiatry*, 134:556-558.

Horwitz, A. V. & White, H. R. 1987. Gender role orientations and styles of pathology among adolescents. *J. Health Social Behav.*, 28:158-170.

Hunt, D. E. 1990. Drugs and consensual crimes: Drug dealing and prostitution. In M. Torny & J.Q. Wilson, Eds., *Drugs and Crime*. Chicago: University of Chicago Press.

James, J. & Thornton, W. 1980. Women's liberation and the female delinquent. *J. Research in Crime and Delinquency*, 17:230-244.

Kalter, N., Riemer, B., Brickman, A., & Woo Chen, J. 1985. Implications of parental divorce for female development. *J. Amer. Acad. Child Psychiatry*, 24:538-544.

Kashani, J. H., Daniel, A. E., Reid, J. C., & Sirinek, A. J. 1984. Comparison of delinquent boys and girls in group homes and factors associated with the outcome. *Brit. J. Psychiatry*, 144:156-160.

Kashani, J. H., Manning, G. W., McKnew, D. H., Cytryn, L., Simonds, J. F., & Wooderson, P. C. 1980. Depression among incarcerated delinquents. *Psychiatric Research*, 3:185-191.

Kroupa, S. E. 1988. Perceived parental acceptance and female juvenile delinquency. *Adolescence*, 89:171-185.

Krystal, H. 1988. *Integration and Self-Healing: Affect, Trauma, Alexithymia*. Hillsdale: The Analytic Press.

Leflore, L. 1988. Delinquent youths and family. *Adolescence.*, 13:629-642.

Lewis, D. O., Shanok, S. S., & Pincus, J. H. 1982. A comparison of the neuropsychiatric status of female and male incarcerated delinquents: Some evidence of sex and race bias. *J. Amer. Acad. Child Psychiatry*, 21:190-196.

Lewis, D. O., Yeager, C. A., Cobham-Protorreal, C. S., Klein, N., Showalter, C., & Anthony, B. A. 1991. The follow-up of female delinquents: Maternal contributions to the perpetuation of deviance. *J. Amer. Acad. Child Adol. Psychiatry*, 30:197-201.

Loeber, R. 1991. Antisocial behavior: More enduring than changeable? *J. Amer. Acad. Child Adol. Psychiatry*, 30:393-397.

Marohn, R. C., Locke, E. M., Rosenthal, R., & Curtis, G. 1982. *Adol. Psychiatry*, 10:147-170.

McClelland, A. M. 1982. Changing rates or changing roles—adolescent female delinquency reassessed. *J. Adolescence*, 5:85-98.

McCord, J. 1979. Some child-rearing antecedents of criminal behavior in adult men. *J. Pers. Social Psychol.*, 37:1477-1486.

McCord, J. 1982. A longitudinal view of the relationship between paternal absence and crime. In J. Gunn & D. P. Farrington, Eds., *Abnormal Offenders, Delinquency, and the Criminal Justice System*. New York: John Wiley & Sons.

McManus, M., Alessi, N., Grapentine, W. L., & Brickman, A. 1984. Psychiatric disturbances in serious delinquents. *J. Amer. Acad. Child Psychiatry*, 23:602-615.

Mednick, B. R., Baker, R. L., & Carothers, L. E. 1990. Patterns of family instability and crime: The association of timing of the family's disruption with subsequent adolescent and young adult criminality. *J. Youth Adol.*, 19:201-220.

Miller, M., Chiles, J. A., & Barnes, B. E. 1982. Suicide attempters within a delinquent population. *J. Consult. Clin. Psychol.*, 50:491-498.

Miller, P. Y. 1979. Female delinquency: Fact or fiction. In M. Sugar, Ed., *Female Adolescent Development*. New York: Brunner/Mazel.

Mitchell, S. & Rosa, P. 1981. Boyhood behavior problems as precursors of criminality: A fifteen year follow-up study. *Journal of Child Psychology and Psychiatry*, 22:19-33.

Myers, W. C., Burket, R. C., Lyles, W. B., Stone, L. & Kemph, J. P. 1990. DSM-III diagnoses and offenses in committed female juvenile delinquents. *Bull. Amer. Acad. Psychiatry and Law*, 18:47-54.

Nagel, I. & Hagan, J. 1983. Gender and crime: Offense patterns and criminal court sanctions. *Crime and Justice*, 4:91-143.

O'Brien, R. M. 1985. *Crime and Victimization Data*. Beverly Hills: Sage.

Office of Juvenile Justice and Delinquency Prevention. 1987. *Children in Custody: Census of Public and Private Juvenile Custody Facilities*. Washington, D.C.: U.S. Government Printing Office.

Office of Juvenile Justice and Delinquency Prevention. 1990. *Juvenile Court Statistics:1987*. Washington, D.C.: U.S. Government Printing Office.

Offord, D. R. 1982. Family backgrounds of male and female delinquents. In J. Gunn & D. P. Farrington, Eds., *Abnormal Offenders, Delinquency, and the Criminal Justice System*. Chicester: John Wiley & Sons.

Offord, D. R., Allen, N., & Abrams, N. 1978. Parental psychiatric illness, broken homes, and delinquency. *J. Amer. Acad. Child Psychiatry*, 17:224-238.

Offord, D. R., Abrams, N., Allen, N., & Poushinksky, M. 1979. Broken homes, parental psychiatric illness and female delinquency. *Amer. J. Orthopsych.*, 49:252-264.

Offord, D. R., Boyle, M. H., & Racine, Y. 1989. Ontario child health study: Correlates of disorder. *J. Amer. Acad. Child Adol. Psychiatry*, 28:856-860.

Patterson, G. R. 1982. *Coercive Family Process*. Eugene, OR: Castalia Press.

Pollock, V. E., Briere, J., Schneider, L., Knop, J., Mednick, S. A., & Goodwin, D. W. 1990. Childhood antecedents of antisocial behavior: Parental alcoholism and physical abusiveness. *Amer. J. Psychiatry*, 147:1290-1293.

Price, R. R. 1977. The forgotten female offender. *Crime and Delinquency*, 23:101-108.

Rappenport, J. & Lassen, G. 1966. The dangerousness of female patients: A comparison of the arrest rate of discharged psychiatric patients and the general population. *Amer. J. Psychiatry*, 123:413-419.

Rey, J. M. & Plapp, J. M. 1990. Quality of perceived parenting in oppositional and conduct disordered adolescents. *J. Amer. Acad. Child Adol. Psychiatry*, 29:383-385.

Rutter, M. & Giller, H. 1984. *Juvenile Delinquency: Trends and Perspectives*. New York: Guilford.

Shengold, E. 1989. *Soul Murder: The Effects of Childhood Abuse and Deprivation*. New Haven: Yale University Press.

Simons, R. L., Miller, M. G. & Aigner, S. M. 1980. Contemporary theories of deviance and female delinquency: An empirical test. *J. Crime Delinq.*, 1:42-57.

Simons, R. L., Robertson, J. F., & Downs, W. R. 1989. The nature of the association between parental rejection and delinquent behavior. *J. Youth Adol.*, 18:297-310.

Socarides, D. D. & Stolorow, R. D. 1984/1985. Affects and self-objects. *Annual of Psychoanalysis*, 12/13:115-119.

Steffensmeier, D. 1978. Crime and the contemporary woman: An analysis of changing levels of female property crime, 1960-75. *Social Forces*, 57:566-584.

Stephenson, P. S., Blakely, B., & Nichol, H. 1973. The psychiatric status and treatment needs of a random sample of juveniles charged with delinquency. *Psychiatric Clinics*, 6:257-270.

Teilmann, K. S. & Landry, P. H. 1981. Gender bias in juvenile justice. *J. Research Crime and Delinq.*, 1:47-80.

Thornton, W. E. 1982. Gender traits and delinquency involvement of boys and girls. *Adolescence*, 12:749-768.

Tolan, P. 1988. Socioeconomic, family and social stress correlates of adolescent antisocial and delinquent behavior. *J. Abnorm. Child Psychol.*, 16:317-331.

Velez, C. N., Johnson, J., & Cohen, P. 1989. A longitudinal analysis of selected risk factors for childhood psychopathology. *J. Amer. Acad. Child Adol. Psychiatry*, 28-861-864.

Viale-Val, G., Rosenthal, R. H., & Clay, R. 1986 Child abuse, depression, and suicidal behavior in institutionalized adolescents. Presented at the Annual Meeting of the American Psychological Association, Washington, D.C.

Viale-Val, G., Rosenthal, R., Lynch, J., Jaworski, J., & Nowinski, C. 1991. Prevalence of psychiatric disorders in incarcerated adolescent females. In *Scientific Proceedings for the Annual Meeting*. Washington, D.C.: American Academy of Child and Adolescent Psychiatry.

Wallerstein, J. S. 1991. The long-term effects of divorce on children: A review. *J. Amer. Acad. Child Adol. Psychiatry*, 30:349-360.

Weeks, H. A. 1940. Male and female broken home rates by types of delinquency. *Amer. Sociol. Rev.*, 5:601-609.

West, D. J. 1967. *The Young Offender*. London: Duckworth.

Yeager, C. A. & Lewis, D. O. 1990. Mortality in a group of formerly incarcerated juvenile delinquents. *Amer. J. Psychiatry*, 147:612-614.

Zedner, L. 1991. Women, crime, and penal responses: A historical account. *Crime and Justice: A Review of Research*, 14:307-362.

11 Effects of Secondary School and College Experiences on Adolescent Female Development

Irving H. Berkovitz, M.D.

This chapter will consider how features in American, mostly public, secondary schools and coeducational colleges influence developmental changes in adolescent women. Many diverse factors are involved in the development of all adolescents to determine the kind of adult each will become. Foremost are genetic and familial influences. These are crucial to the development of a basic sense of self, trust of others, comfortable assertiveness, feeling positive about being female or male, and being able to love and be loved. After the family, the most important influence in the lives of all is experience in schools, public or private.

In the school years, one would hope to see enhancment of ego functions such as problem-solving, cognitive skills, occupational choice, and feelings of empowerment and capability, as well as maintaining or increasing the level of self-esteem. Concurrent is the task of integrating the new and powerful sexual energies and making sexual choices and decisions. Many of the factors which determine some of these choices and personality characteristics are already in place by the time a young girl or boy first enters elementary school. However, the school experience can influence many individuals in the process of development.

The preschool and elementary school experience provides crucial early socializing experiences which determine the young person's relation to his/her peer group. Competitive and assertive skills and power relationships between the sexes are reenforced. While the secondary school and college experiences occur late in this developmental sequence, changes do occur after puberty, as well as in adult life. It may seem unfortunate timing to stress the need for changes in schools at a time when public education in the U.S. is financially in trouble and already under severe criticism. Some of the changes to be suggested here may

Thanks for editorial assistance from Martha Kirkpatrick, Joan Zilbach, and John and Marilyn Lindon.

require attitudinal alteration rather than only new funding. Benefits can accrue for all students, but especially for the adolescent females.

I will now focus more on the adolescent woman. The effects of school experience on female students can be divided into a mix of person-related and female-related. Person-related includes the support of self-esteem, feelings of self-worth, pride in one's ability, motivation, sense of mastery, and trust of adults. Every child and adolescent needs these. Female-related refers to effects which are more directly related to female development, namely specific roles, advantages, liabilities, prerogatives, mores, etc. prescribed overtly or covertly for women in the culture of the particular school. The school can be seen as a microcosm and agent of the larger society.

Similarly, effects directly related to male development, i.e., roles allowed and encouraged for men, often involve reciprocal implications for women's roles—emphasis on athletic prowess or the behaviors associated with "macho" or wimp label (Berkovitz, 1979). Also, in a society which features the female body extensively in advertising and other media, the message conveyed to adolescent girls can overpower any other teaching about femaleness provided in schools.

The teaching and mores in schools often cannot go beyond those prevalent in the wider society. Cultural change often has to precede school change. For example, in the 1990s, female role models such as female astronauts, military personnel, priests, rabbis, and heads of state will likely expand what younger women will choose and/or be encouraged to emulate. Certainly, whatever the society will do to improve schools, in general, will rebound, as well, to the betterment of the effects of schools on female development. Many school practices perpetuated inequities for women until the civil rights movement in the U.S. provided the stimulus for passage of Title IX of the Higher Education Act (1972), which mandated equitable provisions for females in our schools. This Act specified:

No person in the U.S. shall, on the basis of sex, be excluded from participation in, be denied the benefits of, or be subjected to discrimination under any educational program or activity receiving Federal financial assistance.

In 1976, Title II of the Educational Amendments implemented the spirit of Title IX, requiring that each state establish policies, procedures, and programs to assure men and women equal access to vocational education.

As of 1981, a number of changes in school practices had occurred as a result of Title IX (National Advisory Council, 1981). Efforts to introduce females into courses once considered unusual for their sex became more visible and successful—for example, architectural drafting, industrial arts, auto mechanics, and carpentry. Changes occurred in school staff attitudes. Many teachers who feared Title IX would create discipline problems found that the more natural coeducational balance in their classes reduced such problems. Instead, competition between the sexes increased and the boys became less "rowdy."

Health services changed. While Title IX did not require schools to provide birth control, family planning services, or counseling, many institutions provided these services. Discrimination based on pregnancy is still present, but decreasing. More high schools allow pregnant girls to stay in school, providing special aids such as nursery care for the infant during class hours, as well as classes in child care for the mothers and occasionally for the fathers. However, in many schools, student health policies still discriminate against pregnant students.

College enrollment changed. In 1979, for the first time since World War II, women college students outnumbered men students. Women are obtaining an increasing number of college degrees at every level, especially in customarily male fields: agriculture, business and management, law, and engineering. More women have entered professional schools: dental, veterinary, law, and medical. Women now receive recognition for abilities in sports once considered the exclusive domain of men, such as sailing, crew, basketball, and distance running. In colleges, administrators are beginning to recognize the revenue potential in women's sports, especially basketball. There has been a notable growth in the availability of athletic scholarships to women.

ETHNIC AND SOCIOECONOMIC FACTORS

In addition to school practices, an important determinant of opportunities and norms for women is related to ethnic and socioeconomic factors. The possibilities open to poverty-level females are very different from those available to women in affluent or middle-class homes. About 25 percent of America's children are living in poverty. African-American and Hispanic children are two to three times more likely to be living in poverty than white children (Lipsitz, 1991). As with so many psychosocial problems, the diversity of roles for women is influenced by multiple conditions in society as a whole, such as poverty, unemployment, availability of divorce, abortion and child care, media stereotyping, level of racial and religious prejudice, war, etc. In many inner-city high schools, some girls are increasingly involved in gang activities. Some of these girls may well be more violently aggressive than the average girl being discussed here.

SELF-ESTEEM AND SCHOOL ACHIEVEMENT

The mix of the person-related and female-related effects is highlighted in a recent nationwide survey of 3,000 children in grades four to 10. The survey,

(American Association of University Women, 1991), found that at age eight to nine, 60 percent of the girls were confident and assertive, with positive feelings about themselves. However, by the time they reached 10th grade in high school, only 29 percent still felt that way. On the other hand, 67 percent of boys were confident at age eight; by age 14, 46 percent still maintained this level of confidence. In other words, 10 percent fewer boys declined in confidence than girls.

Physical appearance was most important for girls in middle school, the time of the greatest decline in self-esteem. Boys viewed the adolescent physical changes positively, as getting bigger and stronger. Girls believed that their changes were leading in a negative direction, reinforcing their declining self-esteem and gender stereotypes. The higher self-esteem of the boys translated into bigger career dreams and they were slightly more likely than girls to believe their own career dreams would come true.

Several studies have found that early developing girls have more problems with body image, self-esteem, and other areas relative to on-time or later developing girls (Tobin-Richards, Boxer & Petersen, 1983). "Early developing girls especially will have rounder, nonpreferred shapes" (Petersen, Sarigiani & Kennedy, 1991). These problems appear to persist at least to 12th grade (Petersen, Kennedy & Sullivan, in press). In addition, experiencing a change in the family (e.g., parental death or divorce) is related to depressed affect for girls but not for boys during early adolescence (Kennedy & Petersen, 1991). A positive tone in this research is provided by the finding that "closeness with parents moderates the negative effects of early adolescent changes on emotional tone and depressive episodes in middle adolescence" (Petersen et al., 1991).

The AAUW researchers connected the decline in girls' esteem with the effects of the schools. To my reading, this was not proven conclusively. Also, the absence of data about changes in self-esteem after age 14 may have overlooked many later positive changes which often do occur for many boys and girls.

Among the students surveyed in the AAUW study, far more black girls were still self-confident in high school, compared with the white and Hispanic girls. White girls lost their self-assurance earlier than Hispanic girls. Gilligan (1991) opined "this survey makes it impossible to say that what happens to girls is simply a matter of hormones. If that was it, then the loss of self-esteem would happen to all the girls and roughly at the same time." To my mind, also, it is not "simply a matter of hormones"! The familial and societal reactions to these hormonal changes provide a crucial positive or negative input. In addition, there are disturbing body changes (for both sexes). For girls, depending on economic level and maternal relationship, there is the additional stress of how to choose the best clothing and cosmetics in the competition about appearance. At this age also, girls become more aware of their muscular strength differences from boys.

The researchers concluded that black girls drew their apparent self-confidence from their families and communities rather than from the school system. As reasons for this, one researcher (Ward, 1991) speculated that "black girls are often surrounded by strong women they admire. Black women are more likely than others to have a full-time job and run a household. Black parents often teach their children that there is nothing wrong with them, only with the way the world treats them."

In a previous study of 7th, 8th, and 9th graders (ages 12-14), the black students had significantly higher (or more positive) self-concept scores than the white students. Those black students having the highest self-concept scores were those in segregated or predominantly black schools (Powell & Fuller, 1970). This may affirm that strong enough positive environmental influences, such as role models in the family or even in the school, can moderate the negative effects of this developmental period on self-esteem.

These findings raise the question of the comparative influence of the school experience. The black girls felt strong pressure from the school system and dropped significantly in positive feelings about their teachers and their school work. The Hispanic girls started with significantly higher levels of self-esteem, but by high school "they plummeted in terms of confidence in appearance, family relationships, school, talents and importance." This study brought out that these young women learned that people, including their teachers, thought that "females cannot do the things they believe they can." Furthermore, teachers were important role models. Nearly three out of four elementary school girls and over half of the high school girls wanted to be teachers. Most of these elementary school teachers were female. Far fewer adolescent boys, at any grade, wanted to be teachers. The importance of teacher attitudes is emphasized by these findings.

The influence of the school milieu was further confirmed by Rutter, Maugham, Mortimore et al. (1979) in England. This group surveyed 12 London urban high schools and concluded that some were demonstrably better than others at promoting the academic and social success of their students. Self-esteem of female students was not studied explicitly, but conclusions about this can be inferred. They reported "the pattern of findings suggested that not only were pupils influenced by the way they were dealt with as individuals, but also there was a group influence resulting from the ethos of the school as a social institution." They regarded "ethos" as including the respect shown students by staff, the expectation of serious application, and the adherence of staff to positive work habits for themselves. The researchers stressed that the quality of a school program can make a difference, despite familial or community factors!

The mix between the influence of schools, the family, and the individual female psyche is obviously complex. For example, socioeconomic factors appeared to have a greater influence on girls' aspirations than mental ability; for boys, the reverse appeared true. Middle-class parents often value educational attainment as a means toward high occupational attainment and as a value in itself, while lower-class parents more often see education only as an instrument toward occupational ends. Also, lower-class families are more sensitive to considerations of cost and length of schooling. High-achieving girls lessened this effect of the family's socioeconomic status on their educational aspiration (Danziger, 1983; Sewell & Shah, 1968).

A significant downward trend in school achievement for girls from grade six onward has been documented for over 50 years. Terman (1930) found that a retest of girls at age 13 showed a considerable drop in scores on the Stanford-Binet from previous high scores in primary grades (Fitzpatrick, 1978). Some have felt that the stereotype which discourages aggressiveness in girls has prevented gifted girls from developing their full intellectual potential and positive self-concept (Olshen & Matthews, 1987). Kirkpatrick (1989) maintains that this described "dropping off of academic performance in adolescent girls, the fear that 'success' will compromise femininity . . . is a pathological inhibition of aggression in the service of social restraint . . . it is not mature femininity.''

OCCUPATIONAL CHOICE AND OPPORTUNITIES

An essential goal of all educational programs should be to help each young person, male and female, achieve the confidence and ability to learn and to develop their resources and skills optimally, so they can pursue desired adult occupational or career opportunities. In psychological descriptions of adolescent development, this entails the ego ideal (Freud, 1914), namely, that part of the mind containing the goals, values, ambitions, hopes, and fantasies for the future.

The level of occupational attainment of a particular group often shows how equitably a society is providing or allowing opportunities. Over the years, women have been underrepresented in many of the professional and high-paying occupations. Some women have not been interested in professional occupations. Other women have been fearful of the social stigma previously attached to female assertiveness and success in the minds of many men (and women). Others were handicapped by the exclusion of women from the "old boy" network.

The differences between occupational choices of women and men may reflect, as well, differences in "self-efficacy" (Hackett & Betz, 1981). This means that one's subjective perception of the possibility of succeeding at a task determines in part the behaviors that one will attempt (Bandura, 1977). High self-efficacy will improve effective career planning behaviors. This is included in the ego ideal. When a group of college undergraduates were evaluated, women reported higher self-efficacy for the traditionally female occupations and lower self-efficacy for the traditionally male occupations (Betz & Hackett, 1981).

Yet, when a group of eighth- and ninth-grade college-bound students were compared with the previous undergraduate sample (Post-Kammer & Smith, 1985), this younger group of girls had perceptions of their abilities to succeed in several traditionally male occupations as well, such as accountant, lawyer, and physician, similar to the boys. This was thought to reflect greater openness among the younger students, social changes in the time lapse between the two studies, or lack of clarity among young students about actual educational requirements and/or job duties. Or, is there actually a decline in many girls' sense of self-efficacy during high school? Several studies suggest this.

One study on the choice of traditional versus nontraditional occupations by girls concluded that "the most consistent predictor of women's career orientation and innovation among girls and young women is their plans for marriage and family" (Fitzgerald & Betz, 1983). Gottfredson (1981) and others (Auster & Auster, 1981) have proposed that in American society an individual's occupational aspirations become permanently circumscribed within a range of acceptable sex-typed alternatives, between ages six and eight. Occupations that fall outside the range will not be reconsidered except under unusual circumstances. This emphasis on the crucial, formative influence of the childhood years is certainly familiar from psychoanalytic and psychiatric writings. This has suggested that the experience in secondary schools does not significantly affect earlier choices. Nevertheless, educators and society do invest heavily in secondary school and college programs.

INFLUENCE OF TEACHERS

Among early influences, nontraditional female students reported that their fathers had the most influence on their career decisions. Peers were the second most powerful. School personnel were third. Among the school personnel, the teacher would be expected to be most influential on young students due to having daily class contact, and being the major source of information and many attitudes.

A very direct influence is the difference in the way teachers talk to female and male students in elementary and secondary school classrooms. "Not only do teachers punish boys more, they also talk to them more, listen to them more and give them more active teaching attention" (Sadker & Sadker, 1986). Boys are eight times more likely than girls to call out the answers to questions. When girls do this, "teachers often remind them to raise their hands." When this prejudicial behavior was pointed out, many teachers "were surprised and shocked at the disparities in interaction."

However, in the average public secondary school, each student has five to six teachers per day. Each teacher usually sees 50-250 students per day, depending on the size of the middle or high school. Opportunities for personal direct contact between teacher and student are not always available. Still, for the most part, the teacher is a prime influence on school children.

COUNSELING PROGRAMS

Counselors in most secondary schools have responsibility for 300-500 students, usually spending more time with those students who are disturbed or disturbing. In some high schools, career and college counselors are able to devote more time to individual students. However, the role of the school guidance counselor was seen to be less contributory to students' career decisions. In some cases, counselors have been known to discourage girls from trying nontraditional choices (Berkovitz, 1979).

In 1982-83, one school district retrained counselors in order to pioneer a program for recruiting more females into nontraditional occupations (Garfield-Scott & LeMahieu, 1984). For example, one female counselor was enrolled in cabinetry and machine operations. A male counselor was enrolled in cosmetology for six weeks. Each experienced the discomforts of these nontraditional activities. This helped them to advise students who wished to try other nontraditional occupations.

In this same program, a vocational awareness unit was presented to all 10th graders. For example, a group of girls gathered from all the city high schools visited and talked with a female bricklayer, while a group of boys visited a cosmetology school. Over the three years, enrollment in the program nearly doubled. The activities of the counselors were considered to have been a crucial factor in this increase. "The additional students recruited and supported by the program were able to realize a sense of safety because of the commitment of school personnel and the assurances provided by an emerging nontraditional peer group" (Garfield-Scott & LeMahieu, 1984). Awareness activities were more effective when conducted in a small group or classroom setting than in individual counseling conferences. Thus, student support was made more visible.

To improve counseling programs, school districts must realize that adolescents need an opportunity to talk about peer, family, and personal problems, along with, and often related to, career choices. While a school cannot become a mental health center, some attention has to be given to emotional factors since these interfere with academic or personal success. If such specialized counseling is not available, career counselors will often find themselves called upon to give help around mental health and emotional issues, where they usually are not as adequately trained.

An adequate counseling program in schools will provide also for assistance to emotional conditions which occur more often in females. Two frequent manifestations of adolescent female disturbance are in the areas of eating disorders (anorexia and bulimia) and suicide attempts. Girls and young women manifest these conditions much more frequently than boys. While family dynamics are causally primary, school events and relationships also impinge on the underlying pathology. Often, these conditions become evident first in the school setting. Some school-based interventions can be helpful as adjuncts to, or prior to, psychotherapy. At times, the school services are the only available source of intervention.

In-service training can help teachers identify the signs of anorexia and bulimia (Chassler, 1985). Group counseling and suicide prevention programs have become more available in schools, especially since the adolescent suicide epidemic of the 1980s (Berkovitz, 1985; Peck, 1985). Many other conditions of psychopathology in both boys and girls first become evident in schools, including mood disorders, psychosis, and the effects of physical and/or sexual abuse. Drug abuse and alcoholism have received, and deserve, greater attention as well.

SEX AND FAMILY LIFE EDUCATION PROGRAMS

Menarche is a crucial formative event in a girl's life. Boys' entry into puberty, with nocturnal emissions and embarrassing, unpredictable erections, brings a similar, but less demanding, confrontation with a new sexual role. For individual young women, menarche may bring joy or fear, depending on attitudes in the family, especially the mother's. Menarche's effect on self-esteem may be crucially determined by these attitudes. Changes take place also in the way the family and males outside the family respect and regard the newly adolescent female. Male reaction is a matter of distress to some and simply of interest to others, increasing self-esteem in some and decreasing it in others.

Unfortunately, few school systems or families provide the kind of opportunities that help girls discuss and become comfortable with these bodily changes. Developing competence in handling the sexual decisions, which now become more pressing, is especially necessary. Group counseling programs in middle and high schools have been useful in helping these needs (Berkovitz, 1987). Since the 1980s, due partly to efforts to reduce the spread of the AIDS epidemic, sex education classes in many high schools have become more frank and explicit, encouraging open discussion of these issues. To promote optimal participation and learning, a nonjudgemental attitude is essential in the group leader. Other programs, such as school-based health clinics, have reduced the pregnancy rate in some high schools. The clinics provide a place for the adolescent to share sexual concerns and receive information from youth-responsive adults. Some clinics also provide contraceptives (Center for Population Options, 1990).

Actually, many American communities, for religious or other reasons, prohibit full consideration of these issues in schools. Significantly, one study showed that sex education courses in middle school delayed the age at which young girls began sexual activity (Zabin, Hirsch, Smith et al., 1986). "In Baltimore, students at two inner-city schools—all of whom were poor and took early sex for granted—participated in a program by the Johns Hopkins School of Medicine. A social worker and nurse gave individual and group counseling; medical and contraceptive services were provided at two nearby clinics. Students at two other schools got only Maryland's required sex education courses. After three years, the pregnancy rate at the first pair of schools had dropped 30%. At the second, it had gone up 58%." Another study (before the AIDS epidemic) showed that parental counseling was slightly more effective than school programs in encouraging use of contraceptive measures. Alas, parental counseling is not available enough. Equally unfortunate is the fact that, according to a 1987 survey, 75 percent of the nation's schools were found to be violating Title IX, as far as not reducing discrimination based on pregnancy and helping mothers to stay in school (NEA Today, 1991).

Some schools attempt to prepare young persons, male and female, for parenthood and family life issues. Several classroom programs have been developed to have students role-play the daily responsibilities of child-raising, as well as discuss some of the long-term issues in resolving marital conflicts. In some cases mental health consultants have been valuable in the classroom (Dunlap & Porter, 1985).

FEMALE PROFICIENCY IN MATH, SCIENCE, AND COMPUTERS

Female students often fail to achieve their academic potential in the areas of math and science (Wentzel, 1988). An early female superiority on math achievement tests often disappeared by the end of the high school years (Lewis & Hoover, 1983). These differences in standardized test scores do not always generalize to classroom performance. "Classroom grades are partly a reflection of social competence, social skills and positive attitudes toward compliance. The use of integrative skills, i.e., social responsibility and cooperation, defines achievement for females, whereas the use of self-assertive skills, i.e., competition and mastery, is considered to define areas of achievement for males" (Ford, 1982).

The attitudes accounting for greater male enrollment in math courses were "greater confidence in themselves as learners of math, more positive perceptions of the attitudes of mother and father toward them as learners of math and greater perceived usefulness of math" (Sherman & Fennema, 1977). Tobias (1978) emphasizes: "it is likely that the mother's math problems are directly passed on to her daughters."

Other authors highlight the influence of the teachers. In grades 9 and 12, the girls who took more theoretical math felt a more positive attitude from teachers toward them as learners of math. Several of the girls would have taken a fourth year of math if not for what they perceived as negative treatment by the teacher. One-third of the girls mentioned this, compared to only one-tenth of the boys (Sherman, 1982). Attraction to science teacher models was positively related to science career commitment among same-sex teacher-student pairs, but not among opposite-sex pairs (Stake & Granger, 1978). "In the average high school, girls with male models were particularly likely not to have other women teachers who could serve as models, since only 23 percent of science teachers were women" (Stake & Noonan, 1985). In college, more female science teacher models are available and many women begin, or renew, their interest in science then.

Math avoidance by women may lead to the narrowing of choices for future careers. "All but five of the 20 majors at Berkeley in the early 1970s required either calculus or statistics. Women, then, were crowding themselves into the remaining five fields (the humanities, music, social work, elementary education, guidance, and counseling) not only because of sex-role socialization but because of math avoidance" (Tobias, 1978). Some advocate that "educators must develop methods to have students experience greater success in mathematics in elementary and junior high school and to make mathematics courses more attractive to students in high school" (Van Blerkom, 1988). Courses have been developed to help women reduce "math anxiety" (Tobias, 1978). Even in the 1980s, the trend continued for women to be the dominant gender in "social-type" college majors in education, nursing, and social work, and for men to be the dominant gender in accounting, business administration, predentistry, and premedicine (Gianakos & Subich, 1988).

The study by the American Association of University Women, 1991, found that as the students learned that they were not good at math and science, their sense of self-worth and aspirations deteriorated. "Half of all elementary school boys, but only one-third of all elementary school girls, say they are good at math. By high school, one in four males, but only one in seven females, still say they are good at math."

Girls interpreted their problems with math as personal failures. Boys projected it more as a problem with the subject matter itself. By small margins, students who liked math and science expressed stronger desires for careers as teachers, doctors, scientists, or other professionals. The researchers concluded that schools and teachers should work harder to encourage girls to like math and science. As has been indicated by other studies, the problem is not just the attitude of the schools, but effects of family attitudes as well.

Similarly there has been low participation of women in scientific and technological programs, including computer science courses. Computing is generally perceived as being technologic and machine-centered, as well as being mathematically oriented. This discourages many women from enrolling. In practice, most computing professionals have extensive dealings with people and with issues that are centered around people. Women perform very well at systems analysis, that is, problem-solving in its broad sense in which the computing professional must interact with the users in the process of designing the system. Communication skills are central to this problem-solving and women are seen traditionally to have strengths in communication (Harding, 1983; Head, 1979). Women who persisted in computer science courses achieved as well as, or better than, men in the final year of the course (Kay, Collings, Lublin, et al., 1989). These researchers felt that ''women's traditionally lower level of confidence interacted with an impoverished background in computing, technology and mathematical expertise.'' They opined that the problem of increasing the number of women in the field lay with the institution, as well as with the broader society.

In some situations, computer access was carefully built into classroom activities; competition was not the basis for opportunity. Attitudes about potential ability were not allowed to determine use. In these situations, the differences between the sexes decreased or disappeared altogether (Smith, 1986; Swadener & Hannafin, 1987). When women were specifically instructed and encouraged, and actually required to use the machines, they were as competent and as confident as the men (Arch & Cummins, 1989).

EXTRACURRICULAR INFLUENCES

The extracurricular life of a school can breed and reenforce many gender-related stereotypes. In a middle school located in a medium-sized midwestern community, the male athletic events were the main social events of the school. This is true in many communities. Both male athletes and female cheerleaders had considerable visibility and were members of an elite group. Male athletes were achievement-oriented, competitive, and aggressive; females were encouraged to smile and be concerned about their appearance. These values became incorporated into the informal peer culture (Eder & Parker, 1987). The authors suggested that administrators and teachers could give greater prestige and visibility to female athletic events or to other achievement-oriented activities to counter these narrow options. Large high schools usually offer more options than athletics and cheerleading, and most colleges offer considerably more.

A relevant question here is: Do girls take more time for friends than boys? In one study among students scoring high on need for achievement, those who scored low on need for affiliation had higher grade point averages than those who scored high on need for affiliation (Schneider & Green, 1977). This was true for males and females. Schneider and Coutts (1985) prefer the term ''person orientation'' since it ''encompasses not only affiliative tendencies—movement toward positive interaction with others—but such variables as empathy, sensitivity to social reinforcement, cooperativeness, and responsiveness to social influence.'' Several writers have stressed that ''girls, more than boys, were likely to rate being popular as more important than doing things well'' (Simmons & Rosenberg, 1975) or achieving in school. However, ''girls were more likely to report they studied with friends, boys reported spending more time involved in sports and organizations'' (Schneider & Coutts, 1985). Thus, girls may be better able to satisfy simultaneously their affiliative and achievement needs.

WOMEN'S STUDIES COURSES

The question raised so far is: How far can schools go in reducing stereotypic attitudes towards male and female roles, including career alternatives? Women's Studies (WS) courses may be one of the most innovative contributions of the feminist movement to school curricula for meeting this goal. In one school, after participating in a 20-unit course on sex roles, students in grades 10-12 perceived the roles of males and females in a ''more socially androgynous context'' (Kahn & Richardson, 1983). Androgyny is a classification used by Bem (1974) to indicate that some women can use masculine or feminine traits as the occasion demanded. This group of androgynous women were considered to be more flexible, better adjusted, more intellectually developed, and more confident.

In the WS course, students analyzed the history and modern development of male and female gender roles. The course materials included ''consciousness-raising exercises, which heighten the awareness of one's attitudes and beliefs; a role reversal of typical sex-typed behaviors; role-play of difficult work and family conflict situations; and assertiveness training for direct, honest communication'' (Kahn & Richardson, 1983). The satisfaction of the students was better in the two schools where the students, largely female, chose the course than in a school where students were assigned.

In follow-up interviews six years after a women's history course in another high school, some students said: ''It opened up another view of history, seeing it from a woman's point of view'' (Tetreault, 1986). The author concluded: ''There is little in the schools which educates female students to think about their rights and responsibilities in shaping their own lives . . . today young women reported resentment about the pressure to work and raise children with few models for how to do it.''

In a small private school, self-concept rose in a group of gifted girls after they increased their awareness of conflicts related to being female (Olshen & Matthews, 1987). A weekly series of twelve 40-minute sessions focused on open-ended self expression. Among other features, ''Written work generated by the subjects included a piece on 'The things I like and dislike about being a girl,' stories about people depicted in photographs (in and out of gender-specific roles), rewriting fairy tales, nursery rhymes, etc. that display gender bias, rewriting newspaper articles that utilize sexist language, and creating new lists of clichés to combat gender bias.'' The group aged 10-11 was enthusiastic about the course. The group aged 12-18 was resistant, but ''there was an observable development of self-assertion and group cohesion.''

Such courses have proliferated in colleges between 1970 and 1982, increasing from two to 432 (Howe, 1983). The courses provide a supportive atmosphere that fosters and encourages women to challenge traditional views of appropriate female roles and behavior, as well as decreasing ''fear of success'' (Horner, 1972) or helping to eliminate other psychological barriers to achievement (Zuckerman, 1983). One study reported an increased willingness to delay marriage in some women (Canty, 1977), a tendency to decrease desired family size, and an increase in self-esteem (Brush, Gold & White, 1978).

In another study, a differential effect of WS courses occurred in college upper- and underclasswomen (Zuckerman, 1983). In the underclasswomen, self-esteem decreased, while it increased in the juniors and seniors. The hypothesis was that the courses generated a new and disturbing awareness of sex discrimination in the younger women, while the older group was already more aware of this. This was not considered an indictment of WS courses for younger women. WS underclasswomen's post-test career expectations were still less traditional than upperclasswomen's pretest responses, and self-esteem scores were comparable to upperclasswomen's pretest responses. The implication was that faculty needed to be aware of the potentially discouraging effects of WS courses on some teenage women, especially in high schools. The suggestion was made to ''integrate these topics into the regular curricula.''

One proposed college curriculum focused on the roles of men as well as women (Carney, Taylor & Stevens, 1986). This is especially relevant, since roles designated for women often involve reciprocal roles for men, and vice versa. Large mixed-sex didactic groups were used along with smaller single-sex discussion groups to help students personalize the impact of sexism in their own lives. Women felt anger toward the patriarchal system, while men experienced guilt toward their own sexist attitudes and behaviors. In the fourth stage of the course, same-sex and mixed-sex formats were combined to promote the integration of old and new value systems and same-sex bonding. There was conscious striving to actualize nonsexist values.

In another college without a WS course, a psychology of women course helped develop ''healthy'' self-perceptions (Harris, 1983). Some suggested that campuses should offer male students opportunities to work in child-care centers, accept dates from women, plan noncompetitive games, and work with female student leaders (Blocher, 1978).

READING MATERIALS

The influence of the content of textbooks and other reading matter requires consideration. Many studies emphasize that gender characteristics of instructional materials influence pupils' sex role attitudes, learning, and interest (Schau & Scott, 1984). For both boys and girls, sex-fair materials produce fewer sex-typed responses about occupations, roles, and personality traits than sex-biased materials (Schau, 1978). For example, children who read instructional materials about girls in nontraditional roles were more likely to think that girls could perform the nontraditional activity of the narrative than children who read the same materials with boys as main characters (Scott & Feldman-Summers, 1979). Fourth- and seventh-grade pupils were less stereotyped than 11th-grade pupils in response to the measures of "who can" perform the sex-typed activities portrayed in the narratives. Seventh- and 11th-grade pupils were more stereotyped than fourth-grade pupils on the "who should" measure (Scott, 1986).

SEXUAL HARASSMENT

While various influential relationships between school personnel and students have been touched on throughout this discussion, there is also sexual harassment by teachers (or other personnel). This often has traumatic consequences for the victim. One study found that "approximately one in every six women" will experience this from teachers (McCormack, 1985). The type of harassment can consist of embarrassing comments, "undressing looks," physical contact, or coerced sexual relations. The initiation of sexual demands upon the student for a "favor" or by a "threat" creates an intimidating environment for the student. This influences the attitude that a woman has about being female and the use or abuse of that femaleness.

While some students may instigate sexual propositions, this does not make involvement by teachers any less sexual harassment. The asymmetric power relationship between teacher and student justifies labeling this involvement as harassment (McCormack, 1985), as in the case of therapists, ministers, or doctors. A formal grievance procedure in the school and support from other faculty, male and female, is essential for lessening the damaging consequences (Dziech & Weiner, 1984).

SUMMARY

It is evident that the influence of schools on female development is but one strand in a multithreaded fabric. Important threads are the individual's genetic inheritance, familial values and nurturing, and conditions in the wider society. Schools transmit the values of the society generally, exerting a person-related as well as female-related influence. A prime female-related influence, unfortunately, has been the promulgation of negative stereotypes about the capabilities of women and the limited vocational opportunities. These were often presented in courses or advocated in counseling. Some of these features have been remedied by Title IX, but constant vigilance and improvement are still required.

A crucial person-related area is that of self-esteem. A recent study (American Association of University Women, 1990) found that girls' self-esteem decreased from age nine to 14 more than did that of boys. Other studies have shown that for many women aspirations decrease with age. It may be unfair to expect the schools alone to reverse this trend, but certainly changes are justified, when schools are compounding the inequities. In this same study, difficulties in performing well in math and science were found to correlate with low self-esteem in boys and girls, but more so in girls.

This points to the need for increased efforts by schools to improve girls' interest and ability in math and science. While attitudes of fathers and mothers are very crucial, the attitudes of teachers as role models or negative voices were found to be highly influential as well. Another factor may well be the finding that teachers often interact more with boys than with girls in the classroom.

High school and college women have been found to be reluctant to choose professional or nontraditional careers, especially if these involved technical or math-related skills. Some schools have been able to lessen this avoidance by promoting more positive attitudes from teachers, greater availability of female role models, and stronger persuasion for women to persevere. Providing more courses in women's studies in high schools and colleges has stimulated many girls to feel more assertive, capable, and willing to develop their abilities.

An important feature of the school's contribution to female self-esteem is the type of sex and family life education programs offered. Openness, honesty, and explicitness in such programs have been found to encourage greater self-respect, self-knowledge, and safer sexual behavior in girls. In some schools such programs have resulted in a delay of beginning sexual activity and a decreased rate of adolescent pregnancy. Other influential school programs are the types of extracurricular activities, types of counseling services, and choice of reading materials used in class. In schools where male sports heroes and female cheerleaders were the most valued peer figures, positive values for all females were not always promoted. Female athletic programs and elevation of other school programs were recommended to counteract this.

While the secondary school counselor was less primary than family and peers as an influence on most young persons, well trained counselors were seen to be less prone to reenforcing stereotypes and more likely to promote nontraditional career choices more strongly. In addition, counselors could use assistance from mental health consultants to provide better counseling assistance to women with eating disorders, suicide attempts, and drug abuse, as well as other psychological problems. Unfortunately, sex harassment of women, especially by college personnel, is too frequent, often with traumatic consequences to school careers as well as to future development of the individual student. Lastly, the role of reading materials cannot be overlooked. If these present women only in traditional roles, rather than in innovative situations, girls are less likely to consider innovative roles for themselves.

This chapter was able to present only a fraction of the writings and research on this topic. Even so, hopefully, the message conveyed will help to improve the abilities of schools and school personnel, at times in alliance with mental health personnel, to provide more school programs and conditions that will advance the development of young women in secondary schools and colleges.

REFERENCES

American Association of University Women. 1991. *Short Changing Girls, Short Changing America*. Washington, D.C.: Presented at meeting.

Arch, E.L. & Cummins, D.E. 1989. Structured and unstructured exposure to computers: Sex differences in attitude & use among college students. *Sex Roles*, 20(5/6):245-253.

Auster, C.J. & Auster, D. 1981. Factors influencing women's choice of nontraditional careers: The role of family, peers and counselors. *Vocat. Guidance Quart.*, 29:253-261.

Bandura, A. 1977. Self-efficacy: Toward a unifying theory of behavioral change. *Psycholog. Rev.*, 84,191-215.

Bem, S.L. 1974. The measurement of psychological androgyny. *J. Consult. Clin. Psych.*, 42:155-162.

Berkovitz, I.H. 1979. Effects of secondary school experiences on adolescent female development. In M. Sugar, Ed., *Female Adolescent Development*. New York: Brunner/Mazel.

Berkovitz, I.H. 1985. Elements of an optimum suicide prevention climate in schools. In I.H. Berkovitz & J.S. Seliger, Ed., *Expanding Mental Health Interventions in Schools*. Dubuque, IA: Kendall/Hunt.

Berkovitz, I.H. 1987. Value of group counseling in secondary schools. *Adol. Psychiatry*, 14:522-545.

Betz, N.F. & Hackett, G. 1981. The relationship of career-related self-efficacy expectations to perceived career options in college men and women. *J. of Counsel. Psych.*, 28:399-410.

Blocher, D.H. 1978. Campus learning envi8onments & the ecology of student development. In J.H. Banning, Ed., *Campus Ecology: A Perspective for Student Affairs*. Cincinnati, OH: Nat. Assoc. of Student Personnel Administrators.

Brush, L.E., Gold, A.R., & White, M.G. 1978. The paradox of intention and effect: A women's studies course. *Signs*, 3:870-883.

Canty, E.M. 1977. Effects of women's studies courses in women's attitudes and goals. Paper presented at the Am. Psychological Assn. meeting, San Francisco, 1977.

Carney, C., Taylor, K., & Stevens, M. 1986. Sex roles in groups: A developmental approach. *J. Special. Group Work*, Nov., 11:200-208.

Center for Population Options 1990. *School Based Clinics: Update*. Washington, D.C.

Chassler, L.L. 1985. The school's role in the detection and management of students with anorexia and bulimia. In I.H. Berkovitz & J.S. Seliger, Eds., *Expanding Mental Health Interventions in Schools*. Dubuque, IA.: Kendall/Hunt.

Danziger, N. 1983. Sex-related differences in the aspirations of high school students. *Sex Roles*, 9(6): 683–695.

Dunlap, D.A. & Porter, D. 1985. Helping adolescents directly: The consultant as co-teacher in a family life curriculum. In I.H. Berkovitz & J.S. Seliger, Eds., *Expanding Mental Health Interventions in Schools*. Dubuque, IA: Kendall/Hunt.

Dziech, B. W. & Weiner, L. 1984. *The Lecherous Professor: Sexual Harassment on Campus*. New York: Beacon Press.

Eder, D., & Parker, S. 1987. The cultural production and reproduction of gender: The effect of extracurricular activities on peer-group culture. *Sociol. Educat.*, 60:200-213.

Fitzgerald, L.F. & Betz, N.E. 1983. Issues in the vocational psychology of women. In W.B. Walsh & S.H. Osipow, Eds., *Handbook of Vocational Psychology*. 1:83-159. Hillsdale, N.J.: Erlbaum.

Fitzpatrick, J.L. 1978. Academic achievement, other directedness and attitudes toward women's roles in bright adolescent females. *J. of Educ. Psych.*, 70:654-660.

Ford, M.E. 1982. Social cognition and social competence in adolescence. *Dev. Psych.*, 18:323-340.

Freud, S. 1914. On narcissism: An introduction. *Standard Edition*, 14:73-102. London: Hogarth (1957).

Garfield-Scott, L. & LeMahieu, P. 1984. Targeting non-traditional students: A study of chance process in vocational education. *Vocat. Guid. Quart.*, 33(2):157-168.

Gianakos, I. & Subich, L.M. 1988. Student sex and sex role in relation to college major choice. *Career Develop. Quart.*, 36:259-268.

Gottfredson, L.A. 1981. Circumscription and compromise: A developmental theory of occupational aspirations. *J. Counsel. Psych.*, 28:454-479.

Gilligan, C. 1991. Little girls lose self esteem in school. *New York Times*. January 9, B6. Magazine Section.

Grinder, R.E., 1966. Relations of social dating attractions to academic orientation & peer relations. *J. Educ. Psych.*, 57:27-34.

Hackett, G. & Betz, N.E. 1981. A self-efficacy approach to the career development of women. *J. of Vocat. Behav.*, 2:142-153.

Harding, J. 1983. Switched off: The science education of girls. *Longman, for Schools Coun.*, 57 pp (Australia).

Harren, V.A., Kass, R.A., Tinsley, H.E.A., & Moreland, J.R. 1979. Influence of sex role attitudes, and cognitive complexity on gender-dominant career choices. *J. Counsel. Psych.*, 26:227-234.

Harris, R.M. 1983. Changing women's self-perceptions: Impact of a Psychology of Women Course. *Psych. Reports*, 52:314-318.

Head, J. 1979. Personality and the pursuit of science. *Studies Science Educat.*, 6:13-18.

Horner, M.S. 1972. Toward an understanding of achievement related conflicts in women. *J. Social Issues*, 28:157-175.

Howe, F. 1983. New teaching strategies for a new generation of students. *Women's Studies Quart.*, 11(2):7-11.

Hutt, C.H. 1983. College students' perceptions of male and female career patterns. *J. College Stud. Personnel*, 19:240-246.

Kahn, S.E. & Richardson, A. 1983. Evaluation of a course in sex roles for secondary school students. *Sex Roles*, 9:431-440.

Kay, J., Collings, P., Lublin, J., Poiner, G., Prosser, M., Bishop, R., & Watson, K. 1989. *Investigation of the Women at Early Stages of Professionally Accredited Tertiary Computer Science & Data Processing Programmes.* Report to Evaluations and Investigations Programme, Commonwealth Tertiary Education Commission. (Australia).

Kennedy, R.E. & Petersen, A.C. 1991. Stressful family events and adjustment among young adolescents. Unpublished manuscript. The Pennsylvania State University, University Park, PA.

Kirkpatrick, M. 1989. Society plays significant role in labeling of women as masochistic. *Psychiatric Times*, (May):19-21.

Lewis, J. & Hoover, H.D. 1983. Sex differences on standardized academic achievement tests—A longitudinal study. Paper presented at meeting of Am. Educ. Research Assn. Montreal, Quebec, Canada, April.

Lipsitz, J. 1991. Public policy and young adolescents. *J. of Early Adol.*, 11:20-37.

Maccoby, E.E. & Jacklin, C.N. 1974. *Psychology of Sex Differences.* Palo Alto, Ca.: Stanford University.

McCormack, A. 1985. The sexual harassment of students by teachers: The case of students in science. *Sex Roles*, 13:21-31.

NEA Today. 1991. p. 6. Washington, D.C.: Publication of National Education Association.

New York Times. 1991. The husband vanishes (editorial). Tuesday, February 19, 1991. 140: A 14.

Olshen, S.R. & Matthews, D.J. 1987. The disappearance of giftedness in girls: An intervention strategy. *Roeper Rev.*, 9:251-254.

Peck, M.L. 1985. Youth suicide: Programs for prevention intervention & postvention. In I.H. Berkovitz, & J.S. Seliger, Eds., *Expanding Mental Health Interventions in Schools.* Dubuque, IA., Kendall/Hunt.

Petersen, A.C., Sarigiani, P.A., & Kennedy, R.E. 1991. Adolescent depression: Why more girls? *J. Youth & Adol.* 20:247-272.

Petersen, A.C., Kennedy, R., & Sullivan, P. (in press) Coping with adolescence. In M.E. Colten & S. Gore, Eds., *Adolescent Stress, Social Relationships, and Mental Health.* New York: Aldine.

Post-Kammer, P., & Smith, P.L. 1985. Sex differences in career self-efficacy consideration, and interests of eighth and ninth graders. *J. Counsel. Psych.*, 32:551-559.

Powell, G.J. & Fuller, M. 1970: Self concept and school desegregation. *Am. J. Orthopsychiat.*, 40:303-304.

Rutter, M., Maugham, B., Mortimore, P., & Oustan, J. 1979. *Fifteen Thousand Hours*. Cambridge, MA: Harvard Univ.

Sadker, M. & Sadker, S. 1986. Sexism in the classroom of the 80's. *Psychology Today*, March.

Schau, C.G. 1978. Evaluating the use of sex-role reversed stories for changing children's stereotypes. Paper presented at meeting Am. Educ. Research Assoc., Toronto.

Schau, C.G. & Scott, K.P. 1984. The impact of gender characteristics of instructional materials. An integration of the research literature. *J. of Educ. Psych.*, 76:173-183.

Schneider, F.W. & Coutts, L.M. 1985. Person orientation of male and female high school students: To the educational disadvantage of males? *Sex Roles*, 13:47-63.

Schneider, F.W. & Green, J.E. 1977. Need for affiliation and sex as moderators of the relationship between need for achievement and academic performance. *J. of School Psych.*, 15:269-277.

Scott, K.P. 1986. Effects of sex—fair reading materials on pupils' attitudes, comprehension & interest. *Am. Educ. Research J.*, 23:105-116.

Scott, K.P. & Feldman-Summers, S. 1979. Children's reactions to textbook stories in which females are portrayed in traditionally male roles. *J. of Educ. Psych.*, 71:396-402.

Sewell, W.H. & Shah, V.P. 1968. Social class, parental encouragement and educational aspirations. *Am. J. of Sociol.*, 13:559-572.

Sherman, J. 1982. Mathematics, the critical filter: Look at some residues. *Psych. Women Quart.*, 6:428-444.

Sherman, J. & Fennema, E. 1977. Study of mathematics by high school girls and related variables. *Amer. Educat. Research J.*, 14:159-168.

Simmons, R.G. & Rosenberg, F. 1975. Sex roles and self image. *J. of Youth & Adol.*, 4:229-258.

Smith, S.E. 1986. Relationships of computer attitudes to sex, grade level & teacher influence. *Education*, 106:334-338.

Stake, J.E. & Granger, C.R. 1978. Same-sex and opposite-sex teacher model influences on science career commitment among high school students. *J. of Educ. Psychol.*, 70:180-186.

Stake, J.E. & Noonan, M. 1985. The influence of teacher models on the career confidence and motivation of college students. *Sex Roles*, 12:1023-1031.

Swadener, M. & Hannafin, M. 1987. Gender similarities and differences in sixth graders attitudes toward computors. An exploratory study. *Educat. Technol.*, 27:37-42.

Terman, L.M. 1930. *Genetic Studies of Genius*. Palo Alto: Stanford Univ.

Tetreault, M.K.T. 1986. "It's so opinioney." *J. of Educat.*, 168:78-95.

Title IX of the Education Amendments of 1972. Washington, D.C.: U.S. Government Printing Office.

Title IX: A Practical Guide to Achieving Sex Equity in Education. 1988. Washington, D.C.: National Coalition for Women and Girls in Education.

Tobias, S. 1978. *Overcoming Math Anxiety*. New York: Norton.

Tobin-Richards, M.H., Boxer, A.M., & Petersen, A.C. 1983. The psychological significance of pubertal change: Sex differences in perceptions of self during early adolescence. In J. Gunn and A.C. Petersen, Eds., *Girls at Puberty and Psychosocial Perspectives*. New York: Plenum.

Van Blerkom, M.L. 1988. Field dependence, sex role self-perceptions, and mathematics achievement in college students: A closer examination. *Contemp. Educat. Psych.*, 13:339-347.

Ward, 1991. Little girls lose self esteem in school. *New York Times*, Jan. 9, B6.

Wentzel, K.R. 1988. Classroom goals and academic competence in adolescence. *J. Educat. Psych.*, 81(2):131-142.

Wilson, J., Weikel, W.S., & Rose, H. 1982. A comparison of non-traditional career women. *Vocat. Guidance Quart.* 31:109-116.

Zabin, L.S., Hirsch, M.B., Smith, E.A., Streett, R., and Hardy, J.B. 1986. Evaluation of a pregnancy prevention program for urban teenagers. *Fam. Plann. Perspect.*, 18:119-126.

Zuckerman, D.M. 1983. Women's studies, self-esteem, and college women's plans for the future. *Sex Roles*, 9:633-640.

12 Adolescent Motherhood and Development

Max Sugar, M.D.

In the mind of some, any mother, age notwithstanding, is adult, mature, capable, and caring. However, many studies of pregnant adolescent mothers have raised questions about the maternal capability and maturity of these young women (Furstenberg, Brooks-Gunn & Morgan, 1987; Hayes, 1987; Jones, Forrest, Goldman, et al., 1986; Nickel & Delany, 1985; Sarrel & Davis, 1966; Sugar, 1979). This chapter discusses some of the relevant factors.

CURRENT ASPECTS OF ADOLESCENT MOTHERHOOD

Until several decades ago, the single, white, pregnant adolescent usually went off to a home for unwed mothers away from her area and gave the child up for adoption after delivery. In the last quarter century, this has become an infrequent pathway and about 90 percent of white adolescents who go to term keep their baby. Now we have a clearer picture of the frequency of single, white, adolescent pregnancy and motherhood. The rate of increase of single teen fertility from 1955 to 1984 is 300% among whites and 12% among blacks. However, among black single teens, the fertility rate is 4.6 times that in whites, i.e., "one-quarter of all unmarried blacks will become a mother by age 18 compared to about one in twenty whites" (Furstenberg, 1987).

Since 1960, the number of births per 1,000 women and the birth rate to mothers age 15 to 24 have decreased (U.S. Bureau of the Census, 1990, p. 63) as indicated in Table 12.1, but there has been an increase in the birth rate for those age 10 to 14.

The fertility rate for teenagers in the U.S.A. is the highest of the industrialized nations despite the fact that the level of their sexual activity is the same as in these other countries (Jones, et al., 1986). Ethnicity, employment, geography, and income affect the fertility rate which Table 12.2 shows.

213

TABLE 12.1
Births and Birth Rates 1960–1987*

	1960	1970	1980	1985	1987
Libe Births (in 1,000's)	4258	3831	3612	3761	3809
White	3601	3091	2899	2991	2992
Black	602	572	590	608	642
Birth Rate per 1,000 Women (all ages)	118	87.9	68.4	66.2	65.7
White	113.2	84.1	64.7	63.0	62.0
Black	153.5	115.4	88.1	82.2	83.8
Age of Mother					
10-14 years	0.8	1.2	1.1	1.2	1.3
15-19 years	89.1	68.3	53.0	51.3	51.1
20-24 years	258.1	167.8	115.1	108.9	108.9

*Modified from Table 82, p. 63.
U. S. Bureau of the Census 1990
Statistical Abstract of the United States 1990

Twenty-five percent of all first births in 1987 were to unmarried women. Of those, seven percent were to under 15s; 31 percent were to adolescents age 15 to 19; and 36 percent were among 20 to 24-year-olds (U.S. Bureau of the Census 1990, Table 90).

The figures for adolescent pregnancy vary by ethnic and SES groups, but they are largely sorted out into black, Hispanic, and white groups (U.S. Bureau of the Census 1990). Nevertheless, they show a consistent pattern in the past three decades in that adolescents and young adults have higher contraceptive use than other age groups. Although the popular media may indicate otherwise, the percent of blacks using contraceptives is more than twice that of the whites, as Table 12.3 shows (U.S. Bureau of the Census 1990, p. 70).

Sexual and other risk-taking continues unabated in female adolescents. From 1971 to 1987, the percent of 15- to 19-year-old girls who ever had intercourse increased from 28 to 50 (Hayes, 1987). Eighty-eight percent of teenage clinic patients had intercourse before seeking contraceptive help. The first use of any prescription method for contraception is 11 months (mean) after intercourse in clinic patients, and 13 months (mean) in private patients (Jones et al., 1986).

Sixty-three percent of sexually transmitted diseases (STD) occur in the under 25s, and two and a half million teenagers are infected with an STD; pelvic inflammatory disease (P.I.D.) is 10 times more frequent in the adolescent than

TABLE 12.2
Factors Affecting Fertility Rate 1988 (Per 1,000 Women)*

| | Total Births per 1,000 Women | |
	Age 18-44	Age 18-24
All Women	69.7	87.1
White (84% of population)	66	76
Black (12% of population)	87	151
Hispanic (8% of population)	94	117
Not high school graduate	87	129
In labor force	48	54
Unemployed	85	114
Not in labor force	128	181
Family income <$10,000	106	166
Family income >$50,000	50	23
In the South	72	104
In the Northeast	68	74

*U. S. Department of Commerce Current Population Reports. Modified from pp. 2 & 3, 1989. *Fertility of American Women: June 1988.* Population Characteristics Series, p. 20, 436. Washington, D.C.: U. S. Government Printing.

TABLE 12.3*
Contraceptive Use Among Sexually Active Women—1982
Percent Distribution per 1,000

	All Wmn	15-24	25-34	35-44	White	Black	Never Married	Married	Formerly Married
All Wmn (1,000)	54099	20150	19644	14305	45387	6985	19164	28231	6704
Sexually Active Wmn % Contraceptors	7.4	9.2	6.5	6.0	6.4	13.5	10.1	4.8	10.4

*Modified from Table 89, p. 70, U.S. Bureau of the Census 1990.

the adult, and nearly one in eight sexually active girls will develop it (Washington, Sweet & Schafe, 1985). Twenty-six percent or more of AIDS patients in the U.S.A. are women, but only 28 percent of sexually active women, age 11 to 25, had partners using condoms (Grace, Emans & Woods, 1989). Substance abuse continues in female adolescents at high rates, with greater frequency in the sexually active than in the virgins (Zabin, Hardy, Smith & Hirsch, 1986).

ETHNIC FACTORS

In an earlier chapter (Sugar, 1979), the pregnant teenager was presented as having a stereotypical syndrome of failure ascribed to, and predicted for, her (Sarrel & Davis, 1966). Since then, the features of the pregnant adolescent have become less global, with many individual considerations beyond being black, on welfare, unmarried, and having another teen pregnancy. The uniform picture from that time does not apply anymore. The pregnant girl's situation is affected by many factors such as SES, ethnicity, family and family support, crises, employment, geography, education, the boyfriend who impregnates her, and the government.

Salguero (1984) noted a contrasting pattern of the black adolescent mother and the Hispanic adolescent mother in New Haven. The black female initiated intercourse at age 15.5 years and was approximately 15.8 years of age when first pregnant. Zabin, Hardy, Streett and King (1984) found that the age of first intercourse in their Baltimore study was 14.5 for the black female and 12.2 for the black male. In their sample, 50 percent of the pregnancies occurred within six months of the first heterosexual experience. At one year after delivery, a slight majority of these black adolescents were not attending school.

In Salguero's group, the Hispanic adolescent mother was 15.5 years of age, and was about to enter high school in the ninth grade while leaving her family of origin at the time of conception. In 39 percent of cases, she was living with her partner. She had initiated intercourse at age 14.7 years (Smith, McGill & Wait, 1987) and was married in 63 percent of cases for an average of 12 months when seen prenatally or within 48 hours of delivery. The relationship of the Hispanic female adolescent to her mother changes after the delivery since she is now a mother and is expected to be home. She is usually involved with a man who is five or more years older (Salguero, 1984). This contrasts with the black female impregnated by an adolescent three to four years older than she, who leaves her soon afterwards (Smith et al., 1987).

Several recent studies have observed that return to school for the youngster is not a prerequisite or an indicator of suitable functioning, being a contraceptor, or limiting her family. The rate of return to school in one study varied from 65 percent in Mexican-American pregnant females to 27 percent in whites, to 7 percent for the black females, and a return to school was not a necessary feature of a low recidivism rate (Stevens-Simon, Parsons & Montgomery, 1986).

When a group of Mexican-American, white, and black females of low SES from San Diego were compared (Felice, Shragg, James, & Hollingsworth 1987), 50 percent of the blacks were in school on the occasion of the first prenatal visit, in contrast to 18 and 32 percent of Hispanics and whites, respectively. Here, 61 percent of the black females lived with at least one natural parent in contrast to only 29 percent each of the whites and Hispanics; also, 46 percent of the Hispanics lived with their boyfriend or spouse in contrast to 43 percent of the whites and 9 percent of the blacks. The white teenagers came from the most troubled families with many reports of psychiatric illness in a parent or sibling, runaway behavior, or a deceased parent. In contrast, the black pregnant adolescents were more likely to have good mother-daughter relationships and have a family history of other out-of-wedlock births. Thus, using school enrollment as an indicator of better functioning, or as a predictor of being a contraceptor is not very well-supported since the blacks in this study had the highest school enrollment and also the largest number of repeat pregnancies.

Youngsters in rural areas have not been studied much compared to those in the inner city, and there probably are significant subcultural variations between those groups. The study by Lamb, Elster, Peters, et al. (1986) of a cohort from Utah indicates a further cultural variant that indicates more heterogeneity of adolescent mothers.

PSYCHIATRIC CONSIDERATIONS

Recently, McGee, Felhan, Williams, et al. (1990) found that 26 percent of 15-year-old girls had a DSM-III disorder, while boys had an 18 percent rate of disorder. Despite such rates, there is no basis for considering that all girls who get pregnant have a psychiatric disorder, since many get pregnant without a disorder. Teenage pregnancy is not a psychiatric condition.

Abortions do not cause any significant long-term emotional difficulty (Family Plann. Perspect, 1990; Koop, 1989; Psychiatric News, 1990)

The different stages of adolescence involve developmental tasks that lead to adulthood. The end of adolescence is viewed by some as having arrived when the ego-ideal and superego have been cathected (Blos, 1977). The development of the teenager's ego and ego-ideal are incomplete (Blos, 1977; Jacobson, 1964) and a mature superego is not available before age 30 (Pearson, 1959).

The capacity for abstract thinking may not be attained in adolescence or even in adulthood due to inadequate intellectual stimulation, innate lack of ability, being a migrant, or having an otherwise disadvantaged environment (Piaget, 1972).

For the adolescent female, especially in the early and middle stages, the issues of mothering needs or the wish to be mothered relate to her second individuation development where these have not been satisfactorily settled; further, she has not settled her negative oedipal conflicts (Blos, 1974). The adolescent mother often has been thrust into the mother-to-be role with little preparation, thought or plan at a time when she herself is in need of a mother.

To Williams (1974), the pregnant teenager seemed unconcerned about having a baby, but was anxious about marriage, even if she had been a mother for some time. This emulates denial about the importance of motherhood to her and corroborates Jacobson's (1964) notions about the use of primitive defenses. The conscious attitude and the actual behavior leading to pregnancy seem to connect with a lack of fidelity—the presence of distance instead of intimacy (Erikson, 1968). The girl feels a very intensified rivalry with her own mother, since her physical sexual maturity is self-evident and may pose a threat to her mother, who is now nearing or facing the end of her own reproductive life. Rivalry may be brewing between them over the maternal role; this may become focused on whose baby it really is that this girl is having, and who will care for it.

There are some distinct psychodynamic features that may be found in three large groups, but do not exclude other dynamics. One group consists of those who are psychologically deprived, possibly profoundly damaged girls. By becoming pregnant and having an infant, they find some fulfillment of a deep narcissistic need that is related to a faulty self-concept and primitive object ties to the mother, along with strong urges for contact and affirmation. These are the girls at highest risk for pregnancy, age nine to 14. Another group is composed of those who are somewhat better integrated and become pregnant in an effort to resolve an oedipal conflict. In a third group are those girls for whom the pregnancy is an attempt at maturation, an expression, and confirmation, of their connection to their relatives (Fisher, 1984). These three constellations are not necessarily binding to all pregnant adolescents since there are subtleties attendant on them as illustrated earlier by the ethnic and cultural issues.

Fisher (1984) described two industrialized towns where the generations were compressed among the working class and there were no career plans for these girls who for generations had copied their mother, become pregnant, married in their teens and raised children. A pregnancy amongst this group did not interrupt, but furthered the youngster's career since she was only doing as her mother had done and modeled for her. Here, pregnancy appeared to represent an effort at mastery, growing up and becoming part of the community. This is also often the case in rural communities. From another view, they may have an identity foreclosure (Marcia, 1980).

CRISES

Another feature that may be involved in some adolescents' pregnancies is the occurrence of crises, one of whose resolutions may be a pregnancy. In my study (Sugar, 1976) of 481 mothers (of whom 90 percent were black and 10 percent white, with an age range of 13 to 46, and 91 percent in lowest SES, nine percent in the middle SES group), there was a significant difference in the number of

TABLE 12.4
Comparison of Crises in Pregnancies of Adolescent and
Adult Mothers by Infant's Birth Weight

Infants	Birth Weight in gm		Crises in: Adol. Mother	Adult Mother	x2	df	p*
Prematures	≤2500	Number	161	160			
		Percent	56.5	35.6	12.33	2	0.002
Full Term	≥2501	Number	53	107			
		Percent	55.7	33.6	8.41	1	0.004
All Infants		Number	21.4	267			
		Percent	56.3	35.2	20.74	3	<0.001

*If p <0.05, the percentages are significantly different.

crises in the pregnancy between different groups of mothers by birth-weight of the infant and by the mother being an adolescent or an adult. Adult mothers had a significantly lower percentage of crises (35 percent) than adolescent mothers (56 percent), whether the infant was full-term or premature, as shown in Table 12.4.

The development of crises is partly self-arranged, involving particular emotional patterns or dynamics. The greater percent of crises in adolescent pregnancies may be related to the adolescents' incomplete education and emotional development, ambivalence, unsettled life situation and lack of experience. Many of the crises are beyond the individual's control, e.g., death of a loved one, loss of a job, etc. However, many crises follow from a particular decision the individual makes, e.g., dropping out of school, quitting a job, marrying, moving, resuming school, or starting a new job. These figures coincide with the findings of Holmes and Rahe (1967) and Heisel, Ream, Raitz, et al. (1973). Exclusive of multiple births, it would appear that for the adolescent with a crisis in pregnancy, there may be a greater chance of a premature birth.

PROBLEMS IN MOTHERING BY ADOLESCENTS

At present, one in five inner city infants are born to drug-abusing mothers annually for a total of 400,000. This often results in prematurity, respiratory disease syndrome, and learning disabilities. A significant number of these mothers are adolescents. Adolescent mothers have a higher than average number of premature infants.

Brain-damaged, blind, or premature infants are at greater risk for poor mothering or becoming battered children than normal infants (Klein & Stern, 1971; Robson & Moss, 1970).

Frommer and O'Shea (1973) found that mothers who had problems in managing their infants were very depressed, had many physical complaints, and were polarized into either being anxiously perfectionistic in their pursuits or not caring at all for the infant. They felt that the basis for this was the common feature among these mothers of having had a permanent separation from one or both of their parents before age 11 years.

In their study of failure-to-thrive children from a low socioeconomic background, Evans, Reinhart, & Succop (1972) found that a majority of the mothers were depressed adolescents who had experienced a severe object loss within four months of the baby's hospitalization, or had received very poor mothering in their own childhood, or had been failure-to-thrive infants themselves. Possibly, these findings are similar to the neonatal deprivation of mothers of prematures, and tally with the findings of Hudgens, Chilgren and Palardy (1972).

Some review of ethnic factors seems pertinent here since they contribute to the infant's status and caretaking efforts by the mother. For instance, Puerto Rican neonates of teenage mothers had a superior outcome in the first year compared to infants of black teenage mothers of the same SES in the U.S.A. (Field, Widmayer, Adler & deCubas, 1990; Lester, Coll & Sepkoski, 1983). Field and Widmayer (1981) noted that Cuban-U.S. mothers were more affectionate and talked continuously to their infants, in contrast to black teenage mothers who talked very little to them. Moreover, the face-to-face interactions of Cuban-U.S. mothers and infants were more harmonious. At one year, the Cuban-U.S. youngsters were touched, looked at, talked to, smiled at, laughed with, played with more, had more toys demonstrated and more books read to them than did the black infants of teen mothers. The black young mother directed her infant's play while ignoring the infant more. In contrast, the Cuban infants were much more engaged interactively with their mothers in smiling, vocalizing, and laughing. In the Cuban nuclear families, the teen mother and infants did better socially. However, in the second year, the play by all mothers decreased and there was a drop in the Bayley developmental and language scores, so that all cultural differences were insignificant by age two.

MOTHER'S STIMULATION OF HER INFANT

As shown in Table 12.5, my study (Sugar, 1976) found significantly less involvement and less adequate stimulation of the infant in the first six months by the black adolescent mother compared to the black adult mother. This difference was greater among mothers of full-term compared to premature infants. These mothers were ignorant of child development basics and expected unrealistic adult-like behavior of their infants. When their infants attained locomotor ability, they often felt the need to punish the youngster as if a teenager.

TABLE 12.5
Comparison of Adequate Stimulation of Infant by
Mother's Age and Infant's Birth Weighty

Infants	Birth Weight in gm		Adequate Stimulation by:		$x2$	df	p*
			Adol. Mother	Adult Mother			
Prematures	≤2500	Number	160	161			
		Percent	73.4	85.2	6.72	2	0.035
Full-term	≥2501	Number	53	107			
		Percent	83.6	94.3	4.38	1	0.036
All Infants		Number	214	267			
		Percent	76.3	89.4	11.10	3	0.011

*If p <0.05, the percentages are significantly different.

The lesser stimulation given by both adolescent and adult mothers to prematures might be a reflection of their neonatal deprivation and delay in bonding, since the prematures stayed in the nursery one to two months. The percentage of adequate stimulation by adolescent mothers of prematures vs. adult mothers of prematures was 73 vs. 85, which supports the idea that there might be a special problem in mothering of premature infants. The above-average percent of prematures born to adolescents makes this a significant problem.

Adolescent mothers of full-term babies also provided significantly less adequate stimulation compared to adult mothers of full-terms, i.e., 84 percent vs. 94 percent.

Twenty-four percent of all the adolescent mothers gave inadequate stimulation to their infants in the first six months. Contributing to this apparently are the adolescents' narcissism, inadequate preparation for motherhood, neonatal hospitalization, divided mothering, and unresolved dependency, as well as hostility displaced from the maternal grandmother (on whom the adolescent mother is dependent) onto her mate or infant. These figures indicate inadequate mothering and problems in bonding between the infant and the mother.

Many of these mothers shared the mothering with the grandmother, aunt, or cousins. Only seven percent of adolescent mothers actually care for their infant (Smith, Mumford, Goldfarb & Kaufman, 1975).

Clarke-Stewart (1973) found that a highly significant relationship was present for both sexes between children's competence at age 9 to 18 months in all areas of development and affectionate, responsive maternal care, and that the child's behavior influenced the mother's. Broussard (1979) focused the issue of maternal perception of the infant as a delicate and very significant issue in terms of the youngster's development, and more so with adolescent mothers.

The mother's emotional availability is critical in the rapprochement subphase of separation-individuation at age 14 to 24 months, when the beginning capacity for self-regulation allows the child to cope to some extent with stresses due to the normative periods of mother's decreased attentiveness or brief separations. When the toddler's failure at self-regulation leads to distress, it turns to the mother in an appeal cycle to obtain her attention and involvement. Then the emotionally available mother responds suitably (Settlage, Rosenthal, Spielman et al., 1990). These authors concluded that the child who copes well identifies with such abilities in the mother, her regulatory abilities, and interventions. This is similar to the observations made by Werner and Smith (1989) that the offspring of stable mothers in the at-risk population were at less risk than the others.

Osofsky and Eberhart-Wright (1989) observed that young mothers and infants have less positive affect and more negative affect than those in a normative group and that their infants' affective responses are often not reciprocated by the mother. At 13 months, less maternal physical and emotional availability, along with negative and non-affect sharing by the mothers, predicted inappropriate empathic behavior at 20 months with aggressive behavior to the victims.

THE CONFLICT BETWEEN THE YOUNG MOTHER AND THE GRANDMOTHER

Fineman and Smith (1984) found that among some single teen mothers there was acting out of a primary struggle with their mothers, the wish for fulfillment of early regressive needs and a defense against them. Among these youngsters, there was an absence of an internalized experience of their own earliest emotional separation and ego solidarity. As a result, they failed to resonate unconsciously with their own infant's passage through the early separation-individuation phase and could not experience the infant's passage through this phase as normal and indicative of growth and development. With this group of young mothers, living in the maternal grandmother's home led to confrontations and rivalries between the mother and grandmother over the baby. This involved an alternating wish by the mother to be nurtured by the grandmother just as grandmother was providing for the baby, and to nurture the baby herself.

Ooms (1984) pointed out that the women's movement, privacy, confidentiality, and individual rights imply adulthood, maturity, independence, and being in charge of one's fertility. She feels that pregnancy may be a way of getting back into the family or a way of showing the grown-up status of the young parent. She also feels that the family should be very much involved in the decision-making and support offered to the young mother in her decision to keep the baby, since the youngster has to know if she and her baby are acceptable so that she can plan for the future.

DEPENDENCY FEATURES

In my study (Sugar, 1976) there seemed to be a connection between the infant sleeping in the mother's bed and the mother being very dependent on the maternal grandmother with whom she had a rivalrous relationship, which involved maternity rights to the infant. When a father was present, he was often the target of the teenage mother's marked hostility whether he lived with her or not. She used the infant as a barrier against him. Both these aspects of the mother's behavior seem to reflect some measure of arrest in her development, which was most obviously manifest in her symbiosis with the maternal grandmother.

There were frequent situations, as noted above, where the maternal grandmother shared in the mothering whether the mother was working, in school, or at home, with the mother feeling part child and part mother, dependently hostile, and at the same time not interested in a commitment to any male. Some of these mothers had repeated pregnancies and their dependency problem was quite clear and significant, but they had no wish to have a man take care of them. They seemed to accept the dependency on their own mother or on state welfare. This condition precludes a sense of fidelity (Erikson, 1968) and commitment to a heterosexual object, which involves a further stage of progress in adolescent development presaging a move toward closure. The symbiosis would explain Williams' (1974) findings of problems about attachment to a man and leaving mother.

Many of the youngsters in my study were raised in one-parent matriarchal families and/or had witnessed repeated separations and reconciliations in their parents' unstable marriage. These features may have contributed to the infants' inadequate stimulation by the adolescent mothers and would fit the data from Frommer and O'Shea (1973).

There has been a fear that giving aid to families with dependent children discourages marriage or prolongs welfare dependency. Duncan and Hoffman (1990) noted that only a minority of women who are single heads of households have a long welfare history, with a group younger than 25 having a higher percentage (45 percent) than those above 25 (14 percent) who received welfare for as long as nine years. In addition, the receipt of welfare does not worsen the individual's attitude about locus of control.

Adolescent motherhood seems to augment dependency in terms of having to be supported by someone—boyfriend, spouse, maternal grandparents, or the state. Along with this, there is decreased opportunity for academic learning (unless the youngster returns to school) and there is decreased capacity for self-observation. However, since the young mother may now be in the work force as a mother and housekeeper, she has an opportunity for increased consolidation of character and a heightened sense of responsibility. There may also be some increased autonomy, but for the young mother who returns to the grandmother's home, there is regression since she is now feeling, and being, taken care of again. There is also a possibility of regression in the service of further growth.

In contrast, the non-maternal youngster on an academic track has increased dependency (being taken care of by parents or scholarships), but has increased learning opportunities and increased capacity for self-observation. At the same time, there is decreased consolidation of character, decreased autonomy, with more regression available in the service of growth.

INDIVIDUATION EFFORTS

The adolescent's need and conflict about detaching herself from the infantile objects leads to a state of normal adolescent mourning (Sugar, 1968) and there are many varied responses to the loss of an object, which may be intermingled with pathological defenses and maladaptation.

Among the group of adolescent mothers I observed, some seemed to have made an unconscious ambivalent gift to the maternal grandmother in the form of the infant for the maternal grandmother to mother. This also served, perhaps, as a ransom for these mothers who were attempting to individuate from their mothers. This pattern was more obvious among the mothers who deserted their infants. Some of the adolescent mothers of premature infants seemed ambivalent since they returned to care for the infant several months later and shared the mothering with the maternal grandmother. Perhaps their desertion and inadequate mothering were also related to fears about raising a damaged premature infant (Klein & Stern, 1971; Robson & Moss, 1970).

The relation of an adolescent mother with her mother determines much of the girl's mothering behavior. The mothers of these girls seem to have been unable to provide this satisfactorily for them, and perhaps some disturbance or deprivation had occurred in the adolescent's rearing.

The conflict about mothering and wishing to be mothered seems to be regularly unresolved for many of these girls and may continue to the point of the girl acting out by becoming pregnant. The oedipal conflict may be the focal point in this for some, but perhaps less intensely than, or not exclusive of, the symbiotic or other pregenital conflicts in others.

Thus, pregnancy in an adolescent may be: an unconscious effort to effect a separate identity and individuate; an attempt to make up for the loss of the infantile objects; a substitution and avoidance of early separation-individuation conflicts; or part of an ethnic or cultural pattern with modeling after her mother.

These are particular factors involved that have some commonality for the group of adolescent mothers, but the dynamics, defenses, and diagnoses are quite individual.

A PERSPECTIVE

Behaviorally, it may seem that a young adolescent, especially if single, who becomes a mother "is grown up." Psychodynamically, however, she is probably having a developmental arrest of variable degree, since she is psychologically not yet in, or out of, adolescence.

A fortnight before Juliet's 14th birthday, her mother said,

Tell me daughter Juliet,
How stands your disposition to be marry'd?
(William Shakespeare, "The Tragedy of Romeo
and Juliet" Act I. Sc. 3, lines 63-65)

and goes on (Act I. Sc. 3, lines 68-72)

Well, think of marriage now. Younger than you
Here in Verona, ladies of esteem,
Are made already mothers. By my count
I was your mother much upon these years
That you are now a maid.

If these lines are representative of the beginning age of motherhood in Juliet's time, was adolescent development completed at age 14 and different from the current state of affairs? Perhaps, but possibly they were no different from the present-day adolescent mothers.

In the past, the low longevity and high mortality rates for children required early motherhood for survival of the species. Until the child labor laws were passed, children and adolescents were significant contributors to the work force in the field and factory. Since colonial times, the U.S.A. has had earlier childbearing compared to Europe (Wattenberg, 1976). Early motherhood was more appropriate and necessary for those times.

When Juliet's mother discussed marriage, Juliet's nurse was present. This reflects the support given by retainers or surrogate mothers and the extended family in the past to the adolescent mother in all social classes. Their support, I believe, served to mask the immaturity and dependency of the adolescent parents as well as aiding the youngster towards further development. Such considerations may have application to present-day adolescent mothers in other cultures in nonindustrialized nations that have an agrarian economy, a shorter life span, and a close-knit family. With the present high mobility and divorce rates in the United States, the absence of an extended family, and the massive shift of the rural population to urban areas over the past 50 years, the adolescent mother stands exposed, without such a support system, as having incomplete emotional development.

From their research, Furstenberg, et al. (1987) have documented that the black teenage inner city mother was better off than expected when seen 17 years later, and better than when observed at the five-year follow-up. The factors contributing to a successful outcome for these mothers were: the mother's ability to continue her educational goals, limit her fertility, marry and stay married before and after the child's birth. For a negative outcome, the contributing features were: welfare dependency, high fertility, being married and family supported at different periods.

Werner and Smith (1989, pp. 169-170) noted that for resilient youngsters (even though they had earlier difficulties with behavior disorders, mental problems, and teenage pregnancy) the presence of a supportive mother, or mother and father, for the youngster was of positive significance for a good outcome.

Among the various family planning programs, the successful ones (Nickel & Delany, 1985) usually have involved an ombudsman or some person in the role of surrogate mother for the adolescent during her pregnancy and afterwards (Salguero, Schlesinger & Yearwood, 1984). Some programs address the youngster's conflict with, and need for, the maternal grandmother by an effort from the beginning to involve her in prenatal family sessions and regularly scheduled postnatal family sessions (Balk, Roye & Kappgraff, 1990). These efforts provide help for the youngster in dealing with some of the conflicted issues between her and her mother. They may help her to become better integrated with her family of origin.

In Iceland, there are no surnames and the single pregnant girl or single mother are not the objects of criticism. In the U.S.A., currently, the unwed mother has been accorded greater acceptance than several decades ago. This provides her with options for development.

SUMMARY

Motherhood in, and emotional development of, the female adolescent are examined in this chapter. Adolescent motherhood remains a significant problem. Although the birth rates are declining, the early adolescent birth rates are not. It appears that there are a number of antecedent experiences and psychological configurations that may determine if an adolescent will become pregnant and what kind of mother and person she will be if she does. Ethnic and cultural factors, as well as family modeling, are significant components of this. The heterogeneity of adolescent mothers requires stressing that although there are some patterns that emerge statistically and clinically, each youngster must be considered individually for a complete assessment.

The inadequacies of the adolescent mother may be manifest in her inability to provide for herself or her infant, and to relate to a mate satisfactorily, since she is still dependent on, and symbiotic with, her own mother. This indicates she has not consolidated or synthesized her adolescence to become an adult. The difficulties for this young mother may include the increased possibility of having a premature birth, coping emotionally with giving up the baby for adoption, or problems in bonding to her infant. The adolescent mother's symbiotic needs, lack of commitment, and fantasy attitude about her infant are also seen in her less adequate stimulation of her infant, as well as in her dividing the mothering of the infant with her own source of dependence.

Pregnancy may help the girl to separate from her own mother, but she remains dependent on her or some substitute mother if she is unmarried. Thus, for some, the pregnancy may initiate a round of self-defeating behavior instead of leading to a successful separation from home, the development of self-sufficiency and acceptance, and a healthy environment for herself and her baby.

For most adolescents, motherhood confounds their emotional development by engendering or protracting their dependency on their own mothers, delaying their normative development of separation-individuation, psychic structure, and a sense of commitment and fidelity to a heterosexual object. From a practical view, this leads in many to an arrest or a long delay in emotional development and incomplete preparation for self-sufficiency and motherhood.

With present-day longevity and loss of the extended family for support, these features of adolescent motherhood are more apparent than in the past. However, various beneficent ethnic, cultural, and family program features may have an ameliorating effect on the youngster's situation.

REFERENCES

Balk, S., Roye, C., & Kappgraff, M. 1990. The Teenage Mothers' (TAM) Grandmothers' Program. Presented at the American Orthopsychiatric Association Meeting, Miami, Florida, April.

Blos, P. 1974. The genealogy of the ego-ideal. *Psychoanal. Study Child*, 29-43-48.

Blos, P. 1977. When and how does adolescence end: Structural criteria for adolescent closure. *Adol. Psychiatry*, 5:5-17.

Broussard, E.A. 1979. Assessment of the adaptive potential of the mother infant system: The neonatal perception inventories. *Seminars in Perinatol.*, 3-91-100.

Clarke-Stewart, K.A. 1973. Interaction between mothers and their young children: Characteristics and consequences. *Monog. Soc. Res. Child Develop.*, 38:1-109, Level 153.

Duncan, G.J. & Hoffman, S.D. 1990. Teenage welfare receipt and subsequent dependence among adolescent mothers. *Fam. Plann. Perspectives*, 22:16-37.

Erikson, E.H. 1968. *Identity, Youth and Crisis*. New York: W.W. Norton.

Evans, S., Reinhart, J.B., & Succop, R.A. 1972. Failure to thrive. *J. Am. Acad. Child Psychiat.*, 11:440-457.

Family Planning Perspectives 1990. More on Koop's study of abortion, 22:36-39.

Felice, M.E., Shragg, G.P., James, M., & Hollingsworth, D.R. 1987. Psychosocial aspects of Mexican-American, white and black teenage pregnancy. *J. Adol. Health Care*, 8:330-335.

Field, T.M., & Widmayer, S. 1981. Mother-infant interaction among lower SES black, Cuban, Puerto Rican and South American immigrants. In T. Field, A. Sostek, P. Vietze, & A.H. Liederman, Eds., *Culture and Early Interactions*. Hillsdale, N.J.: Erlbaum.

Field, T., Widmayer, S., Adler, S., & DeCubas, M. 1990. teenage parenting in different cultures, family constellations, and caregiving environments: Effects on infant development. *Infant Mental Health J.*, 11:158-174.

Fineman, J.A.B., & Smith, M.A. 1984. Object ties and interaction of the infant and adolescent mother. In M. Sugar, Ed., *Adolescent Parenthood*. New York: Spectrum.

Fisher, S.M. 1984. The psychodynamics of teenage pregnancy and motherhood. In M. Sugar, Ed., *Adolescent Parenthood*. New York: Spectrum.

Frommer, E.A., & O'Shea, G. 1973. Antenatal identification of women liable to have problems in managing their infants. *Brit. J. Psychiat.*, 123:149-156.

Furstenberg, F.F. 1987. Race differences in teenage sexuality, pregnancy, and adolescent childbearing. *Millbank Quart.*, 65 (suppl. 2):381-403.

Furstenberg, F.F., Brooks-Gunn, J., & Morgan, S.P. 1987. *Adolescent Mothers in Later Life*. New York: Cambridge.

Grace, E., Emans, S.F., & Woods, E.R. 1989. The impact of AIDS awareness on the adolescent female. *Adol. & Pediat. Gynecol.*, 2:40-42.

Hayes, C.D. 1987. *Risking the Future: Adolescent Sexuality, Pregnancy and Child Bearing*. Washington, D.C.: National Academy.

Heisel, J.T., Ream, S., Raitz, R., Rappaport, M., & Coddington, R.D. 1973. The significance of life events as contributing factors in the diseases of children. *J. Pediat.*, 83:119-123.

Holmes, T.H. & Rahe, R.H. 1967. The social readjustment scale. *J. Psychosom. Res.*, 11:213-218.

Hudgens, G.A., Chilgren, J.D., & Palardy, D.D. 1972. Mother-infant interactions: Effects of early handling of offspring on rat mothers' open-field behavior. *Develop. Psychobiol.*, 5:61-70.

Jacobson, E. 1964. *The Self and the Object World*. New York: International Universities Press.

Jones, E.J., Forrest, J.D., Goldman, N., Henshaw, S., Lincoln, R., Resoff, J.I., Westoff, C.F., & Wulf, D. 1986. *Teenage Pregnancy in Industrialized Countries*. New Haven: Yale.

Klein, M., & Stern, L. 1971. Low birth weight and the battered child syndrome. *Am. J. Dis. Child*, 122:15-18.

Koop, E. 1989. A measured response: Koop on abortion. *Fam. Plann. Perspect.*, 21:31-32.

Lamb, M.E., Elster, A.B., Peters, L.J., Kahn, J.S., & Tavare, J. 1986. Characteristics of married and unmarried adolescent mothers and their mothers. *J. Youth & Adol.*, 15:487-496.

Lester, B.M., Coll, C.T.E., & Sepkoski, C. 1983. A cross cultural study of teenage pregnancy and neonatal behavior. In T. Field & A. Sostek, Eds., *Infants Born at Risk: Perceptual and Physiological Processes*. New York: Grune and Stratton.

Marcia, J. 1980. Identity in adolescence. In J. Adelson, Ed., *Handbook of Adolescent Psychology*. New York: Wiley.

McGee, R., Felhan, M., Williams, S., Partridge, F., Silva, P.A., & Kelly, J. 1990. DSM-III disorders in a large sample of adolescents. *J. Am. Acad. Child & Adol. Psychiatry*, 29:611-619.

Nickel, S.P., & Delany, H. 1985. *Working With Teen Parents: A Survey of Promising Approaches*. Chicago: Family Resource Coalition.

Ooms, T. 1984. The family context of adolescent parenting. In M. Sugar, Ed., *Adolescent Parenthood*. New York: Spectrum.

Osofsky, J.D. & Eberhart-Wright, A. 1989. Risk and Protective Factors for Parents and Infants. Presented at Cornell Symposium on Human Development. Future Directions in Infant Development Research. October, Ithaca, New York.

Pearson, G.H.J. 1959. *Emotional Disorders of Childhood*. New York: Norton, pp. 62-63.

Piaget, J. 1972. Intellectual evolution from adolescence to adulthood. *Hum. Dev.*, 15:1-12.

Psychiatric News 1990. Jan. 19. Washington: Am. Psychiatric Assoc.

Robson, K.S. & Moss, H.A. 1970. Patterns and determinants of maternal attachment. *J. Pediat.*, 77:976-985.

Salguero, C. 1984. The role of ethnic factors in adolescent pregnancy and motherhood. In M. Sugar, Ed., *Adolescent Parenthood*. New York: Spectrum.

Salguero, C., Schlesinger, N., & Yearwood, E. 1984. A mental health program for adolescent parents. In M. Sugar, Ed., *Adolescent Parenthood*. New York: Spectrum.

Sarrel, P.M. & Davis, C.A. 1966. The young unwed primapara. *Am. J. Obstet. & Gyn.*, 95:722-725.

Settlage, C.F., Rosenthal, J., Spielman, P.M., Gassrier, S., Afterman, J.R., Bemesderfer, S., & Kolodny, S. 1990. An exploratory study of mother-child interaction during the second year of life. *J. Am. Psychoanal. Assoc.*, 38:705-731.

Shakespeare, W. *The Tragedy of Romeo and Juliet*. Fourth printing. Edited by R. Hosley, New Haven: The Yale Shakespeare, Yale University Press, 1964.

Smith, F.B., McGill, L., & Wait, R.B. 1987. Hispanic adolescent conception and contraception profiles. *J. Adol. Health Care*, 8:352-355.

Smith, P.B., Mumford, D.M., Goldfarb, J.L., & Kaufman, R.H. 1975. Selected aspects of adolescent post partum behavior. *J. Reproductive Med.*, 14:159-165.

Stevens-Simon, C., Parsons, J., & Montgomery, C. 1986. What is the relationship between post-partum withdrawal from school and repeat pregnancy among adolescent mothers? *J. Adol. Health Care*, 7:191-194.

Sugar, M. 1968. Normal Adolescent Mourning. *Am. J. Psychother.*, 32:258-269.

Sugar, M. 1976. At risk factors for the adolescent mother and her infant. *J. Youth & Adol.*, 5:251-270.

Sugar, M. 1979. Developmental issues in adolescent motherhood. In M. Sugar, Ed., *Female Adolescent Development.* New York: Brunner/Mazel.

U.S. Bureau of the Census 1990. *Statistical Abstract of the United States 1990.* Washington, D.C.: U.S. Government.

U.S. Department of Commerce 1989. Fertility of American women: June 1988. *Current Population Reports. Population Characteristics Series*, No. 436, P. 20. Washington, D.C.: U.S. Government.

Washington, A., Sweet, R., & Schafe, M. 1985. Pelvic inflammatory disease and its sequelae in adolescence. *J. Adol. Health Care*, 6:298-310.

Wattenberg, B.J. 1976. Ed. *The Statistical History of United States: From Colonial Times to the Present.* New York: Basic.

Werner, E.E. & Smith, R.S. 1989. *Vulnerable But Invincible.* Honolulu: U. Press of Hawaii.

Williams, T.M. 1974. Childrearing practices of young mothers. *Am. J. Orthopsychiat.*, 44:70-75.

Zabin, L., Hardy, J.B., Smith, E.A., & Hirsch, M.B. 1986. Substance abuse and its relation to sexual activity among inner-city adolescents. *J. Adol. Health Care*, 7:320-331.

Zabin, L.S., Hardy, J.B., Streett, R., & King. T.M. 1984. A school- hospital- and university-based adolescent pregnancy prevention program. *J. Reproductive Medicine*, 29:421-426.

Name Index

Subject Index